Lincoln Christian College

P9-DFN-156

The Christian World Mission

TODAY and TOMORROW

J. Herbert Kane

BAKER BOOK HOUSE
Grand Rapids, Michigan 49506

Copyright 1981 by
Baker Book House Company

ISBN: 0-8010-5426-5

PHOTOLITHOPRINTED BY CUSHING - MALLOY, INC.
ANN ARBOR, MICHIGAN, UNITED STATES OF AMERICA

266.02
K16c

To
Our dear friends
KENNETH AND RUTH KANTZER
Faithful servants of Jesus Christ
Loyal supporters of the Christian mission

and

People helpers *par excellence*

62133

Foreword

In the annals of the Christian mission one can readily discover some of the most outstanding examples of self-giving service the world has yet witnessed. One would be hard pressed to equal, in any sphere of human accomplishment, the devotion and altruism of men and women possessed of great missionary hearts.

It may come as a surprise to some, but what can be said concerning Christian deeds can also be said with respect to Christian thought. Not a few men and women of mission have bequeathed to the church and the world the fruit of prodigious mental effort. To follow the trail of missions is to encounter some of the great minds of the church.

What is rare is to find a person who possesses both a great missionary heart and a superior missionary mind. Most generations of Christians produce a few of them—but only a few. Professor J. Herbert Kane is one such man. A successful missionary to the China of another day, a beloved teacher of literally hundreds of missionaries, a missionary-conference speaker who has challenged thousands, and an author whose books on missions have been read with great profit by other thousands, Dr. Kane's influence on his generation has been of signal importance.

Now we are blessed with still another book from Dr. Kane's prolific pen. In *The Christian World Mission: Today and Tomorrow*, he reminds us of the true sources of the missionary motivation and message, he traces the missionary current through the geographical and ideological spheres of our contemporary world, he sheds light upon mission issues within the church, and he alerts us to problems outside the church which will continue to challenge the mission of tomorrow. No matter what his or her responsibility or sphere of service, every Christian leader, pastor, missionary, student, and lay person who reads this book will benefit. And, even more importantly, the cause of Christ will be furthered as readers allow the spirit and knowledge herein contained to become part of their commitment to Christ and the world.

Beyond that which is written in the Preface, another word should be mentioned concerning Dr. Kane's wife, Winnifred. Readers who are not fortunate enough to know the Kanes personally will be prone to skip over the author's words concerning his wife rather hurriedly, attributing them to politeness and decorum. But those of us who best know how the Kanes live and labor together will see on every page, not only the clear thinking of the author, but also the unmistakable reflection of his wife "Winnie." Theirs has been a labor of love in which two hearts beat as one.

Take up this book then. Read its words. Study its ideas. Pray about its challenge. Here you will find both the heartthrob and the clear thinking that should characterize the Christian world mission—today and tomorrow.

David J. Hesselgrave
Deerfield, Illinois

Preface

During the Battle of Britain in the summer of 1940, Winston Churchill in the House of Commons paid public tribute to the brave men of the Royal Air Force in these words: "Never in the field of human conflict was so much owed by so many to so few."

A similar statement could be made of the missionary movement of the last two centuries. Tens of millions of people in all parts of the world are what they are today because a comparatively small number of gallant men and women risked their lives to give them the gospel with all the fringe benefits pertaining thereto. It is doubtful whether a single country in Black Africa would be independent today were it not for the contribution made by the pioneer missionaries, who established churches, opened hospitals, and operated schools, thereby setting Africa on the path to modernization. Indeed, but for the missionary translators most of the languages and dialects of Africa would still exist only in oral form.

Things are changing, however. The Third World is on the march and the church in that part of the world has come of age. The problems we now encounter are more subtle and therefore more difficult to solve than those of the nineteenth century. At the same time we are faced with unprecedented

5

opportunities undreamed of a hundred years ago. Consequently we are torn between two extremes: to see only the problems and give way to discouragement, or to see only the opportunities and do nothing to solve the problems.

If the Christian world mission is to continue to the end of the age, we must do our best to avoid both extremes. We must rejoice in the unprecedented opportunities; at the same time we must realistically face up to the unprecedented problems. The day is gone when we could naively assume that because God is in His heaven, all therefore must be right with the world—or at least with the church. It is still true, as Adoniram Judson said on one occasion, that "the future is as bright as the promises of God." But we must remember that His ways are not always our ways, nor His thoughts our thoughts (Is 55:8). He often acts in ways we deem strange. William Cowper's words were never truer:

> God moves in a mysterious way
> His wonders to perform;
> He plants His footsteps in the sea
> And rides upon the storm.

When we look around at the turmoil in the world and realize to what extent it is affecting the Christian mission, we should remember that the "storm" that threatens to engulf us is the very thing that buoys Him up and carries Him along to sure and certain victory. The psalmist said that God is able to make the wrath of man to praise Him (Ps 76:10). If that is so, perhaps we should be grateful for all the wrath there is in the world.

In any case, we can be certain that God knows the end from the beginning, that He has a purpose for both the church and the world, and that He is working all things after the counsel of His own will, by His own power, for His own glory (Eph 1).

Surely the Christian mission is at the very center of that purpose; and if we want to be identified with Him in its outworking, we had better understand and support missions at home and abroad.

As with my other books, I am deeply indebted to my wife for her cheerful, unfailing support in all phases of production, from the preparation of the manuscript to proofreading the galleys. She has always been my companion in the Lord's service, but for a while last month she became my "galley slave"!

March, 1981

J. Herbert Kane
Deerfield, Illinois

Contents

TODAY

Part I *Biblical Basis of Missions*

1. Jehovah a Missionary God 15
2. The Bible a Missionary Book. 25
3. The Gospel a Missionary Message .....,...... 35
4. The Church a Witnessing Community 45
5. Every Christian a World Christian 57

Part II *Global Dimension of Missions*

6. The Demographic Dimension 73
7. The Social Dimension 93
8. The Economic Dimension 109
9. The Political Dimension 121

TOMORROW

Part I *Crucial Issues*

10. Definition of Mission 139
11. Humanization or Salvation? 155
12. Demand for Moratorium 173
13. Contextualization of Theology 185
14. The Dynamics of Church Growth 201

Part II *Continuing Problems*

15. The Decline of the West 215
16. The Rise and Spread of Nationalism 233
17. The Resurgence of the Non-Christian
    Religions 247
18. The Charismatic Movement 261

Bibliography 277
Subject Index 283
Scripture Index 291

TODAY

Biblical Basis of Missions

CHAPTER 1

Jehovah
A Missionary God

The missionary movement did not originate with Francis Xavier or William Carey or the apostle Paul or even with the Lord Jesus Christ. It began with God the Father Himself. Robert E. Speer wrote: "The supreme arguments for missions are not found in any specific words. It is in the very being and character of God that the deepest ground of the missionary enterprise is to be found. We cannot think of God except in terms which necessitate the missionary idea."[1]

The missionary movement of the last two centuries was built and maintained on the Great Commission in Matthew 28. There were historic reasons for this. The Protestant Reformers had declared that the Great Commission applied only to the twelve apostles and that they had taken the gospel to the ends of the then known world. The Great Commission had been fulfilled by them, and the church in later generations had neither the authority nor the responsibility for the evangelization of the world. As a result the Protestant churches of Europe failed to engage in world missions for over two hundred years.

1. Robert E. Speer, *Christianity and the Nations* (New York: Revell, 1910), pp. 17-18.

When William Carey appeared, he first had to refute this false doctrine in order to get the churches to support world missions. To accomplish this he wrote a treatise called *The Obligation of Christians to Use Means for the Conversion of the Heathen*. In it he clearly defined and defended the duty of the churches in the West to take the gospel to the ends of the earth. From that day to this the emphasis in mission circles has been on the Great Commission as the rationale for world missions. Hundreds of books, articles, and sermons have concentrated on the Great Commission. As recently as 1976 a book appeared with the title, *The Great Commission for Today*.

Harry Boer in his book, *Pentecost and Missions*, insists that the Great Commission played little or no part in the missionary activity of the early church: "There seems to be no warrant to believe that awareness of the Great Commission played a role in the mind of the Church at Jerusalem when she undertook the great decision to acknowledge the equal share of the gentiles in the gospel and to validate Peter's baptism of the household of Cornelius."[2]

Even the great apostle Paul seems not to have been motivated by the Great Commission. Boer goes on to say that "there is no evidence that the apostles or anyone else ever communicated the command of Jesus to Paul."[3] After referring to the many times in the Book of Acts that Paul mentions his missionary calling, Boer concludes: "In all these statements of motivation and the manner in which he came to his missionary calling we search in vain for any indication that the Great Commission was the moving factor or even a moving factor in Paul's witnessing ministry."[4]

To base the world mission of the Christian church solely on the Great Commission is to miss the whole thrust of biblical revelation. From Genesis to Malachi Jehovah is portrayed as a missionary God. The Jesus of the New Testament is the Jehovah of the Old. He was the first and great Missionary— called "Apostle" in Hebrews 3:1. From Matthew to Revelation

2. Harry R. Boer, *Pentecost and Missions* (Grand Rapids: Eerdmans, 1961), p. 42.
3. Ibid., p. 44.
4. Ibid., p. 45.

the New Testament is concerned with Christ's mission to the world. Bible history is salvation history because God is the God of salvation. The Bible is simply the story of His saving acts. "Salvation," says the prophet, "is of the Lord" (Jonah 2:9).

The cross, therefore, was not an afterthought with God; neither was it a stopgap measure introduced when the original plan went wrong. Long before the creation of the world, long before the fall of man, God devised a plan for the salvation of the world. At the heart of that plan was the cross of Christ. Jesus was the only one who seemed to understand this. Even His apostles missed the point entirely. They considered the cross to be an unmitigated tragedy, and Peter tried to use force to save Jesus from His enemies. Jesus would have none of it. He rebuked Peter, telling him to sheathe his sword, adding, "The cup which my Father hath given me, shall I not drink it?" (John 18:11). It was only after the resurrection and the ascension that the apostles came to understand this great truth; and in their prayer in Acts 4:27-28 they acknowledged that the human agents associated with the crucifixion—Herod, Pontius Pilate, Jews, and Gentiles—were unwittingly carrying out God's eternal plan.

It is a mistake, therefore, to think that the missionary mandate is restricted to the Great Commission. The missionary obligation of the church would be just as imperative if Jesus had not spoken those words. The missionary mandate antedates the incarnation and is rooted in the very nature of God. Indeed, if Jehovah were not a missionary God, there would have been no incarnation.

Man was created in the beginning not only by God but for God. Just as man cannot get along without God, so God will not get along without man. God then becomes the Hound of Heaven. Once on the sinner's scent He follows him to the end of the trail. The reason for this is not hard to discover. Man is endowed with a divinely created soul that will live as long as God lives, either in fellowship with Him or alienated from Him. Because of this, man is infinitely precious in the sight of his heavenly Father, who will have all men to be saved and to come to a knowledge of the truth (1 Tim 2:4).

God is a God of love, and His heart goes out to the sinner in his sin and longs for his return. He loves the sinner because it is His nature to love; it requires no special effort on His part. If the sinner rejects God's love and persists in his rebellion, God has to deal with him in judgment; but even then His act is an act of love. God's mighty acts are always redemptive, designed to show not only His creative power but also His redeeming grace. As for judgment, it is His "strange" work (Is 28:21). He takes no pleasure in the death of the wicked (Ez 33:11). When He acts in judgment, it is to bring men and nations to their senses, to deliver them from self-destruction. In wrath He always remembers mercy (Hab 3:2). In judgment He always makes a way of escape. If the sinner continues to be recalcitrant and finally ends up in hell, even there he will be the object of God's love.

> There's a wideness in God's mercy
> Like the wideness of the sea;
> There's a kindness in His justice
> Which is more than liberty.
>
> For the love of God is broader
> Than the measure of man's mind;
> And the heart of the Eternal
> Is most wonderfully kind.

God's missionary concern was by no means confined to Israel. He was equally interested in the welfare of the heathen nations. They too belonged to Him even though they were not part of the covenant. They too were required to repent and acknowledge the universal rule of Jehovah. In the whole of the Old Testament there is no more moving story than the account of Jonah's calling upon the wicked city of Nineveh to repent. They repented and the city was spared. This had been Jonah's problem in the beginning. He had a hunch that, if God were given a good reason, He would show mercy to Jonah's enemies the Ninevites, so he headed for Tarshish instead of Nineveh. Actually, God did exactly what Jonah feared

He would; so Jonah became angry with God and sulked outside the city.

To Jonah, preaching judgment was an end in itself; and he would have been happy to see Nineveh destroyed, just as Sodom and Gomorrah had been. With God it was different. To Him the preaching of judgment was a means to an end. He intended that it should lead to repentance and salvation.

The Old Testament is a melancholy story of man's moral and spiritual declension. Left to himself he always goes astray. He has no homing instinct; consequently he goes farther and farther away from God and deeper and deeper into sin and idolatry. Even Israel, God's covenant people, lapsed time and again into idolatry; but God never completely gave them up. He had set His love upon them and had promised Abraham that through him all the nations of the world would be blessed (Gen 12:3). His choice of Abraham was unconditional (Deut 7:7-8). He would keep His end of the bargain even if Israel proved unfaithful.

When man persists in his rebellion, he is allowed to go only so far and then God intervenes in judgment. But judgment is never simply punitive; it is also redemptive. That is why in every instance God has made a way of escape. When He was about to destroy the world with the flood, He instructed Noah to construct an ark "to the saving of his house" (Heb 11:7). That only eight persons availed themselves of the salvation provided by the ark was man's fault, not God's intention. When He destroyed Sodom and Gomorrah, He sent an angel to deliver Lot and his family. Both cities would have been spared if God had been able to find ten righteous persons in them (Gen 18:32).

Certain Bible scholars have depicted the God of the Old Testament as cruel, vindictive, and bloodthirsty, demanding the last pound of flesh and the last drop of blood. Such a characterization is a libel on the nature of God. Manasseh, one of Judah's most wicked kings, was spared when at the end of his life he repented and confessed his sin. In the Psalms God is described as "slow to anger and plenteous in mercy"

(Ps 103:8). His lovingkindness is better than life (Ps 63:3) and His tender mercies are over all His works (Ps 145:9).

Time and again throughout history God sent His messengers to call Israel back to Himself. Under the theocracy He raised up judges who defeated their enemies and led the people of Israel back to the worship of the one true God. During the monarchy He raised up good and godly kings, such as David, Josiah, Hezekiah, and others, who ruled in the fear of God and brought revival and prosperity to Israel. Even during the captivity He sent His prophets and leaders, Daniel in Babylon, Jeremiah in Egypt, Nehemiah in Persia, to exhort the captives to accept their God-ordained fate and to pray for the peace and prosperity of their captors. Only in this way would they enjoy a measure of peace themselves.

Always God wanted to do His people good. When they deliberately turned their backs on Him and went after other gods, He never completely gave up on them. No one made this plainer than did Isaiah when he cried: "Let the wicked forsake his way, and the unrighteous man his thoughts; and let him return unto the Lord, and he will have mercy upon him; and to our God, for he will abundantly pardon" (Is 55:7).

And what shall we say about the God and Father of our Lord Jesus Christ as portrayed in the New Testament? The central fact of the New Testament is the incarnation, and it is very clear that the incarnation was God the Father's idea, not man's, not even Christ's. Consistently Jesus reminded His hearers that He did not come of His own volition but was sent by the Father. The words He spoke were not really His, but the Father's (John 12:49). The works He did were not really His, but the Father's (John 5:19). In short, it was the Father who sent the Son, and He sent Him to be the Savior of the world (1 John 4:14). Jesus Christ was God's love gift to a sinful world. "God so loved the world, that he gave his only begotten Son" (John 3:16).

In the New Testament God is described as a giving God. He is always on the giving end. Living water (John 4:10), heavenly manna (John 6:32), sun (Mt 5:45), rain (Acts 14:17), faith (Eph 2:8), grace (James 4:6), wisdom (James 1:5), peace

(2 Thess 3:16), and eternal life (Rom 6:23) are all gifts from God. Paul says: "He giveth to all, life and breath and all things" (Acts 17:25); and James tells us that "every good gift and every perfect gift . . . cometh down from the Father of lights" (James 1:17).

God's most precious gift was Jesus Christ. "God so loved the world, that he gave his only begotten Son, that whosoever believeth in him should not perish, but have everlasting life" (John 3:16). With this great truth in mind Paul says: "He that spared not his own Son, but delivered him up for us all, how shall he not with him also freely give us all things?" (Rom 8:32).

In the greatest and best known of all the parables Jesus depicted God as the heavenly Father who waits, looks, and longs for the return of the prodigal. When the familiar figure appeared on the horizon the father ran to meet him and fell on his neck and kissed him. He escorted him into the old home and gave orders to the servants to provide the ring, the robe, and the shoes, so that the wayward boy might sit at his father's table not as a servant but as a son. Such love and forgiveness are alien to the human spirit, so much so that the elder brother refused to join in the merriment but sulked outside in the field. He thought in terms of justice, so the father's action did not make sense to him. The father, on the other hand, thought in terms of love; and love goes far beyond justice or reason or any other human calculation.

God not only "sent" Jesus into the world to be its Savior, but in the person of Christ He wrapped Himself around with the mantle of our humanity and appeared on earth in the humble guise of a human being, so completely and perfectly human that only a few enlightened disciples recognized Him for who He really was. The others regarded Him simply as the son of Mary and Joseph.

Jesus came as the supreme expression of God's love for a fallen world, and He demonstrated that love in word and deed. Peter summed up that matchless life of perfect love in one sentence: He "went about doing good, and healing all that were oppressed of the devil; for God was with him" (Acts 10:38).

The climax of the gospel story came at the end of Jesus' life when He went to the cross. His death, like His birth and His life, was unique. He died as no one else before or since has ever died. He died "the just for the unjust" (1 Pet 3:18). He bore "our sins in his own body on the tree" (1 Pet 2:24). Paul says: "He hath made him to be sin for us, who knew no sin; that we might be made the righteousness of God in him" (2 Cor 5:21). One must adamantly reject the notion that the cross was an expression of God's anger against the world and that Jesus, of His own volition, came between the sinful world and an outraged God and thus secured our salvation for us. The cross was a declaration of God's righteousness, not an expression of His wrath (Rom 3:25). The cross was God's idea in the first place. Pilate thought he could intimidate Jesus: "Speakest thou not unto me? knowest thou not that I have power to crucify thee, and have power to release thee?" Jesus replied: "Thou couldest have no power at all against me, except it were given thee from above" (John 19:10-11). As the Roman procurator, Pilate held in his hands the power of life and death; and in his time in office he had sent many a man to the cross. The signing of a death warrant was a regular part of the day's routine. To sign another was a simple matter. So Pilate thought. But Jesus, knowing that His death was not only a manifestation of God's love (1 John 4:9), but also the realization of God's eternal purpose (Acts 4:27-28), reminded Pilate that in this case he was quite helpless to do anything on his own. Jesus refused to accept the cup from any hand but the hand of the Father (John 18:11). This death was no mere incident, much less an accident, of history. It was part of God's eternal purpose and as such it could be brought about only in God's time, in God's way, and with God's consent.

Paul had a deeper understanding of the cross than did any of his contemporaries. He preached about it; he wrote about it; he gloried in it. It was he who made the profoundest statement in the New Testament regarding the cross. He said: "God was in Christ, reconciling the world unto himself" (2 Cor 5:19).

If the God of the Christian revelation is this kind of God, we can rest assured, in spite of all evidence to the contrary, that this universe is in the hands of a God who is love and whose love, like Himself, is eternal, inscrutable, and unchangeable. That is why we say that this God is a missionary God. No modern writer has summed it up better than James S. Stewart, who wrote: "There is no argument for missions. The total action of God in history, the whole revelation of God in Christ—this is the argument."[5]

5. James S. Stewart, *Thine Is the Kingdom* (New York: Scribner's, 1957), p. 11.

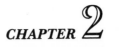

The Bible
A Missionary Book

The Bible is a missionary book. It alone contains all revealed truth concerning God, man, sin, salvation, and judgment. It alone is able to make men "wise unto salvation" (2 Tim 3:15). From it the missionary derives his message, his mandate, his motivation, and his methodology. Apart from the Bible the missionary enterprise has neither meaning nor sanction.

Rightly understood the Bible is a veritable mine of truth on all aspects of the Christian mission. One does not have to *hunt* for missionary passages. The entire Bible from beginning to end is concerned with man and his salvation, and that is what missions is all about. One essential difference between the Bible and other sacred scriptures is that they describe man's search for God, whereas the Bible describes God's search for man.

The Bible opens with the majestic statement: "In the beginning God created the heaven and the earth." Surely this verse establishes solid grounds for the Christian mission. It reminds us of the fact that this world belongs to God. He made it. He sustains it. He controls it. He judges it. He loves it. He intends to redeem it. The psalmist expressed this fact in these words: "The earth is the Lord's, and the fulness thereof; the world, and they that dwell therein" (Ps 24:1). This message runs through the entire Bible from Genesis to Revelation.

The Bible portrays God as the moral governor of the universe. He has established His throne in the heavens and His kingdom rules over all (Ps 103:19). Day by day He opens His hand and supplies the need of every living thing (Ps 145:16). One day He is going to judge the world (Acts 17:31). All men, good and bad, will stand before Him to be judged (John 5:29), as will all nations, great and small (Mt 25:32).

One does not read very far into Genesis before discovering the missionary motif. God's search for Adam after the fall (Gen 3), His expostulation with Cain regarding the murder of Abel (Gen 4), His solicitude for the safety of Noah and his family (Gen 6), His intervention at the Tower of Babel (Gen 11), His call to Abraham in Ur of the Chaldees and His purpose to bless the nations through him (Gen 12) all point to God's concern for the welfare of the human race.

Abraham's intercession on behalf of Sodom and Gomorrah (Gen 18), Joseph's sojourn in the land of Egypt (Gen 39-47), Moses' role in the exodus (Ex 1-12), Mordecai's intervention when his compatriots were doomed to genocide (Esther 1-10), Daniel's intercession for captive Judah (Dan 9), Nehemiah's concern for the rehabilitation of Jerusalem (Neh 1-6), and Jonah's preaching to the people of Nineveh (Jonah 3-4) all have missionary overtones.

The call of Abraham in Genesis 12 marks a turning point in God's dealings with the world. Abraham and Israel were not chosen by God for their own sakes but for a much wider purpose, the salvation of the world. The promise, "In thee shall all the nations of the earth be blessed," was made twice to Abraham (Gen 12:3; 22:18) and once to Jacob (Gen 28:14). Though weaker and smaller than the other nations Israel was indispensable to God's overall scheme of redemption. God's plan to redeem the world centered in Israel. The history of redemption began not with Adam or Noah or Moses, but with Abraham.

God had a threefold purpose in the election of Israel. *First,* Israel was to be the recipient and guardian of God's special revelation to the world (Heb 1:1-3). *Second,* Israel was to be the channel through which the Redeemer was to enter the stream of human history. *Third,* Israel was to be God's servant (Is 44:1-2) and witness (Is 43:10) in the midst of the nations.

The election of Israel was not an end in itself, but a means to an end. Election not only confers privilege; it involves responsibility as well. God dealt with His covenant people both in grace and in judgment. In either case Israel was a witness to the nations. When obedient, Israel was delivered from the hand of its enemies and thus became a witness to the saving power of Jehovah (Ps 66:1-7; Is 52:10). When disobedient, Israel came under the judgment of God and became a witness to the moral character of Jehovah, who is righteous in all His ways and holy in all His works (Ps 145:17). Whether God dealt with Israel in grace or in judgment, it was always with the expectation that His name would be declared throughout the earth (Ex 9:16; Ps 67:1-2).

The Psalms are replete with references to God's worldwide rule and His ultimate purpose to extend His kingdom to the ends of the earth. "Ask of me, and I shall give thee the heathen for thine inheritance, and the uttermost parts of the earth for thy possession" (Ps 2:8). The Messiah will have dominion from sea to sea and from the river to the ends of the earth; and all kings will fall down before Him and all nations will serve Him (Ps 72:8, 11).

What was the message of the prophetic books? "Whether we study the words of the early prophets, Elijah, Amos, and Hosea, or the Messianic hope voiced in the time of Isaiah, we find a missionary message in God's announced purpose in Israel and in His love and purpose, which, reaching beyond Israel, seeks to bless all men."[1]

Isaiah has more to say about salvation than has any other Old Testament prophet. Frequently Jehovah is referred to as

---

1. Edmund F. Cook, *The Missionary Message of the Bible* (Nashville: Publishing House M.E. Church, South, 1924), p. 33.

the Savior and Redeemer, the Holy One of Israel (43:3; 49:7; 54:5). Israel was to be a light to the Gentiles. Through Israel God was to reach out in saving power to the other nations. "I will also give thee for a light to the Gentiles, that thou mayest be my salvation unto the end of the earth" (49:6). Jehovah claims to be the only God (45:22) and the only Savior (43:11) in the world. As such He makes His appeal not only to Israel, His covenant people, but also to the heathen nations. "Look unto me, and be ye saved, all the ends of the earth; for I am God, and there is none else" (45:22). The temple in Jerusalem was to be a house of prayer for all nations (56:6-7) and God's glory was to be declared among the nations (66:19).

Jeremiah spoke of a day when all nations will gather in Jerusalem (3:17). Habakkuk predicted that the time will come when the knowledge of God will cover the earth as waters cover the sea (2:14). Through Malachi, the last of the prophets, God said: "From the rising of the sun even unto the going down of the same my name shall be great among the Gentiles; and in every place incense shall be offered unto my name" (1:11).

Coming to the New Testament we find the idea of mission on almost every page. The note of universality is clearly sounded in the opening words of the Lord's Prayer: "Our Father which art in heaven, Hallowed be thy name. Thy kingdom come. Thy will be done in earth, as it is in heaven" (Mt 6:9-10). Commenting on this passage one writer says: "Before we pray for the daily bread on which our physical life depends, or the forgiveness of sins on which our spiritual life depends, we are to pray for the worldwide hallowing of God's name, the worldwide coming of God's kingdom, and the worldwide doing of God's will."[2]

Jesus' favorite title for Himself was not "Son of Abraham" or "Son of David," but "Son of Man." By adopting this title He indicated the universality of His mission and message. It is true that in the beginning of His ministry He claimed to be

2. Egbert W. Smith, *The Desire of All Nations* (New York: Richard R. Smith, 1930), p. 7.

sent only to the lost sheep of the house of Israel, but it was only right and proper that the offer of the kingdom first be made to Israel. When Israel rejected both the king and the kingdom, He began to speak in wider and more universal terms.

Nowhere is the universal character of Jesus' mission clearer than in His teaching concerning the kingdom. It was to be virtually closed to the wealthy (Lk 18:25) and the worldly-wise (Mt 11:25), but wide open to the meek (Mt 5:5), to the poor (Lk 6:20), and even to the publicans and harlots if they repented (Mt 21:32). It was to be a spiritual kingdom (Lk 17:21), universal in scope (Mt 25:31-36), cosmopolitan in composition (Mt 8:11), and eternal in duration (Lk 1:33). It was to be founded on truth, not power (John 8:31-32); governed by love, not law (Rom 13:8-10); dedicated to peace, not war (John 18:33-38). Its rulers were to be servants, not lords (Mt 20:25-28). Its citizens were to be meek, merciful, peaceful, and forgiving (Mt 5:5-11).

According to Jesus, the field was the world (Mt 13:38) and the kingdom was to extend to the ends of the earth (Acts 1:8). By His death He drew all men to Himself (John 12:32), and by His resurrection and ascension He triumphed over all the powers of death and hell (Eph 1:20-23; Col 2:14-15). His last command was to preach the gospel to every creature and to make disciples of all nations (Mt 28:19-20).

What about the other books of the New Testament? "The rest of the Bible is but the continued carrying out of the Great Commission: first, the record in Acts of the ever-widening missionary travels; second, the 21 epistles to ever-multiplying missionary churches and converts; and third, the prophetic picture in the Revelation of the world-wide success of missionary effort."[3]

The Acts of the Apostles occupies a strategic place in the New Testament canon. It forms a bridge between the Gospels, which are biographical and deal with the ministry of Christ, and the Epistles, which are hortatory and deal with the life of

3. Ibid., p. 4.

the church. Without the Book of Acts we should know nothing of the origin of the churches to which the Epistles were addressed.

The key verse is Acts 1:8: "But ye shall receive power, after that the Holy Ghost is come upon you: and ye shall be witnesses unto me both in Jerusalem, and in all Judea, and in Samaria, and unto the uttermost part of the earth." The book divides into three clearly defined parts and traces the expansion of Christianity in concentric circles, beginning with Jerusalem (1-8), progressing to Judea and Samaria (8-12), extending ultimately to the ends of the earth (13-28). The two important words are "power" and "witnesses." These two words form the motif for the entire book. The resurrection made the disciples witnesses; Pentecost provided them with the power to make their witness effective.

Luke, the author, is concerned only with those events which contributed directly or indirectly to the spread of the gospel and the growth of the church. The book begins with 120 timid disciples in an upper room in Jerusalem and ends thirty years later with vibrant Christian communities in all the major cities in the eastern half of the empire.

The missionary motif is evident in the Epistles also. Most of them were written by Paul, who was both a missionary and a theologian. He was a better missionary because he was a theologian, and he was a better theologian because he was a missionary. As a theologian he emphasized the *truth* of the gospel (Gal 2:14). As a missionary he emphasized the *power* of the gospel (Rom 1:16). These two things are needed if the world is to believe the gospel: a declaration of truth and a demonstration of power. Paul brings them together in 1 Corinthians 2:1-5.

We usually think of Romans as a profound theological treatise on the gospel which Paul called "my gospel" (e.g., 2:16). Its original purpose, however, was not theological but missionary. That comes out in chapter 1 (vv. 8-15) and again in chapter 15 (vv. 23-33). So successful had been Paul's missionary labors in the eastern half of the empire that he could report: "From Jerusalem, and round about unto Illyricum, I have fully preached the gospel of Christ" (15:19). Now he had his eyes set on Spain and wanted Rome to replace Antioch as his base of operations in that part of the world. He hoped that the church in Rome would give him the kind of support he had previously received from the church in Antioch. That was the real reason for his writing the Epistle to the Romans, though most commentators seem to have missed the point.

In Romans 9-11 Paul gives his philosophy of history. Here he deals with the election, rejection, and restoration of Israel. Certainly these three chapters are missionary in their thrust. Through Israel's rejection of the Messiah salvation is come to the Gentiles, for now "there is no difference between the Jew and the Greek: for the same Lord over all is rich unto all that call upon him. For whosoever shall call upon the name of the Lord shall be saved" (10:12-13).

Paul goes on to pose four questions: "How then shall they call on him in whom they have not believed? and how shall they believe in him of whom they have not heard? and how shall they hear without a preacher? And how shall they preach except they be sent?" (10:14-15). As for Israel, in spite of her unbelief and her rejection by God, the day will come when "all Israel shall be saved" (11:26).

Most of Paul's letters were written to mission churches which he himself had helped to establish, or to missionary colleagues (Timothy and Titus) who had been associated with him in his missionary work. Philippians was Paul's bread-and-butter letter to a young mission church, thanking them for their financial support in the spread of the gospel. The first letter to the Corinthians was written to correct the abuses peculiar to a young church in a pagan environment. Colossians was written to warn against the dangers of syncretism. Hebrews, though probably not of Pauline origin, warns Christian converts not to apostatize in the face of persecution. All of these epistles deal with problems that are distinctly missionary in character and can be fully and correctly understood only in that context.

How about the Revelation? It is preeminently a missionary book because it describes the ultimate triumph of the Christian cause and the destruction of the demonic power structures which through the centuries have opposed God and oppressed man. When Jesus gave the Great Commission, it was tantamount to a declaration of war on the powers of evil; and the struggle between the kingdom of light and the kingdom of darkness is clearly seen in four places in the Book of Acts—chapters 8, 13, 16, and 19—where there is a power struggle between the messengers of the cross and the emissaries of Satan. On each occasion the power of God proved to be greater than the power of the devil.

Jesus made it clear that the power struggle will continue until the gospel is preached in *all* the world; at that time the end will come (Mt 24:14). Will the risen and exalted Lord ever realize His missionary purpose for the world? The answer is found in the Book of Revelation. He surely will, for in the depiction of the first worship scene in heaven, the redeemed sing a new song, saying: "Thou art worthy to take the book, and to open the seals thereof; for thou wast slain, and hast redeemed us to God by thy blood out of every kindred, and tongue, and people, and nation" (Rev 5:19).

To make disciples of all nations—that is the church's task, and what a task it has turned out to be! Can the church in its own strength win the victory and bring in the kingdom? Certainly not! It has therefore been given a hope to go with the task. That hope is the second advent, and it is with this stupendous event that the Book of Revelation is concerned.

Jesus Christ will come again, this time in power and glory, to rapture the church, to judge the world, and to establish the kingdom. In the process He will avenge the blood of the martyrs, answer the prayers of His long-suffering saints, and vindicate the faith and patience of His followers. Then shall be heard the shout of triumph for which the church has waited, lo, these many centuries: "The kingdoms of this world are become the kingdoms of our Lord, and of His Christ; and he shall reign for ever and ever" (Rev 11:15).

The new Jerusalem is not to be the home of Israel or the church alone, but of the nations as well; for "the nations of them which are saved shall walk in the light of it: and the kings of the earth do bring their glory and honor into it"

(Rev 21:24). The tree of life will yield its fruit every month, and the leaves of the tree will be for the healing of the nations (Rev 22:2).

The last great summons in the book is a summons to salvation: "And the Spirit and the bride say, Come. And let him that heareth say, Come. And let him that is athirst come. And whosoever will, let him take the water of life freely" (Rev 22:17).

There is no doubt about it. "The Bible is a missionary book from start to finish. Its theme is the great movement of God to man, in creation, in incarnation, in redemption, in sanctification and eternal salvation, a movement involving Father, Son, and Holy Spirit, a distinctly purposive movement, not just *a* mission but *the* mission of God in history from the beginning to the end."[4]

---

4. Douglas Webster, *Local Church and World Mission* (London: SCM Press, 1963), p. 53.

CHAPTER 3

The Gospel
A Missionary Message

The word *gospel* means good news—any kind of good news, religious or otherwise; but in the New Testament it has theological connotations and refers to the Good News of salvation in Christ.

The word is used in various ways. In Romans 1:1 it is the gospel of God. In Romans 1:16 it is the gospel of Christ. In Romans 2:16 it is Paul's gospel. There is no contradiction here. God is the author of the gospel. Christ is the theme of the gospel. Man is the recipient of the gospel.

The Content of the Message

The gospel is God's Good News concerning Christ, who is its central theme. To preach the gospel is to preach Christ; to preach Christ is to preach the gospel. It was said of the early disciples that they "went everywhere preaching the word" (Acts 8:4), but the very next verse says that Philip went down to Samaria and "preached Christ" to the people. Later, in the same chapter, when Philip encountered the Ethiopian eunuch, he "preached unto him Jesus" (v. 35). Paul concludes his address in the synagogue at Antioch (in Pisidia) with these words: "Be it known unto you therefore, men and brethren, that through *this man* is preached unto you the forgiveness of sins: and *by him* all that believe are justified from all things, from which ye could not be justified by the law of Moses" (Acts 13:38-39).

As a theological term the word *gospel* means many things. In its narrowest sense it means John 3:16, John 14:1, Matthew 11:28, and Romans 10:9. In its widest connotation it includes *all* that Jesus taught His disciples (Mt 28:20), including the Sermon on the Mount, the Olivet Discourse, the Parables of the Kingdom, and the Discourse at the Last Supper. Reduced to its simplest meaning it refers to the death and resurrection of Christ. Paul makes this clear in 1 Corinthians 15:1-4: "Moreover, brethren, I declare unto you the gospel which I preached unto you, which also ye have received, and wherein ye stand; By which also ye are saved, if ye keep in memory what I preached unto you, unless ye have believed in vain. For I delivered unto you first of all that which I also received, how that Christ died for our sins according to the scriptures; and that he was buried, and that he rose again the third day according to the scriptures."

The death and resurrection of Christ constitute the core of the gospel message. We may preach more but we dare not preach less. Paul wrote to the Corinthians: "I determined not to know any thing among you, save Jesus Christ, *and him crucified*" (1 Cor 2:2). To believe in Christ is not only to believe in His person but also in His work. Rightly understood the work of Christ includes two unique events: His atoning death and His bodily resurrection. He died, Peter wrote, "the just for the unjust, that he might bring us to God" (1 Pet 3:18). Paul says He "was delivered for our offences, and was raised again for our justification" (Rom 4:25).

One does not have to believe all of the Thirty-nine Articles of the Church of England in order to be saved; but he must believe the core of the gospel, the death and resurrection of Christ (Rom 10:9; 1 Thess 4:14).

The Teachings of Christ

At first glance it might appear that Jesus' message was intended only for the Jews. When He sent out the Twelve He told them they were to go to the lost sheep of the house of Israel, and He warned them against sharing the message with the Gentiles, or even the Samaritans.

These instructions appear to completely preclude the Gentiles, but we must bear in mind that this was a particular mission with an immediate and limited goal. Jesus had to begin *somewhere*, and the most natural place to begin was with His own people. To have sent the apostles *at that time* on a worldwide preaching mission would have been premature and would have served no purpose. What message did they have *at that time* for the Gentile world? Obviously, none. The offer of the messianic kingdom had to be made first to God's covenant people. If they rejected the offer, they would forfeit their prior claim to both the covenant and the promises. What is more, their rejection of the kingdom would involve the death of the King. This would open the way for the gospel to be preached to the Gentiles (Rom 11:25).

Jesus' treatment of the Syrophoenician woman is the strangest episode in His ministry. On the surface it seems that Jesus was completely out of character. His remark, "It is not meet to take the children's bread, and to cast it to dogs" (Mt 15:26), seems uncharacteristically callous. But Mark in his Gospel adds a significant word not found in Matthew: "Let the children *first* be fed" (Mk 7:27). This places the whole episode in an entirely different light. Even here Jesus implies that the Gentiles were to be included. It was simply a matter of time.

It seems clear from the Gospel of John that Jesus thought of His mission in worldwide terms. The word *kosmos* (world) is used seventy-seven times. The opening verses set the tone for the entire book. "That was the true Light, which lighteth every man that cometh into the world. He was in the world, and the world was made by him, and the world knew him not" (1:9-10). John the Baptist pointed Him out as the Lamb of God who takes away the sin of the world (1:29). The Samaritans acknowledged Him not simply as the Messiah of Israel but as the Savior of the world (4:42).

Equally clear are the sayings of Jesus Himself. He said: "God sent not his Son into the world to condemn the world; but that the world through him might be saved" (John 3:17). He claimed to be "the light of the world" (8:12). He also claimed to be "the bread of life," and He promised that He would give this bread "for the life of the world" (6:51). Referring to His death Jesus said: "And I, if I be lifted up from the earth, will draw all men unto me" (12:32). He promised to send the Holy Spirit to convict the world (John 16:8). He prayed that through the witness of the disciples the world might come to a knowledge of the one true God (John 17:21-23).

In His parable of the wheat and the tares Jesus declared that "the field is the world" (Mt 13:38). The temple, He said, was intended to be a house of prayer for all nations, not the Jews only (Mk 11:17).

The significant turning point in the ministry of Christ was His death and resurrection. All four Gospels give prominence to these two events. Having obtained by His death and resurrection eternal redemption (Heb 9:12) for the sins of the whole world (1 John 2:2), Jesus Christ is now the "Savior of the world" (1 John 4:14) and the "heir of all things" (Heb 1:2). As a reward for His life of perfect obedience He was exalted by God to His own right hand (Phil 2:9-11), far above all principality and power and might and dominion (Eph 1:21).

The clearest statement of all is found in the Great Commission, which is given in five different forms (Mt 28:18-20; Mk 16:15-18; Lk 24:45-49; John 20:19-23; Acts 1:4-8). The substance, however, is the same. During the forty days between the resurrection and the ascension Jesus continued His instruction concerning the kingdom of God (Acts 1:3). It is safe to assume that the Great Commission was a major part of that instruction. The earliest announcement came on Easter Day (John 20:19-23); the last one occurred on Ascension Day (Acts 1:8). On the first occasion Jesus said, "As my Father hath sent me, even so send I you" (John 20:21). Matthew's version is the fullest and the clearest: "All power is given unto me in heaven and in earth. Go ye therefore, and teach all nations, baptizing them in the name of the Father, and of the Son, and of the Holy Ghost; Teaching them to observe all things whatsoever I have commanded you: and, lo, I am with you alway, even unto the end of the world" (Mt 28:18-20).

There was never any doubt in Jesus' mind that the Great Commission *could* be carried out. Indeed, He declared that the gospel of the kingdom *shall* be preached in all the world for a witness to all nations, and only then shall the end come (Mt 24:14).

The Universal Appeal of the Gospel

The great word of the gospel is "whosoever." It was used by Jesus (John 3:16), Paul (Rom 10:13), and John (Rev 22:17). The gospel is based on two great truths: that God loved the world (John 3:16) and that Christ died for all (2 Cor 5:15). In God's sight there is no difference between the Jew and the Greek, for "the same Lord over all is rich unto all that call upon him. For whosoever shall call upon the name of the Lord shall be saved" (Rom 10:12-13).

Not only did the gospel appeal to men of all races; it appealed likewise to men of all classes. Jews and Gentiles in all walks of life and at all levels of society were welcomed as full members of the Christian church. Therefore Paul boasted that in Christ there is neither Jew nor Greek, there is neither slave nor free, there is neither male nor female; all are one in Christ (Gal 3:28).

The enemies of Christianity faulted it for gathering converts from the dregs of humanity. Celsus described the Christians as "worthless, contemptible people, idiots, slaves, poor women and children."[1] We make no apology in answer to the accusation. Jesus led the way by fraternizing with publicans and sinners and appealing to the burdened and oppressed (Mt 11:28). The church was the only institution in the Roman world whose doors were open to high and low, rich and poor, slave and free. Even in sophisticated Corinth most of the believers came from the lower strata of society. Paul wrote: "Ye see your calling, brethren, how that not many wise men after

---

1. Origen, *Contra Celsum* 3. 49-55.

the flesh, not many mighty, not many noble, are called: But God hath chosen the foolish things of the world to confound the wise" (1 Cor 1:26-27).

The gospel message has universal appeal for four basic reasons: (1) The fact of sin is universal (Rom 3:23). (2) The offer of salvation is universal (1 Tim 2:4). (3) The command to repent is universal (Acts 17:30). (4) The invitation to believe is universal (Rom 10:9-11).

Evangelism in the Early Church

The Great Commission as recorded in Acts 1:8 is as explicit as words can make it, but somehow the apostles did not quite get the point. They were instructed to begin in Jerusalem and from there to take the gospel to Judea, to Samaria, and to the ends of the earth. As far as Jerusalem was concerned, they did an excellent job. In no time at all they were accused of filling Jerusalem with the doctrine (Acts 5:28). Alas, they were unwilling to leave Jerusalem. Even when the other disciples fled at the martyrdom of Stephen, the apostles remained behind in Jerusalem (Acts 8:1). Instead of taking the gospel to the ends of the earth, as Jesus commanded, they stayed close to Jerusalem; if they did leave the city, it was only for short visits. Even those who were scattered abroad preached the gospel to the Jews only (Acts 11:19). It was with the greatest reluctance that the church leaders, including Peter, finally agreed to include the Gentiles in their plans (Acts 10:9-20).

Philip broke the ice by going to Samaria (Acts 8). Peter set a precedent when he preached the gospel to Cornelius (Acts 10). It was not until Paul came on the scene, however, that the gospel was made available to the Gentiles on anything like a universal scale. Paul came to be known as the Apostle to the Gentiles. He declared himself to be a debtor both to the Greeks and to the barbarians, both to the wise and to the unwise (Rom 1:14).

At the same time Paul, like his Master before him, regarded the Jews as having prior claim on the gospel. The gospel, he said, is the power of God to salvation to everyone who believes, to the Jew first, and also to the Greek (Rom 1:16). Wherever in his travels he found a synagogue, he made that the center of his activity. Only when the Jews rejected the message did he turn to the Gentiles. To the recalcitrant Jews in Antioch (in Pisidia) he said: "It was necessary that the word of God should *first* have been spoken to you: but seeing ye put it from you, and judge yourselves unworthy of everlasting life, lo, we turn to the Gentiles" (Acts 13:46). When the Jews in Corinth resorted to opposition and blasphemy, Paul shook his raiment and said: "Your blood be upon your own heads; I am clean: from henceforth I will go unto the Gentiles" (Acts 18:6). His last appeal, at the close of his ministry, was to the Jews in Rome. When they too rejected his message, he said: "Be it known therefore unto you, that the salvation of God is sent unto the Gentiles, and that they will hear it" (Acts 28:28).

Almost single-handedly Paul laid the foundation of the church in the Roman Empire. In twelve to fifteen years he planted churches in four of the most important provinces: Galatia, Asia, Macedonia, and Achaia. Though an orthodox Jew, he was a native of Tarsus, one of the more cosmopolitan cities of the empire. His rabbinical training at the feet of Gamaliel in Jerusalem, coupled with his background as a Roman citizen, made him uniquely qualified to become the Apostle to the Gentiles. So thoroughly had Paul achieved his objective that he was able to remind the Colossians that his gospel had been preached "to every creature which is under heaven" (Col 1:23).

The Proclamation of the Gospel

The gospel involves certain propositional truths concerning Jesus Christ. Before one can exercise saving faith, he must understand the meaning of those truths. Paul says: "Faith cometh by hearing, and hearing by the word of God" (Rom 10:17). Only shortly before this he had asked the critical questions: "How then shall they call on him in whom they have not believed? and how shall they believe in him of whom they have not heard? and how shall they hear without a preacher?" (Rom 10:14).

Cornelius was instructed by the angel: "Send men to Joppa, and call for Simon, whose surname is Peter; who shall tell thee words, whereby thou and all thy house shall be saved" (Acts 11:13-14). The apostles were not content to "live" the gospel. The truths were too profound and the issues too momentous to expect that men would be able to understand them without some sort of explanation. The truths had to be articulated, line upon line and precept upon precept, to enable men to understand. Only then could they really "believe in Christ." Hence the emphasis in the Acts and in the Epistles of Paul on the importance of preaching. Presence evangelism is right and proper and has its place, but it is no substitute for proclamation evangelism.

The proclamation of the gospel should not be left to professionals—elders, deacons, pastors, or even apostles. Laity and clergy must be involved in the spread of the Good News. A superficial reading of the Acts of the Apostles might give the impression that in the early church all the evangelistic work was done by professionals, full-time workers as we would call them. That is not so. The missionary enterprise of the early church was based on two assumptions that everyone took for granted: (1) the chief task of the church is the evangelization of the world; (2) the responsibility for carrying out this task rests with every member of the Christian community.

In those early times there was no organized missionary endeavor such as characterized later periods. Certainly there was nothing comparable to the hundreds of missionary agencies we have today. For the most part the gospel was spread by laymen who in the course of their daily life "gossiped the gospel" with friends, relatives, neighbors, and even strangers. Will Durant observed: "Nearly every convert, with the ardor of a revolutionary, made himself an office of propaganda."[2] Edward Gibbon wrote: "It became the most sacred duty of a

2. Will Durant, *Story of Civilization*, vol. 3, *Caesar and Christ* (New York: Simon and Schuster, 1944), p. 602.

new convert to diffuse among his friends and relations the inestimable blessing which he had received."[3]

This kind of evangelism is characteristic of the "preaching" found in the New Testament. Both John the Baptist and Jesus came "preaching." Peter and the other apostles preached so extensively in Jerusalem that they were accused of "filling the city" with their doctrine (Acts 5:28). What shall be said about the apostle Paul, the greatest preacher of them all? Immediately upon his conversion he preached Christ in the synagogue at Damascus (Acts 9:20). A whole generation later we find him in his own hired house in Rome preaching the kingdom of God (Acts 28:31). To the Corinthians he wrote: "Christ sent me not to baptize, but to preach" (1 Cor 1:17). Again he said: "Woe is unto me, if I preach not the gospel" (1 Cor 9:16).

If the gospel is indeed a missionary message, the church, which is the custodian of the gospel, is duty bound to share it with the world. "The very heart of the gospel lies in its mission to the world. The church's main task is to stand on the street corners of the world and shout: 'The good news has come.'"[4]

---

3. Edward Gibbon, *The Decline and Fall of the Roman Empire* (New York: Harcourt, Brace and World, 1960), p. 147.

4. John E. Skoglund, *To the Whole Creation* (Valley Forge, PA; Judson Press, 1962), p. 94.

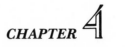

The Church
A Witnessing Community

What is the function of the Christian church? To this question there are many answers. The church has several functions, which include worship, teaching, fellowship, service, and witness; but the *prime* function of the church, at least in her mundane existence, is witness. The church will have all eternity to worship and serve and praise. Witness is the one activity that is restricted to her life here on the earth. Her witness is to extend to the ends of the earth (Acts 1:8) and to continue to the end of time (Mt 28:20).

The Nature of the Church

The validity of the Christian mission is rooted, as we saw in the first chapter, in the character of God. There is also a sense in which it is related to the nature of the church.

What is the essential nature of the church? What kind of community did God intend the church to be? Harry Boer in *Pentecost and Missions* has this to say:

The Great Commission derives its meaning and power wholly and exclusively from the Pentecost event. It does so in terms of a deeply organic relationship. . . . The proclamation of the

45

gospel is therefore not one activity among many in which the
Church of the New Testament engages; but it is her basic, her
essential activity. It is for this reason that the preaching office
is the central office in the Church.[1]

When Emil Brunner said that the church exists by mission
as fire exists by burning, he expressed a profound truth not
always recognized even by missionary-minded churches. Lesslie Newbigin said that a church that has lost its missionary
vision no longer has the right to call itself a New Testament
church. Such a church has denied the faith and betrayed its
trust.

There are two mandates in Scripture, the cultural mandate
given by God in Genesis and the gospel mandate given by
Christ in the Gospels. One is physical, the other spiritual; but
the underlying principle is the same in both, namely, reproduction. God's word to Adam was: "Be fruitful, and multiply,
and replenish the earth" (Gen 1:28). Jesus said to the apostles:
"Go into all the world and make disciples of all nations."

In the physical realm the law of reproduction runs through
all of nature—plant life, animal life, and human life. Adam
was endowed with a God-given instinct called sexuality, and
he reproduced without instruction, inducement, or coercion,
which means that he reproduced instinctively, naturally, and
spontaneously. This was the law of his physical nature. The
same is true of the church in the spiritual realm. She too is
expected to reproduce instinctively and spontaneously by virtue of the life and power of the Holy Spirit within her. Proclamation is, therefore, an essential expression of her life.

When a given activity is not accidental to the life of an organism, but an essential manifestation of it, that activity may be
said to be an expression of the organism's being. It is an expression of its deepest nature. It is in this way that we must regard
the witnessing activity of the Church. The kerygmatic activity
of the Church is an expression of the law that governs the

1. Harry R. Boer, *Pentecost and Missions* (Grand Rapids: Eerdmans, 1961), p. 119.

discharge of her task in the world. This law is the Great Commission. At Pentecost this law went into effect. The Great Commission is the mandate to witness universally. . . . At Pentecost the Church became a witnessing institute because the coming of the Spirit made Christ's mandate an organic part of her being, an essential expression of her life.[2]

The modern missionary movement, dating back to William Carey, had its theological roots in the Great Commission. That has been the driving force, but this was not true of the early church. It is noteworthy that, after Christ's announcement in Acts 1:8, the Great Commission is not mentioned in the Acts of the Apostles, not because the Great Commission was not important, but because it was not necessary to mention it. The church had no need of an external command. She was constituted a witnessing community by the nature conferred on her at Pentecost; after that it was natural and inevitable that she should witness. In Acts 2:4 we read: "And they were all filled with the Holy Ghost, and began to speak with other tongues, as the Spirit gave them utterance." It is a thousand pities that Bible expositors have had such a hassle with the "tongues" and have thereby missed the real point of the passage. "They were all filled with the Holy Ghost, and began to speak . . ."—and they kept on speaking, speaking, speaking, until they had "filled Jerusalem with [their] doctrine" (Acts 5:28).

So powerful was the witnessing of the early church that it provoked severe reaction and repression on the part of the Sanhedrin. Peter and John were commanded not to speak or teach in the name of Jesus. Their reply was significant: "We *cannot* but speak the things which we have seen and heard" (Acts 4:18-20). When the Sanhedrin forbade the apostles to witness, they were asking them to violate a basic law of their nature. Hence their reply: "We *cannot* but speak."

In Acts 1:8 Jesus said: "Ye shall be witnesses unto me." Not "Ye shall witness," but "Ye shall *be* witnesses." He was not in-

2. Ibid., pp. 119-20.

terested so much in what they would *do*, but in what they would *be*. What they would do would grow out of what they were. In the Gospels He had said, "I will make you fishers of men," not "I will teach you to fish." I will *make* you *fishers*. After that they would have the *desire* to fish, the *urge* to fish, the *ability* to fish.

Asking a Spirit-filled believer to refrain from witnessing is like asking a duck to stay away from water or a bird to stop flying. They will do this only if restrained by some outside force. Left to themselves they will gravitate to the water or soar into the sky because that is an expression of the nature they possess.

John Skoglund, speaking of the church's obligation to share the gospel with the world, says:

> We cannot escape this obligation by ignoring it; neither can we delegate it to others. Church and mission are one, and cannot in any way be broken apart. To break them apart is to make both cripples. . . . Mission can never be thought of as only one of the marks of the church. It is *the* mark of the church. All other so-called marks, if legitimate, are but explication of mission. The only power which Christ promises to the church is the power to witness. All other church activities are derived from this essential task and must be judged by it.[3]

To what is the Christian church to give her witness? The New Testament leaves us in no doubt on this point. The early disciples were living witnesses to the central fact of the gospel: the resurrection. Indeed, one of the qualifications of an apostle was that he be a witness of the resurrection (Acts 1:22; 1 Cor 9:1); and wherever the apostles went, they preached Jesus and the resurrection (Acts 4:2).

In their preaching the apostles emphasized the death of Christ, but that was not the *burden* of their testimony. The fact of Christ's death was never in dispute. That Jesus died under Pontius Pilate is simply a fact of history. Nobody denied it. But

3. John E. Skoglund, *To the Whole Creation* (Valley Forge, PA: Judson Press, 1962), p. 94.

the resurrection was a different matter. Such an unlikely event was regarded by many as "incredible" (Acts 26:8). Consequently it called for unusually strong evidential support.

The Truth of the Resurrection

Christianity stands or falls with the resurrection. Deny the resurrection, and the virgin birth, instead of being a beautiful miracle, becomes a biological monstrosity. Deny the resurrection, and the words of Christ, instead of being the truth of God, become the pious platitudes of a provincial prophet. Deny the resurrection, and the miracles of Christ, instead of being the natural outgoing of omnipotence, become the legerdemain of a master magician. Deny the resurrection, and the death of Christ, instead of being the atoning death of the Lamb of God slain before the foundation of the world (Rev 13:8), becomes the untimely death of a religious reformer. This being so, it is impossible to exaggerate the importance of the resurrection.

The twelve apostles spent three years with Jesus. During that time they saw Him under every conceivable circumstance of life, and in the end even doubting Thomas came to the conclusion that He was the Son of God (John 20:28). They witnessed every miracle He performed; they heard every major address He gave. They were persuaded that both His words and His works were from God. They had no need to invent a story or propound a theory, still less to concoct a lie. As for the resurrection, it was no "Easter story" that they believed. As far as they were concerned, it was an indisputable fact that Jesus rose from the dead. They were there when it happened. They saw the empty tomb. They met the risen Lord, and they were completely transformed as a result of the experience.

The apostles had no axe to grind. They had nothing to gain and everything to lose by preaching Jesus and the resurrection. In the biblical record there is nothing to suggest that these men were consciously propagating a false report. They were simple, open-minded, warmhearted individuals who had seen the glory of God in the face of Jesus Christ and had a consuming passion to share the good news with the rest of the world. To the end they regarded themselves as witnesses—no more, no less. Even Paul said toward the close of his life: "Having therefore obtained help of God, I continue unto this day, *witnessing* both to small and great . . . That Christ should suffer, and that he should be the first that should rise from the dead, and should shew light unto the people, and to the Gentiles" (Acts 26:22-23).

The resurrection of Jesus Christ from the dead is the greatest event in the history of mankind. No other person, before or since, ever rose from the dead in the power of an endless life. This one event, more than anything else, places Jesus Christ in a class by Himself. It was the supreme event that changed the course of history and ushered in the kingdom age. The fact that it was totally unexpected on the part of the disciples served only to enhance its significance in their eyes. For the first time it dawned on them that Jesus was in truth what He claimed to be, the resurrection and the life (John 11:25).

The apostles believed that in the gospel of Christ they possessed the truth concerning God, man, sin, and salvation. This is what Paul called "the truth of the gospel" (Gal 2:5). Paul believed that when he preached the gospel he was preaching the truth. So sure was he of his conviction in this matter that he pronounced a curse on anyone, man or angel, who dared to preach what he called "another gospel" (Gal 1:8).

There is a direct connection between the resurrection and the Christian mission. It is expressed most clearly in the words of the angel to Mary Magdalene and the other Mary on the first Easter day: "Fear not ye: for I know that ye seek Jesus, which was crucified. He is not here; for he is risen, as he said. Come, see the place where the Lord lay. And go quickly, and tell his disciples that he is risen from the dead" (Mt 28:5-7). *Come and see*; *go and tell*. The connection is obvious, essential, and imperative. *Come and see*. That is the challenge to investigate. *Go and tell*. That is the command to propagate.

To accept the challenge but refuse the command is a contradiction. One cannot seriously believe in the resurrection without at the same time believing in the Christian mission. Archbishop Richard Whately said on one occasion: "If your religion is false you ought to change it. If it is true you ought to propagate it." The early church would have agreed with Stephen Neill, who said: "The only reason for being a Christian is the overwhelming conviction that the Christian faith is true."[4]

Someone has said that the difference between Hollywood and the Christian church is that Hollywood presents fiction as if it were truth, while the church often presents truth as if it were fiction. Even in our pulpits we have men of the cloth who no longer believe in the bodily resurrection of Jesus; yet they go on year after year celebrating the "Easter story," which they regard as a beautiful myth.

The Power of the Resurrection

It is fair to ask: Is a declaration of the truth *all* there is to the gospel message, especially when that message is presented for the first time to non-Christian people who have no previous knowledge of the Christian faith? Is truth *always* self-authenticating, or does it need to be backed up with a demonstration of power? Paul admits that the Jews demand a sign and the Greeks seek after wisdom (1 Cor 1:22). When he preached the gospel, he endeavored to make it relevant to both groups. He wrote: "We preach Christ crucified, unto the Jews a stumblingblock, and unto the Greeks foolishness; but unto them which are called, both Jews and Greeks, Christ the *power* of God, and the *wisdom* of God" (1 Cor 1:23-24).

Western thought is concerned primarily with truth and the Western mind is intrigued by reason. Hence our emphasis on logic. We vainly imagine that if we can win the argument we will make a convert. The Oriental mind, on the other hand, is not particularly interested in truth, still less in logic. System-

4. Stephen Neill, *Call to Mission* (Philadelphia: Fortress Press, 1970), p. 10.

atic theology as taught in our seminaries has emphasized truth to the neglect of power. The Oriental religions have emphasized power to the neglect of truth. Both are right in what they include but wrong in what they omit. Religion to be viable must be vital as well as valid.

Paul was both a theologian and a missionary. The missionary in him kept him from being completely occupied with truth; the theologian in him kept him from being enamored solely of power. As a missionary-theologian he maintained a healthy balance between truth and power. He spoke not only of the "truth of the gospel" (Gal 2:5), but also of the "power of the gospel" (Rom 1:16). "I am not ashamed," he said, "of the gospel of Christ, for it is the power of God unto salvation to every one that believeth." This he wrote to the Christians in Rome, the center of imperial power.

Paul brings the two concepts together in the opening verses of 1 Corinthians 2: "And I, brethren, when I came to you, came not with excellency of speech or of wisdom, *declaring* unto you the testimony of God. . . . And my speech and my preaching was not with enticing words of man's wisdom, but in *demonstration* of the Spirit and of power" (vv. 1, 4).

The New Testament has as much to say about the power of the gospel as about the truth of the gospel. It all began with the ministry of Christ, who was anointed with the Holy Spirit and power (Acts 10:38). Paul says that He was "declared to be the Son of God with power, according to the spirit of holiness, by the resurrection from the dead" (Rom 1:4). Jesus claimed to possess all power in heaven and in earth, including power to forgive sins (Mk 2:10), to impart eternal life (John 17:2), and to execute judgment (John 5:22, 27). When He sent out the Twelve and again when He sent out the Seventy, He gave them power over evil spirits and all manner of disease (Lk 9:1; 10:1, 9, 17). When He commissioned His apostles, He warned them to stay in the city of Jerusalem until they were endued with power from on high (Lk 24:49). Again, in the same connection, He said: "Ye shall receive power, after that the Holy Ghost is come upon you: and ye shall be witnesses unto me both in Jerusalem, and in all Judea, and in Samaria, and unto the uttermost part of the earth" (Acts 1:8).

Stephen is described as a man "full of faith and power" (Acts 6:8). So evident was the power of God in the apostles' hands that Simon Magus offered them money, saying, "Give me also this power" (Acts 8:19). Luke informs us that "with great power gave the apostles witness of the resurrection of the Lord Jesus" (Acts 4:33). Paul declared that the "kingdom of God is not in word, but in power" (1 Cor 4:20). He prayed for the Ephesian believers that they might know "the exceeding greatness of his [God's] power to us-ward who believe, according to the working of his mighty power, which he wrought in Christ, when he raised him from the dead" (Eph 1:19-20). Paul's own ambition was that he might know Christ "and the power of his resurrection" (Phil 3:10).

All Bible expositors agree that Acts 1:8 is the key to the entire book. In that verse there are two words which go a long way towards explaining the contents of the book: *power* and *witnesses*. The apostles were witnesses, and their witness was effective because it was accompanied by power. Throughout the book the apostles speak and act with conscious power. They heal the sick (3:1-10) and cast out demons (16:16-18). One word from Peter, and Ananias and Sapphira fall down dead at his feet (5:1-10). Peter pronounced a curse on Simon Magus in Samaria (8:20-23) and Paul cursed Elymas in Cyprus (13:10-12) with devastating results. In Joppa Peter raised Dorcas from the dead (9:36-42). At the first church council the whole assembly listened to Paul and Barnabas as they related the signs and wonders which God had wrought through them among the Gentiles (15:12). It is no exaggeration to say with J. B. Phillips that the Book of Acts "throbs with power."

The gospel is not only the truth of God (Col 1:5); it is also the power of God (Rom 1:16). Both ideas were present in the kind of witness described in the Book of Acts. "And the people with one accord gave heed unto those things which Philip spake, *hearing* and *seeing* the miracles which he did" (Acts 8:6). There was a similar situation at the outset of Paul's first missionary journey. "Then the deputy, when he *saw* what was

done, believed, being astonished at the *doctrine* of the Lord"
(Acts 13:12). In both instances it was a demonstration of power
that led to the acceptance of the truth.

We see these two ideas—a declaration of the truth and a
demonstration of power—brought together in the ministry of
Christ. Jesus said to a man sick of the palsy: "Thy sins be
forgiven thee" (Mk 2:5). The scribes standing by objected, asking: "Why doth this man thus speak blasphemies? Who can
forgive sins but God only?" So Jesus answered: "Why reason
ye these things in your hearts? Whether is it easier to say to
the sick of the palsy, Thy sins be forgiven thee; or to say, Arise,
and take up thy bed, and walk? But that ye may know that
the Son of man hath power on earth to forgive sins (he saith
to the sick of the palsy,) I say unto thee, Arise, and take up
thy bed, and go thy way into thine house."

The initial statement made by Jesus was a declaration of
truth, but because it was in the realm of the metaphysical it
could not be proved—or disproved. It was not susceptible to
tangible proof. But the miracle that followed was different.
That the scribes could see and understand, and they could
not refute it. When the declaration of truth was followed by
a demonstration of power, the people were all amazed and
glorified God, saying, "We never saw it on this fashion."

Rightly or wrongly the people of the Third World identify
religion with power. They live close to nature and the veil
between the seen and the unseen worlds is very thin. The
natural and the supernatural are both a very real part of human existence. As a result the people of the Third World do
not have all the "hang-ups" that we in the West have when it
comes to religious experience. In their traditional religions
they have the medicine man, the witch doctor, and the sorcerer, to whom they go in times of drought, disease, disaster,
and death.

Some years ago an extended family of forty persons in Vietnam was about to embrace Christianity as a group, when the
patriarch of the family said to the missionary: "Before we
make up our minds we have one more question. Can your
God make rain?" That sums it up in a nutshell. If religion

works, the people want it. If it does not work, they do not want it. They are not interested in a religion that promises them "pie in the sky by and by." They want something which will meet their needs and solve their problems here and now.

Sarvepalli Radhakrishnan, former president of India, addressing a group of missionaries said quite frankly: "It seems to me that you Christians are a group of ordinary people making extraordinary claims for yourselves." The missionaries replied: "We don't make these claims for ourselves; we make them for Christ." The president was not impressed.

A missionary sailing up the Nile River was sharing Christ with a devout Muslim when the latter turned and asked: "Tell me, what can your Jesus do that our Mohammed cannot?" Again the emphasis is on power and not truth. The world has heard millions of sermons in the present century, many of them containing the truth of the gospel. *What the world is waiting to see is a demonstration of the power of the gospel.*

In the first century the church had access to only one form of power, the power of the Holy Spirit referred to so often in the New Testament. By the latter half of the second century the church was running out of spiritual power and substituted ecclesiastical power for it. In the first century Paul said: "Where the Spirit of the Lord is, there is liberty" (2 Cor 3:17). By the end of the second century it was said: "Where the bishop is, there is the church." In the third century, between A.D. 260 and 300, pagans flocked into the church in large numbers, bringing their paganism as well as their patrimony, and the church became one of the wealthiest institutions in the empire. Thus the church acquired another kind of power—economic power. With the conversion of Constantine in the fourth century the church added political power. From that time to this the Christian church, including the Protestant branch, has depended largely on these carnal forms of power. Only in times of great revival has the church regained the spiritual power so characteristic of her life in the first century.

Few organizations have been more successful in the last twenty-five years than Campus Crusade for Christ. First at home and more recently overseas its staff members have achieved results that are the envy of other organizations. How are we to account for their success? All Campus Crusade staff members must go through an orientation program in which the emphasis is on *living* the victorious life. Bill Bright really believes that Christianity is a supernatural religion. He urges his staff members to think supernatural thoughts, make supernatural plans, pray supernatural prayers, and expect supernatural results. And they get them! That explains the phenomenal growth of Campus Crusade. Unfortunately, this emphasis is largely missing in other Christian organizations.

One can hardly deny that Paul was one of the most successful missionaries of all time. Note how he explains his success: "For I will not dare to speak of any of those things which Christ hath not wrought by me, to make the Gentiles obedient, by *word* and *deed*, through mighty signs and wonders, by the *power of the Spirit of God*" (Rom 15:18-19).

It is regrettable that the modern missionary movement, with few exceptions, has failed to demonstrate the *power* as well as the *truth* of the gospel.

Every Christian
A World Christian

The Christian who is a true follower of Christ is a world Christian. By calling he belongs to a universal fellowship—the Christian church. By conviction he shares a universal message—the Christian gospel. By commitment he owes his allegiance to a universal king—Jesus Christ. Of necessity he is part of a universal movement—the Christian mission.

Not all Christians, however, live up to their high calling as world Christians. The vast majority are content to be "national" Christians—American, Canadian, German, or Japanese, as the case may be. Or they may be "denominational" Christians—Presbyterians, Lutherans, Methodists, Baptists. Few are world Christians.

What a World Christian Is

1. *A world Christian is one who acknowledges the universal fatherhood of God.* "In the beginning God created the heaven and the earth" (Gen 1:1). That makes Him the God above all gods—the creator, sustainer, and controller of the universe. The psalmist narrows it down and says: "The earth is the Lord's, and the fulness thereof; the world, and they that dwell

therein" (Ps 24:1). That makes Him the King of the nations and the Father of the human race.

Jesus taught His disciples to pray: "Our Father which art in heaven, Hallowed be thy name" (Mt 6:9). If there is only one Father in heaven, it stands to reason that there can be only one family on earth—the human family. Anthropologists have a way of dividing mankind into races. At one time they spoke of seven races. Later they reduced the number to three. Now it is thirty-two! But whether it is seven, or three, or thirty-two makes no difference to God. As far as He is concerned, there is only one race—the human race.

Paul made this abundantly clear in his address to the philosophers in Athens. "God that made the world and all things therein . . . hath made of one blood all nations of men for to dwell on all the face of the earth . . . For in him we live, and move, and have our being; as certain also of your own poets have said, For we are also his offspring" (Acts 17:24-28).

If this is so, then every man is my brother and every woman is my sister, regardless of race, class, color, culture, or any other human factor. When the question is asked, "Am I my brother's keeper?" I have to answer with a resounding "Yes, I am my brother's keeper." I may live in affluent America and he may live in poverty-stricken Bangladesh. It makes no difference; we are children of the same Father (Eph 4:6) and members of the same family (Eph 3:15). We have a common origin—Adam (1 Cor 15:45-49). We share a common problem—sin (Rom 5:12). We face a common destiny—death (Heb 9:27). These are fundamental, indisputable, unchanging facts that cannot be altered by such incidental factors as ethnic origin, social status, cultural mores, or linguistic differences.

2. *A world Christian is one who acknowledges the universal lordship of Christ.* In our well-meaning but ill-advised manner of speaking we often talk of "making Jesus Lord." No man, not even a Christian, can "make" Jesus Lord. That is something that God did when He raised Him from the dead and set Him at His own right hand, far above all principality and power and might and dominion, and gave Him to be the head over all things to the church (Eph 1:21-22).

Julius Caesar is always the Roman; Socrates is always the Greek; Confucius is always the Chinese; but Jesus Christ is not to be identified with any one race, people, or culture. Pilate referred to Him as the "King of the Jews," but His own favorite title was "Son of Man."

The earliest and simplest creed of the church was summed up in four words: "Jesus Christ is Lord" (Phil 2:11). "Jesus" speaks of His humanity as the Son of Mary. "Christ" refers to His divinity as the Messiah of Israel and the Son of God. Put the two together and you get a unique person—the God-man.

The early church understood this phrase in its widest connotation. Jesus Christ is not only the Head of the church; He is also the Lord of history, the King of the nations. He is the one and only Lord. He occupies a solitary throne. All authority in heaven and on earth has been given to Him (Mt 28:18). Sooner or later all men must come to terms with Him (John 5:28-29); and all nations, large and small, must own His sway (Rev 11:15). He is the Son of God who in the incarnation became the Son of Man that through His death, resurrection, and ascension He might become the only Savior and Sovereign of the world (1 Tim 6:15); and the day is coming when every knee will bow and every tongue confess that Jesus Christ is Lord to the glory of God the Father (Phil 2:10-11).

3. *A world Christian is one who recognizes the cosmopolitan composition of the Christian church*. Jesus came into a divided world. The Greeks, on the basis of culture, divided it into two groups—Greeks and barbarians. The Romans, on the basis of politics, divided it into two groups—citizens and slaves. The Jews, on the basis of religion, divided it into two groups—Jews and Gentiles. It was just too bad for the person who happened to be a barbarian, a slave, or a Gentile. He was beyond the pale and doomed to be a second-class person as long as he lived.

Jesus adamantly refused to endorse such arbitrary, man-made distinctions. He came to seek and to save the lost, and they were found in all races and cultures. For obvious reasons His first offer of the kingdom was made to the Jews, but it was never His intention that the kingdom should be restricted

to them. He scandalized the self-righteous Pharisees by fraternizing with publicans and sinners. He incurred the wrath
of the hierarchy by exposing their hypocrisy. He raised the ire
of His fellow townsmen by giving honorable mention to two
Gentiles in Old Testament history (Lk 4:24-29). When He
died He was fittingly placed between two malefactors, one of
whom He saved—His last majestic act before He expired.

The apostles took their cue from Him. They preached a
new gospel based on the love of God and the death of Christ,
and they practiced what they preached. If God loved the
Greco-Roman world with all its sin, debauchery, and licen-
tiousness, they would do the same. If Christ died for all, they
would gladly open their doors to Jews and Gentiles, scribes
and Pharisees, priests and Levites, rabbis and zealots—any
and all who would embrace the faith.

The disciples were first called Christians at Antioch, the
most cosmopolitan city in the Roman Empire; and the church
was as cosmopolitan as the city. The little mission church in
Philippi was a microcosm of the church universal. Among its
charter members were three persons with little or nothing in
common: the jailor, Lydia, and the slave girl. The jailor was
a callous, uncouth Roman without faith or feeling until the
gospel reached him. Lydia was an aristocratic, prosperous
businesswoman, equally at home in commerce or culture. The
slave girl was a poor, benighted youngster who belonged body
and soul to her unscrupulous masters, whose sole purpose in
life was to make a quick profit. These three found one another
when they found Christ.

Michael Green in *Let the Earth Hear His Voice* has this to say
about the cosmopolitan character of the early church:

> Master and slave ate together. Jew and Greek ate together;
> unparalleled in the ancient world. Their fellowship was so vital
> that their leadership could be drawn from different races and
> cultures and colors and classes. Here was a fellowship in Christ
> which transcended all natural barriers. There was nothing like
> it anywhere—and there isn't still.[1]

1. Michael Green, "Evangelism in the Early Church," in *Let the Earth Hear His Voice*, ed. J. D. Douglas (Minneapolis: World Wide Publications, 1975), p. 175.

4. *A world Christian is one who recognizes the prime importance of the Christian mission.* It is a melancholy fact that after two thousand years of church history two-thirds of the people of the world are still without a knowledge of Jesus Christ. The world Christian is not happy about this sad state of affairs. He knows that the Christian mission rightly begins at Jerusalem, but he also knows that for too long most of our ministry has been to our Jerusalem. He deplores the fact that 90 percent of all full-time Christian workers are located in the Christian world, where churches abound on every hand and where the Bible is a best seller year after year. He knows and deplores the fact that as far as world evangelization is concerned we are not even keeping up with the population explosion in the Third World. He knows and deplores the fact that there are more non-Christians in India and China than there are Christians in the entire world. He knows and deplores the fact that the average church member in the United States gives less than ten dollars per year to home and world missions, which makes it the smallest item in the family budget.

It is for these reasons that the world Christian believes in and is totally committed to the speediest possible evangelization of the world. He will not, he cannot, rest until every member of the human race has had an opportunity to accept or reject the gospel.

5. *A world Christian is one who recognizes his own personal responsibility for all phases of the Christian world mission.* This does not mean that he will necessarily become a full-time professional missionary. He may never go overseas. That is beside the point. By his attitude, understanding, and commitment he will, even here at home, be personally and vitally involved in home and foreign missions.

Being a world Christian is not an empty profession or a token gesture or a passing hobby. It is not a matter of words but of deeds; and the deeds involve much more than making a faith promise at the annual missionary conference, or signing a check once a month, or writing the occasional letter to a missionary in Africa. It is a total commitment to all aspects of the Great Commission as outlined by Jesus Christ. It is total identification with God in the outworking of His redemptive purpose for the world for which Christ died.

What a World Christian Does

1. *A world Christian will seek to increase his knowledge of world affairs.* Americans are among the most parochial people in the world, and this in spite of the fact that there are more college graduates in America than anywhere else in the world. The average American is woefully ignorant of happenings in other parts of the world. When he picks up his daily newspaper, he goes first to the sports section, then to the comics, and then back to the important news on the front page. He seldom bothers to look at the editorial page.

I once asked fifty-four college graduates how many provinces there are in Canada. Only four knew the answer. Any fifth-grade child in Canada could tell you that there are fifty states in the United States. On one occasion I went to the local post office to mail a paperback to Singapore. The postal clerk did not know the airmail rate and consulted the directory, but she could not find Singapore in the directory. When I asked where she was looking, she replied, "Under 'Africa' "! That is typical here in the United States. Other people know ten times more about us than we know about them, yet we do not seem to be at all embarrassed.

Our educational system is doing nothing to improve the situation. A presidential commission made a recent study of the teaching of foreign languages in our schools and reported that "Americans' incompetence in foreign languages is nothing short of scandalous."[2]

Only 15 percent of our high-school students study a foreign language, down from 24 percent in 1965. Only 8 percent of our colleges and universities require a foreign language for admission, down from 34 percent in 1966. This is in stark contrast to the practice in other countries. Japan has an esti-

2. *Chicago Tribune*, 8 November 1979, section 1, p. 11.

mated ten thousand business representatives in the United States, all of whom speak English. There are nine hundred American counterparts in Japan, "only a handful" of whom can speak Japanese.

The world Christian will not be satisfied with that sorry state of affairs. He will make every effort to increase his knowledge of world affairs, not only church and religious affairs but political, economic, and social affairs as well, knowing that they have a direct or indirect bearing on the progress of world missions. Only in this way will he be able to function effectively as a world Christian.

2. *A world Christian will broaden his view of the church.* One of the most powerful forces in organized Christianity in the twentieth century has been the ecumenical movement. An unprecedented number of church mergers have taken place, especially among the "younger" churches of the Third World. In spite of this the average church member in the United States knows little and cares less about what is happening along interdenominational lines. The average Presbyterian has never been inside a Lutheran church except for a funeral service or a union service on Good Friday. The same can be said of Methodists, Baptists, Episcopalians, and others.

When it comes to Christian activity, there are four concentric circles. The inner circle represents the local church; the second, the denomination; the third, the denomination's work overseas; and the fourth, the wider interests of the kingdom in all parts of the world. The interest of the average church member is confined to the activities of the local church; and if he assumes some personal responsibility in that restricted area, he thinks he is doing well. A few energetic souls go farther and embrace in their thoughts the outreach of the denomination here in the United States. A still smaller number, usually members of the missionary committee, have a knowledge of and interest in missions overseas. As for the fourth circle, it is usually unknown or ignored except at ecumenical gatherings; and there it is often equated with church union rather than world mission.

The world Christian, on the other hand, will be a loyal denominational person and will actively support and promote the work of his own church; but he will never equate his church or denomination with the kingdom of God. The largest and strongest denomination is only a small part of the larger entity, the kingdom. The world Christian in his obedience to Christ, the Head of the church universal, will seek *first* the kingdom of God and His righteousness, knowing that if he does this his denomination will not suffer; rather it will grow and prosper.

Moreover, the world Christian will find himself at home in all denominations where the Word of God is honored, Christ is exalted, and the gospel is preached in sincerity and truth. For the world Christian, denominational labels, while they serve a useful purpose in a divided church, are not really very important. He is quite happy to settle for the appellation first employed in the early church at Antioch—Christian. It is enough for him that he is a Christian. That he is also a Presbyterian, a Methodist, or a Baptist is quite incidental.

3. *A world Christian will want to increase his understanding of the Christian mission.* Evangelical churches in North America have an excellent track record when it comes to supporting missions around the world, which they do generously both by their gifts and by their prayers. Not many church members, however, have anything like an adequate understanding of missions—their history, theology, philosophy, and methodology. Their prayers center around American missionaries and their work. They seldom pray for the indigenous churches and their leaders, for the simple reason that they do not know enough about them to pray intelligently.

In the postwar period the Christian mission has entered a new era with new problems, new difficulties, new dangers, new developments, and new prospects. How many home churches know anything about these new conditions? How many evangelicals bother to read even the paperbacks on world missions that have been published in the last decade? Not a single book on any aspect of world missions has become a best seller in recent years. (*Daktar* is an exception, but it is a biography.[3]) This is one reason why publishers, including evangelical publishers, are reluctant to produce books on missions. They know the market and have good reason to believe the books will not sell.

On one occasion I spoke in a church each Sunday for a month. I taught the adult Sunday-school class and preached at the morning worship service. All eight messages were concerned with some aspect of the Christian world mission. The missionary committee bought, and made available, three copies of my paperback, *Winds of Change in the Christian Mission*.[4] They were displayed on a table in the foyer all four Sundays. At the close of the conference the books were still there! The people seemed to enjoy my ministry, but no one was sufficiently interested in missions to *read a book* on the subject. To listen to a presentation of missions is one thing. To make a serious study of missions is quite another.

Is it possible that the people at home do not want to know what is really happening to missions around the world? Why have missions to the Muslim world been so unproductive? What has happened to the church in China? Has the church in India solved the caste problem? How are we to account for the phenomenal growth of the church in Black Africa? What are the advantages and disadvantages of short-term service? Why are so many missionaries dropping out in mid-career? What does it cost to support a family of four in Japan? What percentage of the 2.6 billion people in Asia are professing Christians? What is the greatest problem facing missionaries today? What factors have led the mainline denominations to retrench? What is meant by theological education by extension, contextualization of the gospel, homogeneous units, moratorium on missions, and so on?

4. *A world Christian will enlarge the scope of his prayer life.* He will embrace in his prayers the whole household of faith—Christian believers on all six continents. He will intercede for

3. Viggo Olsen and Jeanette Lockerbie, *Daktar: Diplomat of Bangladesh* (Chicago: Moody, 1973).
4. J. Herbert Kane, *Winds of Change in the Christian Mission* (Chicago: Moody, 1973).

his brothers and sisters in Communist China, the Soviet Union, and other countries where human rights are denied and where religious persecution is the order of the day. He will pray not only for the peace of Jerusalem, but also for the success of the United Nations, on which, humanly speaking, the hopes of the world depend. He will pray for the president of the United States, the president of the World Bank, the commander-in-chief of the NATO forces. In doing so he will be obeying the admonition of Paul in 1 Timothy 2:1-2. He will pray for the church in Ethiopia, in South Africa, and in other countries where military dictatorships and oppressive regimes hold sway. He will pray not only for his own denomination and his own church; he will pray, "Thy kingdom come. Thy will be done on earth as it is in heaven."

Most mission agencies publish a monthly or quarterly prayer bulletin in which they list one strategic prayer request for each day of the month. Tyndale Publishing House in Wheaton, Illinois, publishes a monthly flyer known as *The Church Around the World*. The Lausanne Committee for World Evangelization publishes a quarterly *Prayer Calendar*. Operation Mobilization has made available a set of 52 cards designed to help the intercessor "pray for 52 spiritually needy nations." Each card contains pertinent information regarding the country, population, people, religions, and so forth, and on the back of the card are four or five strategic requests for that particular country. All of these publications are exceedingly helpful to anyone wishing to broaden the scope of his prayer life and at the same time be specific rather than general in his intercession. Some denominations publish their own prayer calendars. One of the finest is the *Mission Yearbook for Prayer and Study* put out by the United Presbyterian Church in the U.S.A. If our prayer life remains narrow and sterile and seldom goes beyond the immediate concerns of the local church and our own family, we can no longer plead ignorance. There is available today ample material to stimulate effective, intelligent prayer on a worldwide scale.

5. *A world Christian will go abroad if opportunity affords.* If he cannot live abroad he will certainly travel as much as he can,

since travel is the finest form of education. While abroad he will see for himself what the Holy Spirit is doing in and through the churches in the Third World. He will thrill to visit South Korea, where six new churches are springing up every day; or Brazil, where three thousand new churches are formed each year; or Africa, where there are five times as many persons at church on Sunday morning as there are members on the rolls.

The world Christian will also be exposed to the privations and persecutions that the national Christians encounter in a predominantly non-Christian community. He will get some idea of what it is like to belong to a tiny, isolated religious minority that makes up only 2 percent of the population. He will be impressed by the lifestyle of the Christians: the simplicity of their faith, the courage of their convictions, the warmth of their love, the depth of their commitment, their patience in the face of persecution and discrimination. He will come to the conclusion that he is seeing *real* New Testament Christians for the first time.

The world Christian will also see firsthand the appalling poverty of the Third World, where hundreds of millions of persons live and die without ever seeing a bar of soap, a toothbrush, a roll of toilet paper, or a cup of clear water. Such sights will make an indelible impression on his mind and he will never be the same again. He will be a different person, less preoccupied with creature comforts, more concerned for the welfare of others, and more determined to do his part, however small, for the betterment of mankind.

6. *A world Christian will change his lifestyle.* Having seen the poverty, disease, and illiteracy of the Third World, he will take more seriously the words of Jesus: "A man's life consisteth not in the abundance of the things which he possesseth" (Lk 12:15). He will learn to get along with less and enjoy it more. He will adopt John Wesley's philosophy of wealth: Make as much as you can. Save as much as you can. Give away as much as you can.

Wesley practiced what he preached. During the first year of his ministry his income was thirty pounds. He lived on twenty-seven and gave the other three to the Lord's work. Later, when his income doubled, he continued to live on twenty-seven pounds and gave the remainder to the Lord. Still later, when he earned ninety pounds a year, he lived on twenty-seven pounds and gave the rest away. It was no idle boast when Wesley declared: "The world is my parish." He was in every sense of the term a world Christian.

A world Christian believes that it is more blessed to give than to receive, to serve than to be served, to endure hardness for Christ's sake than to enjoy pleasure. He is prepared to buy one suit of clothes every two years instead of two suits every year. He will not drive a Mercedes-Benz or even a Cadillac. The money he saves by his frugality he will give away, not as a gesture of charity but as an act of justice. He will be prepared to live at home at the same level as the missionary lives abroad. In this way he will be identifying himself with the people he supports with his gifts and his prayers. He may never be a missionary in name, but in God's sight he will certainly be a missionary at heart.

To help him adjust to this more modest lifestyle the world Christian will find the following books helpful: *Global Living Here and Now*, by James Scherer; *What Do You Say to a Hungry World?* by Stan Mooneyham; and *Rich Christians in an Age of Hunger*, by Ron Sider.[5] No serious-minded Christian can read these books and not be moved to do something about his own lifestyle.

7. *A world Christian will recognize his personal responsibility for world missions.* He is part of the church universal and is vitally concerned with all aspects of that church—its victories and defeats, its trials and tribulations, its schisms and mergers, its leadership and organization, its finances and facilities, its medical and educational institutions. Nothing that concerns the church in the Third World is outside his sphere of interest.

5. James A. Scherer, *Global Living Here and Now* (Cincinnati: Friendship Press, 1974); W. Stanley Mooneyham, *What Do You Say to a Hungry World?* (Waco, TX: Word Books, 1975); Ronald J. Sider, *Rich Christians in an Age of Hunger: A Biblical Study* (Downers Grove, IL: Inter-Varsity, 1977).

When the world Christian reads the morning newspaper or listens to the six o'clock news in the evening, he concentrates on every scrap of information about the Third World. The news may affect the churches there.

Does anyone want to suggest that this idea is far-fetched? If so I would remind him that the children of this world are wiser in their generation than the children of light (Lk 16:8). When the chairman of the board of one of our multinational corporations picks up the *Wall Street Journal* on Monday morning and learns that over the weekend a civil war has broken out in Zaire, what is his first thought? He instinctively thinks of the hundred-million-dollar investment his corporation has in the copper mines in Shaba province. Immediately he calls his agent in Kinshasa to find out what has happened to the Shaba copper mines.

The world Christian recognizes that he belongs to the oldest and greatest "multinational corporation" in the world, the Christian church. When he learns of the civil war in Zaire, his mind turns instinctively to the many missionaries there and the Christian church with its many pastors, evangelists, and Bible women. How are they faring? What about the churches, schools, and hospitals? Have any of them been occupied or destroyed? He is not interested in copper mines; his interest is in the Christian church with its precious human resources, which is a hundred times more important than any financial empire.

The Christian can no longer afford to restrict his interest or understanding to the fifty states that make up our country. According to *U.S. News and World Report* (March 19, 1979), there are now 2.4 million Americans, including military personnel, living abroad; and we have 250,000 foreign students in our universities and colleges, not to mention the business and professional people who reside here more or less permanently. With jet travel and worldwide satellite communications the world has become a "global village." No one, least of all the Christian, should be willing to live any longer with his head in the sand. Every Christian should be a world Christian.

Global Dimension of Missions

The Demographic Dimension

One of the finest things to emerge during the Kennedy administration was the Peace Corps, which got under way in 1961. In the early years the applications came in so fast that there were not enough staff members to process them. By 1968, when the Peace Corps peaked, there were fourteen thousand volunteers in over sixty countries. Since then there has been a steady decline and today the Peace Corps is no longer a separate entity. With four other organizations it is now part of ACTION and its budget has been slashed from $130 million to less than $100 million. By 1979 the number of volunteers had dropped to 6,185. Unless someone can infuse new life into the Peace Corps, it will probably die for lack of support in the next decade.

In sharp contrast is the modern missionary movement, the Protestant branch of which dates back to the formation of the Danish-Halle Mission in 1705. After 275 years it is still going strong and today is larger than ever. In spite of closing doors in various parts of the world there are today more Christian missionaries in more countries than at any other time in the church's two thousand years of history.

World population is now 4.4 billion, with an annual increase of 1.9 percent. Christians of all confessions account for slightly less than 30 percent. They are divided into three great communions: Roman Catholics (750 million), Protestants (400 million), and Eastern Orthodox (150 million). The majority of these are Christian in name rather than in fact. How many qualify as evangelicals is anybody's guess—perhaps as many as 200 million.

The Home Base

The total number of Protestant missionaries is now about 68,500, divided as follows: from North America, 44,500; from the United Kingdom, 4,200; from Europe, 8,800; from the Third World, 8,000; others, 3,000. That figure of 68,500 has increased 22 percent in the past four years. Not all of them, however, are career missionaries. According to the 1980 edition of the *Mission Handbook*,[1] 19.2 percent are short-term missionaries who serve for one, two, or three years and then return home. Some of these, 25 percent to be exact, return later as career missionaries. This means that the short-term program is a fruitful recruiting agency. If the short-termers are not included in the total, the number of career missionaries has decreased slightly in the last decade.

The North American agencies are divided among six associations: The Division of Overseas Ministries (DOM) of the National Council of Churches, 3,899 missionaries; The Canadian Council of Churches Commission on World Concerns, 315 missionaries; The Evangelical Foreign Missions Association (EFMA), 9,517 missionaries; The Interdenominational Foreign Mission Association (IFMA), 6,496 missionaries; The Fellowship of Missions, 1,283 missionaries; The Associated Missions of the International Council of Christian Churches, 214 missionaries. The greatest growth has occurred in the unaffiliated agencies not included in any of the above-mentioned associations. During the past four years they have reported a huge growth from 12,424 to 23,138. These are mostly conservative, or fundamentalist, missions.

1. *Mission Handbook: North American Protestant Ministries Overseas*, ed. Samuel Wilson, 12th ed. (Monrovia, CA: MARC, 1980).

Included in this category are over four hundred sending and supporting agencies, some of them rather new to the scene. The larger ones include the Southern Baptists, with over 3,000 missionaries; Wycliffe Bible Translators, with over 4,200 missionaries; and New Tribes Mission with over 1,400 missionaries.

The mainline denominations in both Canada and the United States have during the last decade greatly reduced their overseas personnel. An exception is the Southern Baptist Board of Foreign Missions, which plans to have 5,000 missionaries on the field by the year 2000. When it comes to evangelism at home and missions overseas, the Southern Baptists are in a class by themselves. Their monthly magazine, *The Commission*, makes exciting reading in a day when others are pulling back. Some denominations are trying to stage a comeback. The Lutheran Church–Missouri Synod recently voted to increase its missionary staff from 170 to 600 by 1990. The smaller, more conservative denominations, such as the Christian and Missionary Alliance, the Conservative Baptists, the Assemblies of God, and the Evangelical Free Church of America, continue to expand steadily.

Missionary recruitment, however, is a continuing problem. Eighteen thousand young people attended the 1979 Urbana Missionary Convention, but how many of them will actually get to the mission field remains to be seen. The record has been disappointing thus far. There seems to be enormous interest in missions, but we have not yet devised a way to convert *interest* into *action*. The short-term program is increasingly popular, especially the summer missionary programs sponsored by a growing number of colleges and seminaries. Literally thousands of students engage in missionary work every summer and almost all of them get a good impression and return home with glowing reports. But in spite of all the interest and enthusiasm the total number of career missionaries is increasing only very slowly. There are now about 36,300 from North America as against 35,000 some years ago.

The older evangelical societies, due to deaths and retirements, are barely holding their own. When the mark of 1,000 members is achieved, it is difficult to go beyond that. At that point a mission seems to reach a plateau and does well to maintain its personnel at that figure. Just to maintain its existing work a mission needs at least 100 new missionaries every year, and very few societies are getting recruits in those numbers.

Some of the younger societies, the Greater Europe Mission for example, which do not yet have retirement problems, are still forging ahead; but their growth will begin to slow down in the near future.

One distressing feature in recent years has been the increasing number of mid-career dropouts. A generation ago it was a rare thing for an experienced missionary at the peak of his efficiency to resign from missionary service. Some were brought home to fill important posts in the home office, but resignations were unusual. Now, however, mid-career dropouts have reached such proportions that some missions are making a special study of this problem to see what can be done to stem the tide.

There are several contributing factors. One is teen-age children who have outgrown the education available to them on the foreign field. With the rapidly deteriorating situation in our high schools, involving drugs, sex, and vandalism, many parents are understandably reluctant to live half a world away while committing their teen-agers to the tender mercies of the school system here in the United States, especially after the sheltered life they have lived in a mission school. Another factor is discouragement. Missionary work is not easy; Stephen Neill has declared it to be the most difficult of all vocations. After fifteen or twenty years in an unresponsive area, it is easy for the missionary to rationalize and say to himself: "I've given fifteen good years to this kind of hard work; now I deserve a change. It's time for somebody else to put his shoulder to the wheel." When the third or fourth furlough rolls around, there is a great temptation for the missionary to quietly settle down in Christian work at home. Another factor is the prevailing mood in American society. An increasing number of persons, women as well as men, become a little tired of the work they have been doing and want a change; and middle life offers an ideal time to launch out on a new career. Another ten years and it may be too late. For these and other reasons we are facing a relatively new phenomenon, the mid-career dropout.

When a person in the homelands decides to change careers in midlife, it is no big deal. No one suffers any great loss. But with the missionary it is different. It takes the average missionary the best part of ten years to *master* the language and to acquire a genuine love for the people and an adequate appreciation for the culture. Just when he is reaching the peak of his effectiveness as a cross-cultural missionary, he decides to stay at home. This represents an irreparable loss to the mission field, especially to the national church leaders who have been infinitely patient with him through the years when he was making all his blunders. When they finally have a missionary who is perfectly at ease with their language and culture, he decides to go home, where his overseas experience and his knowledge of a foreign language will probably never be of any further use to him.

Third World Missions

The Western world may no longer be considered the home base. The younger churches in the Third World have in recent years shown an increasing interest in world evangelization. In some countries the earliest home and foreign missionary societies began about the turn of the century. The National Missionary Society of India was founded in 1905. Korea sent its first missionary to China in 1912. In the last two decades these churches have come a long way, and today they are making a significant contribution to home and foreign missions, especially in the continent of Asia. Most of the countries have their own national missionary fellowship or alliance which is responsible for promoting missions. The Mar Thoma Church of South India has over 250 missionaries working in a cross-cultural situation in the subcontinent of

India. The churches in Indonesia, the Philippines, Japan, Thailand, and Taiwan are all supporting overseas missionaries.

The churches in Africa, for understandable reasons, got a later start than those in Asia; but here too there has been an upsurge in recent years. One example is the Evangelical Missionary Society of the Evangelical Churches of West Africa, which is now supporting 300 national missionaries in Nigeria and other parts of West Africa. In Latin America the same thing is taking place. In country after country the evangelical churches are sending missionaries to other parts of Latin America. Not a few missionaries from Asia are now located in the West where they are either engaging in evangelism and church planting or serving as pastors in Chinese, Japanese, Korean, Filipino, and other ethnic churches. There is one Quechua Indian in Ecuador who wants to come to the United States to evangelize the Navajos! Altogether there are over 8,000 non-Caucasian missionaries now serving on all six continents of the world. The home base is no longer confined to the West. This is one of the most exciting developments in modern missions and augurs well for the future of world evangelization.

Roman Catholic Missions

Roman Catholic missions antedate Protestant missions by several hundred years. Their first missionaries went to China in 1294. Others sailed to the East Indies and the New World about the year 1500. Protestant missions took another two hundred years before getting under way. To this day the Roman Catholic Church has an enormous investment in overseas missions. One big advantage they have over us is that all their missionaries are single and many of them take vows of poverty as well as chastity and obedience. This means that the Roman Catholic Church has at its disposal hundreds of thousands of dedicated men and women who, devoid of family ties, are prepared to go anywhere and to do anything. Some of the religious orders, especially the Jesuits, Franciscans, Dominicans, Augustinians, White Fathers, Divine Word Fathers, and the Maryknollers, have engaged either largely or exclusively in overseas missions. Today Roman Catholic missionaries are to be found in every country and territory that will receive them.

The precise number of Roman Catholic missionaries (called missioners) is difficult to ascertain. Their definition of a missionary differs from ours. In all countries with which the Vatican has a concordat, missionaries are not known as such. They are called priests or religious. For this reason even the U.S. Catholic Mission Council in Washington, D.C., was unable to provide an estimate of the number of workers whom we would regard as missionaries. The best estimate that I have been able to come up with is 65,000. Of these about 6,000 are from the United States, down from a peak of 9,655 in 1968. American missionaries are sent out and supported by 240 missions and orders. This means that only 10 percent of all Roman Catholic missionaries are from the United States, whereas almost 66 percent of all Protestant missionaries are Americans.

World Christianity

Christianity is by definition a missionary religion. One would expect, therefore, that after two thousand years of history the Christian church would have just about completed the task of world evangelization. Alas, this is not so. It is really only in the last two hundred years that most major denominations of Christendom have taken the Great Commission with any degree of seriousness. Kenneth Scott Latourette, for valid reasons, called the nineteenth century "The Great Century" of Christian missions and devoted three volumes of his seven-volume *History of the Expansion of Christianity* to that century.

In spite of the herculean efforts of the last two centuries and the blood, sweat, toil, and tears of hundreds of thousands of faithful, dedicated missionaries, the net results have been far from satisfactory, at least from a numerical point of view. Today Christians make up about 26 percent of the world's population, and the overwhelming majority of these are found in the so-called Christian part of the world, the North Atlantic community. We are not holding our own in the face of the population explosion, especially in the Third World. The percentage of Christians to non-Christians in the world is slowly but steadily declining, and some prophets of doom are predicting that by the year 2000 Christians may account for only 20 percent of the population.

Asia

The vast, teeming continent of Asia has attracted the lion's share of missionaries, both Roman Catholic and Protestant. It was to this part of the world that the first Catholic missionaries went: to China in 1294, to India in 1500, to Japan in 1549, and to the Philippines in 1565. The Protestants did the same, sending their first missionaries to India in 1705, to China in 1807, to Burma in 1813, and to Japan in 1859. After all this time and labor only 3 percent of the people of Asia make any profession of Christianity.

In India only 2.6 percent of the population is Christian. This includes everyone who by his own profession is a Christian—Roman Catholic, Syrian Orthodox, or Protestant. It is estimated that 60 percent of these Christians come from a background of untouchability, which poses a real problem as far as the image of the church is concerned.

When the Communists came to power in China in 1949 there were three million Roman Catholics and one million Protestants out of a population of about 550 million, less than 1 percent of the population. Nobody knows how many Christians there are in China today, but reports indicate that the number will be a pleasant surprise when it becomes known. In Japan there are about one million Christians, two-thirds of whom are Protestants, out of a population of about 116 million.

Christianity has fared much better in other countries such as Korea, Vietnam, the Philippines, and Indonesia. As far as Protestant work is concerned, South Korea is the showcase of Asia, with six new churches coming into existence every day. According to the latest government census, 18 percent of the people listed themselves as Protestants and 4 percent as Roman Catholics. This is slightly higher than church figures.

There are those who think that if the present rate of growth continues, South Korea may be a predominantly Protestant country by the year 2000.

In Indonesia we have done quite well, ending up after almost four hundred years with about 8 percent of the population professing Christianity. The Philippines is the only predominantly Christian country in Asia. The Roman Catholic Church claims about 72 percent of the population, and another 8 percent belong to various Protestant groups, the Philippine Independent Church, and *Iglesia ni Kristo*. In Vietnam the Roman Catholics at one time represented 10 percent of the people. From 1911 to the early fifties the Christian and Missionary Alliance was the only Protestant mission in the country; when they evacuated in 1975, they left behind the Evangelical Church of Vietnam with 60,000 baptized members. In Thailand the going has been unusually difficult. After 150 years of missionary work only one out of every one thousand persons is a professing Christian. Latourette describes Thailand as the most unresponsive of all the countries of East Asia.

Europe

It is obvious to all students of church history that the continent of Europe, once the heartland of Christendom, is no longer a Christian continent. Kenneth Scott Latourette, Bishop Hans Lilje, and other prominent churchmen and historians have warned that Europe is rapidly becoming de-Christianized.

Several factors have been at work. Secularism and humanism were spawned by the Renaissance. German rationalism and higher criticism attempted to undermine the veracity and authority of the Word of God. The failure of the church in Germany to offer more than token resistance to Naziism hardly enhanced the image of Christianity. The Revolution of 1917, the rise of the Soviet Union, and the emergence of Communist governments in Eastern Europe after World War II have imposed severe restrictions on the activities of the church in those countries. The new theology and the new morality espoused by some Protestant leaders in Western Europe have removed the ancient landmarks and left nominal church members in a spiritual vacuum. Vatican II and the rapid changes taking place in the Roman Catholic Church have thrown the faithful into confusion. With papal infallibility being questioned by leading theologians the church is suffering from a crisis of authority. Non-Christian religions from the East, particularly Hinduism and Buddhism with their mysticism and esoteric rites, are attracting a good deal of attention.

An estimated 175 million people in Europe make no profession of religion. Among those who still claim some affiliation with Christianity there are few who take their religion seriously. One poll indicated that 35 percent of the members of the State Church in Germany no longer believe in a personal God. France, though nominally a Roman Catholic country, is the most pagan country in Europe. In England church membership and seminary enrollment are both down. To aggravate the situation most of the university students in France, Germany, and Italy are Marxists, at least by profession. The two largest confessional groups are the Anglicans in England and the Lutherans in Germany and the Scandinavian countries. About 6 percent of the Anglicans and fewer than 5 percent of the Lutherans attend church regularly.

Wayne A. Detzler in *The Changing Church in Europe* points to several bright spots on the European horizon. Since Vatican II the 250 million Roman Catholics in Europe have been encouraged to read the Scriptures for themselves. An estimated 600,000 charismatic Catholics under the leadership of Leo Cardinal Suenens are sharing their spiritual experiences with fellow Catholics, in this way helping to renew and revive the church. Evangelical minorities are experiencing unprecedented growth. Much of this, especially the Berlin Congress on Evangelism in 1966 and the Lausanne Congress on World Evangelization in 1974, is due to the influence of Billy Graham. The Greater Europe Mission in its ten Bible colleges and seminaries has over the past thirty years trained more than 2,000 students, many of whom are now holding positions of great influence in evangelical circles in Europe. The European Evangelical Alliance, embracing fourteen national alliances, is planning for a decade of evangelism. It declared 1980 to be The Year of Mission, with the aim of bringing together West German state churches, free churches, and independent evangelical groups in a concerted evangelistic outreach. There are signs, however faint, that the Holy Spirit is about to move in a mighty way in the churches of Europe. To help forward that work there are today in Europe 2,300 missionaries from North America and another 700 from other parts of the world.

North America

Here in North America we are barely holding our own. The larger, mainline denominations are losing members year after year. These losses are to some extent offset by the Southern Baptists and the smaller but more vigorous conservative churches, most of which show a healthy increase each year. The result is that overall church membership has remained around 63 percent since the 1960s. This includes Jews, Catholics, and Protestants. The situation in Canada is not so favorable. Dennis Oliver, director of Church Growth Canada, estimates that more than half of the population are without church membership of any kind. The bottom has just about dropped out of Sunday-school attendance, especially in the United Church of Canada, which was formed in 1925.

The United States at the present time seems to be enjoying a religious boom. Religious books are selling well. *The Living Bible* sold 20 million copies in ten years, and *Good News for Modern Man*, published by the American Bible Society, has sold well over 50 million copies since its translation of the New Testament first appeared in the mid-sixties. Private Christian schools, considered to have no future ten years ago, are multiplying so rapidly that by 2000 they will have overtaken the public schools. Christian radio stations, now over 800 in number, are increasing by 50 every year. Even Christian TV stations are thriving, with a new one coming into being each month. Bible colleges are bursting at the seams, as are most of the conservative seminaries. Parachurch organizations, such as Campus Crusade for Christ, which has more than 10,000 staff members worldwide, are forging ahead with unprecedented vigor.

There is, however, another side to the picture. Along with an increase in religious interest and fervor there has been a shocking increase in crime, graft, violence, drug addiction, abuse of sex, pornography, divorce, abortion, and a host of other social evils that threaten the survival of Western civilization as we know it. Racial prejudice, economic exploitation, vandalism and cheating in the schools, graft and corruption in politics, shoplifting and petty thievery in the supermarkets and department stores, poor workmanship and absenteeism in the factories, alcoholism and drug addiction, all indicate that American society is rotting on the inside and in only a matter of time the system will collapse. Will Durant in his book, *Caesar and Christ*, gives seven reasons for the fall of Rome. Six of these are already present in American society. Durant goes on to say: "A great civilization is not conquered from without until it has destroyed itself from within."[2] Unless we experience a genuine revival of religion comparable to the Wesleyan Revival in England in the eighteenth century, we may well be on our way to self-destruction. Even evangelical Christians, estimated at between 30 and 40 percent of the population, are not doing much to halt the moral decay. One thing is certain. We are living in a post-Christian era, and unless we repent we may find our candlestick removed (Rev 2:5).

Billy Graham's crusade in South Korea in June, 1973, was one of the highlights of his twenty-five-year career as the world's best-known evangelist. On his return to this country he made this significant statement: "It may be that the center of spiritual gravity is shifting from the West to the East." It may well be.

Latin America

Latin America is one region of the world where evangelical missions are gaining ground, mostly at the expense of the

2. Will Durant, *Story of Civilization*, vol. 3, *Caesar and Christ* (New York: Simon and Schuster, 1944), p. 665.

Roman Catholic Church, which claims about 90 percent of the population but acknowledges that probably not more than 10 percent of its members are faithful in attending mass. It is from these nominal Catholics that the converts have come. Only a tiny minority of the 30 million Indians in Latin America have been won to personal faith in Christ. In 1900 there were barely 50,000 evangelicals (Protestants) in Latin America. By 1950 the number had climbed to 10 million. Today there are close to 30 million. Of these almost 70 percent are Pentecostals, with the largest concentration in Brazil and Chile. It is estimated that the evangelical community is growing at the rate of 10 percent a year, which means that it doubles every eight years.

Protestant missions got a late start in this part of the world. The first missionaries went to South America in the middle of the nineteenth century, but it was not until the 1870s that the movement built up any momentum. The Big Three were the Southern Baptists, the United Methodists, and the United Presbyterians. As might be expected, the overwhelming majority of the missionaries (10,550) are from North America. Missionaries from the United Kingdom number just under 700. European missions are conspicuous by their absence.

Catholic-Protestant relations have been more strained here than in any other major region of the world, for the simple reason that almost all the Protestant converts have come from a Catholic background and the Roman Catholic Church could hardly be expected to look with favor on that kind of "sheep-stealing." Since Vatican II relations between the two groups have greatly improved. Almost half of all American Catholic missionaries are serving in Latin America. They have done much to enhance the image of the Catholic Church as well as to bring about a great measure of rapprochement between Catholics and evangelicals.

The burning issue of the day in Latin America is politics. Dictatorships of the left and the right are almost universal. At present only five countries can be described as democratic, but that situation might well change almost overnight. Consequently Roman Catholic theologians, and some evangelicals as well, are doing their best to formulate a "theology of liberation." Many of them have been influenced by Marxism and some of them have come to believe that only revolution can solve the social and economic problems of the day. At this time they would prefer to have a nonviolent revolution; but should that prove to be impossible, they would not be averse to a violent one. Their preoccupation with revolution, if they are not careful, may lead them, with or without design, to neglect the important work of evangelism and church planting.

Black Africa

In this section we are concerned only with Africa south of the Sahara Desert, often referred to as Black Africa.

Africa attracted more missionaries from more societies in more countries than any other major region of the mission field, and the investment has paid off. More converts have been won to Christ in Africa than in all the rest of the Third World combined.

The population of Black Africa is approximately 350 million, divided among forty-five independent countries. Most of them are small, having a population of fewer than 10 million. The most populous country is Nigeria, with almost 80 million people. Six countries are considered large: Nigeria (80 million), Ethiopia (28 million), South Africa (26 million), Zaire (25 million), Sudan (18 million), and Tanzania (16 million). Together these countries make up half of the 350 million people in Black Africa.

Accurate statistics are difficult to obtain. Moreover, church growth is so rapid that any estimate is out of date in a year or two. Fifty percent of the people of Black Africa are now Christians. They are divided among four major groups: Roman Catholics (75 million), Protestants (70 million), Separatists or Independents (20 million), and Copts (10 million).

The ratio of Christians to the total population differs from region to region. It is highest in south Africa, lowest in west Africa, and somewhere in between in central and east Africa. Countries with the highest ratio of Christians, including Roman Catholics, are: Zaire (86 percent), South Africa

(83 percent), Angola (83 percent), Uganda (71 percent), Kenya (66 percent), Ghana (63 percent), and Nigeria (46 percent).

One of the greatest problems facing church and mission in Africa is the large number of tribal groups—some 860 in all. This means that in Africa Bible translation, publication, and distribution have been very costly in time and money. One of the major accomplishments of modern missions has been the reduction of most of these languages and dialects to writing. The complete Bible is now available in 110 languages, the New Testament in another 150, and portions (at least one book) in still another 268, making a grand total of 528 for the entire continent.

It is estimated that every day some 20,000 Africans abandon animism and embrace Christianity, about half of them joining the Roman Catholics. The reason for this is not hard to discover. Animism has little attraction for an educated person, and more and more Africans are getting a higher education. The African is a devout person with religion imbedded deeply in his soul. He has no great desire to settle for agnosticism, still less for atheism; so he has two choices—Christianity and Islam. More Africans are choosing the former, with the result that Christians now outnumber both animists and Muslims in Black Africa.

This large influx into the church is good and bad at the same time. It is good in that these Africans have had the courage, in the words of Scripture, to turn from darkness to light (Acts 26:18) to serve the living and true God (1 Thess 1:9). It is bad, on the other hand, in that the new converts are so numerous that it is impossible to give them the kind of instruction they need to make them into strong Christians. As a result many of them bring their old practices with them into the church. Dr. George Peters said, after a trip to Africa, that the gravest danger facing the church in Africa is what he called "Christo-paganism." Byang Kato said the same thing. There is a crying need for more Bible teaching in the churches and more theological education in colleges, universities, and seminaries. There are hundreds of small Bible schools in Africa but only a handful of seminaries operating on the post-college level. Evangelicals opened their first seminary only two years ago in the Central African Republic. It uses the French language. A second seminary, using the English language, is now on the drawing boards. It will be located in Kenya.

Christianity has had a greater impact on Africa than on any other region of the Third World. In addition, Western-based multinational corporations are rapidly changing the economic face of Africa. Many Africans fear that their culture will in time be completely swamped by the West. They are making every effort to preserve all that is good. The Christian church is doing the same. It is trying to indigenize its liturgy, music, theology, and other features of its corporate life. In the words of John Mbiti, leading African theologian, "The missionaries Christianized Africa; now it's time for Africans to Africanize Christianity." The next ten or fifteen years will be crucial for the future of Christianity in that part of the world.

The Muslim World

Islam has 700 million adherents, second only to Christianity as the largest religion in the world. Its heartland is in the Middle East; but faithful followers are also found in North Africa, the subcontinent of India, Malaysia, and Indonesia. In recent years large numbers of Muslims have emigrated to Europe, bringing their number there to 25 million.

Muslims are notoriously difficult to win to faith in Christ. Apart from Indonesia the Muslim world has yielded few converts to Christianity. Several Muslim countries are completely closed to Christian missionaries: Saudi Arabia, Syria, Libya, Somalia, Mauritania, and South Yemen. In other countries missionaries are tolerated largely for their humanitarian activities, hospitals, and schools, though these are being gradually phased out since the countries around the Persian Gulf now have the wherewithal to finance their own schools and hospitals.

Several Arab countries are using their fabulous oil revenues to promote the spread of Islam, especially in Black Africa. Plans are under way to construct a powerful international radio station in Mecca to be known as the *Voice of Islam*. It will blanket Africa and the Middle East with the message of Islam. Back of this movement is a consortium of twenty-five Islamic broadcasting organizations.

There is little doubt that Islam is alive with political as well as religious ferment. The Islamic revolution in Iran in 1979 has attracted worldwide attention. It may well spark similar movements in other Muslim countries. All this comes about at a time when mission leaders in the West are "cautiously optimistic" about the future of evangelical missions to the Muslim world.

The Communist World

Some 1.4 billion persons now live under Communism. All suffer some degree of religious persecution. Missionaries are excluded, but national Christians continue to witness cautiously and courageously. In the Soviet Union there are 40 million Orthodox Christians, 5 million evangelicals, 3 million Roman Catholics, and a million Lutherans. The last two groups are found in Estonia, Latvia, and Lithuania. In addition there are 40 million Muslims, who doubtless have clung to their religious beliefs. Religion, therefore, has not been destroyed in the Soviet Union in spite of over sixty years of discrimination, harassment, punishment, prison, exile, and even death.

In the Communist countries of Eastern Europe the degree of religious liberty differs from country to country. The churches in Poland, Yugoslavia, Hungary, and East Germany enjoy a greater measure of freedom than do those in the other four countries (Albania, Bulgaria, Czechoslovakia, Rumania). In Albania, the first declared "atheist state" in the world, there is no religious freedom at all. Contrary to popular opinion, Bibles are published and distributed openly and legally in small quantities behind the Iron Curtain, but never in sufficient numbers to meet the need. In the whole of Russia and the eight other Communist countries in Europe there are not more than 25 million card-carrying Communists; but their influence, through the party apparatus, is out of all proportion to their numbers. In spite of the untiring efforts of these governments to eradicate religion from their societies, the churches have been able to maintain a viable existence. In fact, the most virile churches in all of Europe are found behind the Iron Curtain. The Roman Catholic Church in Poland, which claims 95 percent of the population, has such power over the people that the Communist government must handle the delicate situation very carefully lest it spark a revolution. The enormous outpouring of affection for Pope John Paul II during his visit in June, 1979, was an embarrassment to the Communist rulers. Such a display of religious fervor after thirty years of repression affords ample evidence that the Communists the world over have grossly underestimated the power of religion in the life of a people.

When the Communists came to power in China in 1949, the missionaries were obliged to withdraw. The churches lost all their nonreligious institutions: schools, colleges, hospitals, clinics, and so forth. Though the constitution guarantees religious freedom, the churches were reduced to one service a week. During the Cultural Revolution (1966-1969) all religious organizations, Christian and non-Christian, were destroyed. Following the death of Chairman Mao, and more especially since the United States and China reestablished diplomatic relations in 1979, there has been a greater sense of freedom. The Religious Affairs Bureau of the government and the former Three Self Patriotic Movement of the churches have both been revived. One by one church buildings are being handed back to the Christians, and one report indicates that the government will permit as many churches as were functioning at the beginning of the Cultural Revolution. The "house churches," which have flourished underground since 1966, will doubtless be expected to join, or at least support, the recently reopened churches, which to all appearance will again be controlled by the Three Self Movement. Many members of the "house churches" prefer to remain as they are. They do not trust either the government or the Three Self Movement. They had a very bad experience once before— during the "Hundred Flowers" campaign in 1957—and do not want a repeat performance; and no one can blame them.

In North Korea the institutional church was completely destroyed by the Communists shortly after Korea was divided at the thirty-eighth parallel. North Vietnam allowed about as much religious freedom as did China up to the Cultural Revolution in 1966. South Vietnam fell to the Communists in 1975; since that time there has been a continual erosion of religious freedom, with the usual study sessions, indoctrination classes, labor camps, and prison sentences. In Cuba many of the pastors left with the other refugees who fled to the United States in the early 1960s. Since then things have somewhat stabilized and the churches are enjoying a fair degree of freedom. Cuba is the only Communist country to maintain diplomatic relations with the Vatican.

Both Russian and Chinese Communists have been active in Africa. Both groups have been expelled from some countries where they overplayed their hand. Cuba maintains troops and military advisers in twenty African countries. They have been particularly active in Angola and Ethiopia, both of which are now under a Marxist regime, as is Mozambique. It remains to be seen just how successful the Communists will be in their bid for Africa and to what extent Marxism will be modified to meet the peculiar needs and demands of the African leaders. Missionary and church activities in all three of these countries have been greatly restricted. Church leaders have been executed and others have been imprisoned, but in spite of the difficulties the churches are doing their best to maintain at least a modified form of Christian witness.

CHAPTER *7*

The Social
Dimension

Missionaries have often been criticized for their failure to win converts from the upper classes of society. The criticism is a valid one; but before we place all the blame on the missionaries, we should remember that this is hardly a recent phenomenon. In every age and in every culture the lower classes have responded most readily to the gospel invitation. In the Gospels it was the poor who heard Jesus gladly. This did not seem to worry Jesus. He declared on one occasion that "the poor have the gospel preached to them" (Mt 11:5). He saw nothing wrong with that.

It was the same in the early church. Writing to the Christians in Corinth, Paul said: "Ye see your calling, brethren, how that not many wise men after the flesh, not many mighty, not many noble, are called" (1 Cor 1:26). Surely in a city the size of Corinth there must have been a large number of the wise, the mighty, and the noble; but few of them apparently were among the converts.

The New Testament makes it quite plain that there are two classes in society that are difficult to win to faith in Christ: the wealthy and the wise. Jesus spoke of the first in Luke 18:24-25: "How hardly shall they that have riches enter into the kingdom of God! For it is easier for a camel to go through a needle's eye, than for a rich man to enter into the kingdom of God."

Referring to the problem of converting the wise, Paul said: "Where is the wise? where is the scribe? where is the disputer of this world? hath not God made foolish the wisdom of this world? . . . For the Jews require a sign, and the Greeks seek after wisdom; but we preach Christ crucified, unto the Jews a stumblingblock, and unto the Greeks foolishness" (1 Cor 1:20-23). It is not surprising, therefore, that the early church was made up largely of people who were considered to be neither wealthy nor wise.

The Early Missionaries

The missionaries of the eighteenth and nineteenth centuries, like the early disciples, came for the most part from the lower echelons of society. There were exceptions. The first missionaries to India, members of the Danish-Halle Mission, were graduates of the University of Halle, influenced by such intellectual giants as August Francke and Count Zinzendorf. Bartholomaus Ziegenbalg mastered Tamil in eight months and in three years he completed the translation of the New Testament into that language. He was followed by Philip Frabicius and Christian F. Schwartz who together gave almost one hundred years of service to India, where they laid the foundations of the great Lutheran Church. Schwartz's extraordinary linguistic gifts enabled him to master Tamil, Persian, Hindustani, English, and Hindu-Portuguese. He was a scholar of the first order and made a study of Hindu literature, religion, and mythology. He was equally at home with Indian princes, educated Brahmins, and Europeans of all classes.

The Moravians were the other large body of missionaries in the eighteenth century. They were altogether a different breed of men. Almost without exception they were artisans with no formal theological training. Like the early apostles they were "unlearned and ignorant men" (Acts 4:13). The first two missionaries to Greenland were gravediggers. Of the first two missionaries to the West Indies, one was a potter and the other a carpenter. But they were all men of passion and piety. What they lacked in knowledge they made up in zeal. When a man named Sorensen, in the missionary colony of *Herrnhut* in Germany, was asked if he were ready to go to Labrador, he replied: "Yes, tomorrow, if I am only given a pair of shoes." When they went out, they were given enough money to take them to the port of embarkation. After that they were on their own. They usually earned their way across the ocean by working on the ship, and when they reached their destination they were expected to fend for themselves. They were accompanied by their wives and their little ones. They took with them plants, seeds, and tools with which they established agricultural and industrial missions. For years the Moravians bore the stigma of their humble origin. It was only the unanswerable power of their humility, courage, industry, and endurance that gradually overcame the prejudice of the cultured classes of Europe. Within twenty years the Moravian missionaries started more missions than the Anglicans and Protestants had during the two preceding centuries.

The missionaries of the early nineteenth century were from the same humble background. William Carey, regarded as the "father of modern missions," was a cobbler. William Ward, one of his colleagues, was a printer. From 1815 to 1891 the Church Missionary Society of England sent out 650 missionaries, of whom only 240 were college graduates. The first band of London Missionary Society missionaries sailed for the South Seas in 1796. There were thirty in the party. Only four of them were ordained; the rest were artisans. The majority of the two hundred missionaries who went to Northern Rhodesia (now Zambia) before 1924 possessed a minimum of formal education and were predominantly from a working-class background. Fewer than thirty-five had received a university education.

Mission directors saw to it that the better-educated missionaries went to Asia, particularly India and China, where they would encounter "superior" cultures and more sophisticated "heathen." Since Africa was universally regarded as the Dark Continent and assumed (falsely to be sure) to be devoid of history and civilization, its conversion could safely be entrusted to missionaries with less education. So the mission directors thought.

Scotland and the United States were exceptions to the rule. Scotland, with its long-standing veneration for education, sent out some of the best-educated missionaries of the day. The United States, with its numerous church-founded and church-related colleges, likewise sent out missionaries of unusually high caliber. The first group of missionaries to sail (1812) were all seminary graduates and their wives were ladies of some culture. The Congregational missionaries who began going to the Near East in 1819 were all college graduates. They naturally gravitated into educational missions and founded some of the most prestigious schools and colleges in that part of the world. The American University in Beirut, one of the best-known universities in the Middle East, was founded by Daniel Bliss in 1860 as the Syrian Christian College.

The Student Volunteer Movement began in 1886 under the leadership of John R. Mott. During the next fifty years it was instrumental in sending 20,500 college graduates to the field. Most were from the United States. Never before in history had so many highly educated persons, women as well as men, volunteered for missionary service.

When the Faith Mission Movement got under way in the second half of the nineteenth century, most of the missionaries had only a secondary education. One mission, destined to outshine them all, was the China Inland Mission founded by J. Hudson Taylor in 1865. Taylor openly appealed for persons of "little formal education"—and got them in large numbers, so much so that the China Inland Mission eventually became the largest faith mission in the world in the 1900s.

Between 1850 and 1900 faith missions began to emerge on both sides of the Atlantic, but it was not until the first decades of the twentieth century that the movement achieved full momentum. Today it is still going strong.

Along with the Faith Mission Movement came the Bible School Movement, which began in the United States in the 1880s. The earliest schools were Nyack (1882), Moody (1886),

Ontario (1894), and Providence (1900). These two movements, both of them largely but not exclusively American phenomena, began about the same time and for a hundred years ran a parallel course. Without the Bible-school graduates the faith missions would never have been able to grow as rapidly as they did, and the Bible schools would never have attracted so many students had it not been for the many independent Bible and Baptist churches in the United States. Thus a triangle was established. The independent churches sent their young people to the Bible schools. The Bible schools encouraged their graduates to join the faith missions; and the faith missions looked to the independent churches for financial support, making the triangle complete.

For many decades the faith-mission members were nearly all graduates of the three-year Bible schools. In the postwar period most of the larger schools have become degree-granting colleges, and many of their graduates go on for advanced degrees. A few faith missions continue to accept nondegree personnel, but the overwhelming majority now require at least a college degree and one year of theological studies.

It should be said to the credit of the humble Bible schools of bygone days that they had the good sense to include mission courses in the curriculum, which is more than can be said for the seminaries. Also, it would be unwise to assume that the Bible schools did not produce men and women of high spiritual and intellectual caliber. Many of them became outstanding linguists, field superintendents, general directors, and professors of missions. When the missionary movement of the twentieth century is finally evaluated in the light of history, it will be found that the Bible schools and the faith missions, in spite of their humble origin and image, made a unique contribution to world evangelization.

I cannot resist the temptation to single out one school, the Moody Bible Institute. No other educational institution in the world approaches the record set by Moody. Since the 1890s more than 5,600 Moody alumni have served under 245 mission boards, denominational and interdenominational, in 108 countries of the world; and believe it or not, almost 40 percent of these missionaries, after all these years, *are still in active service*! That God continues to "bless the school that D. L. Moody founded" is seen in the fact that year after year approximately one hundred Moody alumni actually go to the mission field. It is a mind-boggling thought that today one out of every fifteen career missionaries from the United States is an alumnus of Moody Bible Institute!

With the advance of higher education at home and overseas, it is more imperative than ever that the Christian missionary get all the education he possibly can; but in getting it there lurks a danger. At home there is an oversupply of Christian workers with a Ph.D., but there are very few missionaries with a Ph.D. Knowledge and zeal do not mix too well in the human personality. Many a sharp young seminarian has started out with the mission field in mind, only to discover that the more he becomes absorbed in study the less interest he has in sharing his faith. Having gained a B.A., he goes for an M.A.; and after the M.A. he gets a Ph.D. In the meantime his missionary call has evaporated. He is now a *scholar*; and scholars, so he thinks, do not become missionaries. It would really be a waste of time and talent for him to proceed to the mission field where he would not have ample scope for the full use of his many gifts. So he is lost to missions. It is a matter of record that every year a person remains at home in search of more education diminishes his chances of eventually getting to the field. Only those hardy souls who make a determined effort to cultivate and strengthen their missionary call ever get to the mission field.

The Missionary Image

The missionary, probably more than anyone else, has come in for his full share of criticism. From the beginning he has had his supporters, most of them in the church, and his detractors, most of them in the world.

In today's world the missionary does not really make much sense. Ever since the apostle Paul was declared by Festus to be beside himself, the emissaries of the cross have been regarded by the world as fools and fanatics. Nathaniel Peffer, in his book *The Far East*, says: "There was fundamentally something unhealthy and incongruous in the whole mission-ary idea. . . . Only men of inner limitation both intellectually and spiritually, can gratuitously thrust their beliefs on others on the assumption that they alone have the truth."[1]

Two common fallacies appear in this statement. One is that, while it is correct to speak of scientific truth, it is wrong to speak of religious truth. Here everything is relative. One re-ligion is as good as another; so the idea of propagating "the truth" is foolish. The second fallacy is equally harmful: that missionaries in their misguided zeal "ram religion down the throats of the unsuspecting natives." If we have heard that accusation once, we have heard it scores of times. It is simply not true. There may have been the occasional missionary fool-ish enough to use force to secure converts, but I personally have never met him. I very much doubt if more than a hand-ful of missionaries, out of hundreds of thousands, have been guilty of this kind of reprehensible behavior; but the image persists and the accusation is still being made.

Merchants, traders, and other businessmen have their own reasons for disliking the missionaries. The British East India Company went out of its way to make life miserable for them, often denying them passage on their boats and residence in their territories. Its officers made no attempt to conceal their contempt for this undesirable breed of men. Said they:

> The sending out of missionaries into our Eastern possessions is the maddest, most extravagant, most costly, most indefensible project which has ever been suggested by a moonstruck fanatic. Such a scheme is pernicious, imprudent, useless, harmful, dan-gerous, profitless, fantastic. It strikes against all reason and sound policy; it brings the peace and safety of our possessions into peril.

We have come a long way since these caustic words were penned; but to this day the missionary is regarded as a curi-

---

1. Nathaniel Peffer, *The Far East: A Modern History* (Ann Arbor: University of Michigan Press, 1958), p. 118.

osity, a "do-gooder" not quite at home in modern sophisticated society.

The Role of Women

One of the problems facing both American society and the American church is the role of women. As this is being written, the Equal Rights Amendment still requires ratification by three states in order to become law. In the meantime the Women's Liberation Movement seems to be running out of steam. What is not generally known is that women in the missionary movement during the last century have been away ahead of women here at home.

Two of the oldest interdenominational missions, the Zenana Bible and Medical Mission (1852) and the Woman's Union Missionary Society (1860), were restricted to women only! Both missions were founded to meet the appalling needs of the women of Asia, many of whom were not to be seen, much less heard. They had their own quarters in the family compound and were completely sealed off from all members of the opposite sex. It was, therefore, impossible for male missionaries to minister to these women. If they were to be reached with the gospel, women missionaries would have to be available in significant numbers.

In the second half of the twentieth century, when the social changes in Asia brought a greater measure of freedom and there was less need for this kind of specialized agency, both missions opened their membership to men; but for over one hundred years the work at home and overseas was staffed and administered solely by women. Women also played a major role in promoting missions and raising funds in the supporting churches in the homelands.

The vast majority of Protestant missionaries have always been married. Even such pioneers as Adoniram Judson, Robert Morrison, and William Carey were all married men; and their wives shared the hardships of missionary life and work. For quite some time, however, mission boards were reluctant to admit single women. Missionary life was considered to be

62133

too difficult and dangerous for them. Little by little restrictions were lifted, though, and single women were admitted, first as companions for the married women and later on their own merits. Many of them achieved fame as doctors, nurses, and teachers. Ida Scudder founded what is today the outstanding medical institution in India, the Vellore Christian Medical College and Hospital.

Single women pioneered in the education of women and girls. Isabella Thoburn opened the first school for girls in India and had to go from door to door imploring the parents to permit their daughters to attend. One Hindu father, indignant at the idea, said: "You want to educate my daughter? Next you'll want to educate my cow."

Among many other well-known single women missionaries are Amy Carmichael, Clara Swain, Mary Slessor, and Edith Brown. It is impossible to overestimate the contribution these single women made to the missionary movement of the nineteenth and twentieth centuries.

It has often been said that women missionaries outnumber men two to one, three to one, and sometimes even four to one. Women do outnumber men on the mission field, but only by a ratio of 55 to 45 percent of the total.

A generation or two ago most missionaries went to the field single. When my wife and I went to China under the China Inland Mission in 1935, we were the only married couple in a group of over forty recruits. Today most of the new recruits are already married, some of them with one or two children. A sizable number of single women still become missionaries, but their number is decreasing. Only a few single men offer for missionary service and they usually get married within the first few years. Unfortunately there are not enough men to go around; consequently many of the single women are "doomed to single blessedness" for the remainder of their lives. In most cases this does not trouble them. They have counted the cost and are prepared to pay the price. A tiny minority who cannot endure the loneliness drop out, but the majority remain in missionary work and show themselves to be amazingly well-adjusted persons. It is difficult to imagine what the missionary

Lincoln Christian College

movement through the years would have been like without the single women. In some instances they engaged in dangerous pioneer work which should really have been done by men.

Churches in the Third World

The existence of a worldwide communion, which now includes the churches in the Third World, is what William Temple called the "great new fact of our era." The presence of these tens of thousands of churches, large and small, in all parts of Asia, Africa, and Latin America, to say nothing of the island world, is one of the outstanding phenomena of the twentieth century. It is a great pity that the average American church member knows so little about them.

With reference to the churches in the Third World, it should be remembered that the situation differs from continent to continent, and sometimes even from country to country. It is, therefore, unwise to make general statements. The Christian church is the most diversified institution in the world. What is true of the churches in Japan (for our purposes in this book we will regard Japan as a member of the Third World, even though it is a highly developed country) would not be true of those in Irian Jaya, which is just emerging from the Stone Age. What is true of the churches in Africa would not be true of those in Latin America or Oceania. The churches in South Korea are decades ahead of those in other countries of Asia. The general problems pandemic to most of the Third World—illiteracy, poverty, disease, malnutrition—differ from place to place, making it impossible to generalize about the church as a whole in the Third World.

There are hundreds of large, strong, well-organized churches in the larger cities that compare favorably with the finest churches in the West. Actually, some of them are in far better shape than the churches in Western Europe, where attendance runs around 3 to 5 percent of the membership. Having said that, we must point out some characteristics common to most of the "younger" churches.

Compared with the well-attended, well-organized, well-equipped, wealthy churches in American suburbia, the churches in the Third World tend to be weak and small. In Japan the average church has anywhere from thirty-five to fifty members. Large churches are practically unknown. In Africa the situation is reversed. At the Sunday morning worship service there is not even standing room! It is not uncommon for attendance to outnumber membership by three to one.

There is a good deal of talk about urbanization these days, but the majority of the people in the Third World still live in the small towns and villages. Apart from Japan, where 90 percent of the churches are located in the cities, the churches are largely rural in character. This is not surprising when one remembers that there are seven hundred thousand villages in India and well over one million in China. Most of the villages, and many of the smaller towns, are without such amenities as running water, electricity, and public sanitation. Missionaries planning on serving overseas should be aware of the situation and prepared to make certain major changes in their lifestyle.

Many of the churches, through no fault of their own, are poorly organized and inadequately equipped, at least by Western standards. Their buildings are a far cry from the beautiful churches now part of suburban America—churches with wall-to-wall carpeting, expensive draperies, and cushions in the pews. Not one pastor in a hundred enjoys the luxury of a study, in either home or church. As for separate buildings for the Christian education program, they are undreamed of. In some places the Christians meet in the open air. If they have a building, it is usually an ordinary house with one or two walls knocked out to provide additional space. The floor is good old mother earth. There is no ceiling, only a thatched roof. Windows, if they exist at all, are merely openings in the wall. The worshipers may squat on the floor. If seats are available, they are usually backless benches—sawhorses we call them. They do have one advantage; few people can go to sleep on such seats!

When it comes to organization, the Western missionary will have to be patient. Non-Western peoples do not have our flair for organization and see little reason why they should change. Most churches have deacons and elders—after all, the New Testament church had them; but they do not always function very effectively. No minutes are kept; no reports are made; no votes are taken. It is enough to achieve consensus. The treasurer may or may not keep written records, and there is no bank in which to put church funds. If a good business venture presents itself or if the treasurer finds himself in financial straits, he may "borrow" church funds for the occasion with every expectation of replenishing the treasury at a later date. By local custom this is not generally regarded as an improper use of funds, provided the funds are available when the church needs them. Sometimes they are and sometimes they are not. Many a church has come to grief over such a situation.

One other feature should be mentioned. There are always more women than men in the churches. That is true here at home, but it is much more so on the mission field. Throughout the world women seem to be more religious than men. This is true also of the non-Christian religions, with the possible exception of Islam. As a result the Christian churches are composed mostly of women. The men always have their excuses. They are "too busy." Shops are open seven days a week and the shopkeepers would lose money if they closed up in order to attend church. In Japan the men are so closely tied in to their business firms that they are virtual slaves to the system. When Sunday comes, they are just "too tired" to go to church with their wives.

The Church Leaders

Included in the category of church leaders are pastors, evangelists, teachers, and Bible women. To this day the churches in the Third World lack adequately trained leadership. Some of this is the result of missionary activity, which emphasized evangelism and church planting rather than leadership training. John R. Mott said that this has been the greatest weakness of the modern missionary movement. We were so busy winning converts that we forgot to train church leaders. Many of the smaller churches on the mission field, because of their size, are without full-time leaders. Their leaders are dedicated laymen who practice their profession, ply their trade, or work their farms six days a week and on Sunday lead the church services.

Christian centers on the mission field fall into three classifications: preaching points, small congregations, and organized churches. Needless to say, the first two do not have full-time workers; they cannot afford them, nor do they really need them. Very few leaders have had any formal theological training. For example, in Brazil only 10 percent of the fifty-five thousand pastors in the Assemblies of God have had even Bible-school training. Indeed, many of them are either illiterate or only semiliterate. They learned to read only after they became Christians. The only books they possess are a Bible and a hymnbook.

Most of the larger and better-organized churches have a full-time pastor, but he is not always fully or even adequately paid. He is usually an older man with a large family. In Africa each pastor has a garden the produce from which enables the family to live on a very small salary. There is very little, if anything, left over for the education of the children.

Of the full-time pastors only a small number are ordained, and these are usually overworked and underpaid. I was informed on one occasion by the moderator of the great Church of South India that each of their ordained pastors has the oversight of from ten to twenty congregations. The same dearth of ordained pastors is seen in the large churches in Indonesia. The Batak Church with two million members has only two hundred ordained pastors.

Even the ordained pastors are not all seminary graduates. Many of them have not gone beyond Bible school. Few of them have the literary tools we in the United States take for granted. The average pastor could put all his books on an eighteen-inch shelf! In some areas Sunday-school and Christian-education materials are in short supply. Even a one-volume Bible dictionary may not be available. For his Sunday morning sermon the pastor must rely on his meager understanding of the Bible and his own interpretation of the passage. To round out the sermon he will need a lot of stories and illustrations, all of them of local coloration.

Few pastors have the intellectual ability or the theological training to minister to an urban congregation, and fewer still can attract and hold university students and professional people. So the pattern is perpetuated; the churches continue to reach only the lower echelons of society.

The National Christians

In most of the countries of Asia Christians form a very small part of the total population, sometimes as low as 2 or 3 percent. Consequently they have no power of any kind—economic, political, social, or religious. Moreover, in many cases they are the objects of discrimination if not outright persecution. Persecution is not always physical. More often it is social, economic, or political. For example, Christian children may be denied access to local schools, especially at the secondary level. In such circumstances it is easy for the Christians to withdraw from the world around them and adopt a ghetto complex.

Christianity seldom fails to uplift its converts. In no time at all Christians want to read so off they go to school. The literacy rate among Christians, therefore, is always higher than among the population as a whole. With a better education they manage, at least in the second generation, to get better jobs. In this way they gradually but steadily ascend the social ladder. They usually make dependable employees. They are punctual, reliable, honest, and industrious. Absenteeism is lower among them than among other workers.

Minority groups, especially displaced persons, are more open to the gospel than are others. Fewer than 1 percent of the Chinese in China proper became Christians, but among the Chinese in other parts of Southeast Asia 10 percent are professing Christians. Many fine Chinese churches are located in that part of the world. The same is true of the Japanese.

In Japan fewer than 1 percent of the people have embraced the Christian faith; but in Brazil, where they are free from family ties and social pressures, 43 percent are professing Christians.

The Third World churches have their share of "rice Christians," persons who manifest an interest in the gospel for what they can get out of it. This is especially true when natural disasters occur and church workers engage in relief work on a large scale. When it becomes known that the church or the mission has relief funds for distribution, Sunday attendance doubles and triples in no time at all. Most of these people come for the "loaves and fishes"—just as in Jesus' day. They are not to be turned away or even despised on that account, but church officers should keep this in mind when large numbers apply for church membership during a famine year. It may be, however, that in their distress they have sought comfort in religion. Having lost all their earthly possessions, they are psychologically prepared to give more attention to laying up treasure in heaven, hence their interest in religion. This is not wholly bad or wrong. Few if any persons, East or West, ever come to Christ from motives which are 100 percent pure.

First-generation Christians are usually the brightest and the best. Christianity is new to them. They are in the glow of their first love and are prepared to follow Christ wherever He may lead. Second- and third-generation Christians are seldom as zealous as the first. Christianity has lost much of its inner drive. Conversion, if it takes place at all, is a process rather than an event. At this point Christianity tends to become more a matter of culture than conviction.

Many of the older churches in India and Indonesia are thoroughly orthodox in their theology but sadly lacking in active, committed members intent on sharing their faith with their neighbors. If these moribund churches could somehow be revived, there is no telling what influence they could have on the evangelization of Asia and the world. In the 1940s John Sung, the Chinese evangelist, toured the Chinese churches in Southeast Asia, and wherever he went revival broke out. Is this one reason why the Chinese churches in that part of the world are so virile?

I firmly believe that local Christians, not Western missionaries, make the most effective evangelists. If the older churches in the Third World could experience a genuine, heaven-sent revival, the evangelization of the world would no longer be the white man's burden. Then Western missionaries could be employed in other strategic areas such as discipling, theological training, literature production, Christian education, and leadership training.

CHAPTER 8

The Economic Dimension

Money apparently did not play a large role in the evangelization of the world in the first century. Our Lord showed the way. In the words of Paul: "He was rich, yet for your sakes he became poor, that ye through his poverty might be rich" (2 Cor 8:9). He traveled the hills of Judea and Galilee virtually as a penniless preacher, dependent for His daily bread on the charity of others. There was a treasurer in the group, but he managed to mishandle the few funds that were available and finally sold his Master for thirty pieces of silver.

When Jesus sent out the Twelve, He warned them against taking along excess baggage. They were not to provide gold, silver, or brass in their purses, nor scrip for the journey; neither were they to take two coats, or shoes, or even staves (Mt 10:9-10). The reason for such rigid instructions was that the workman is worthy of his hire. They were expected to depend on the hospitality of their converts. This apparently worked quite well, for we read of no complaints when they returned.

When we turn to the Acts of the Apostles, there is the same lack of emphasis on the economic aspect of church life. Peter had to confess: "Silver and gold have I none" (Acts 3:6); but this did not limit him one bit. He had something money could not buy—spiritual power which enabled him to say: "In the name of Jesus of Nazareth rise up and walk." And the lame man did just that.

A lot of changes have taken place in the intervening years. Today the church is larger, the problems greater, and life in general more complex. It is no longer possible for the churches, East or West, to get along on a modest budget.

In the Third World the churches tend to be poor, in some areas *very* poor. This is no reflection on either the gospel or the church. In any society the church is made up of a cross section of that society. If the poor predominate—as they certainly do in most parts of the world—the church will be poor. In India the per capita income is $140 per year, and 40 percent of the people are below the poverty level of $90. This kind of economic deprivation will inevitably be reflected in church life. Moreover, the situation in India is further aggravated by the fact that 60 percent of the Christians come from a background of untouchability. This naturally gives the Indian church an image of poverty.

In my day in China the Bible societies published the Bible in three sizes. They sold for 30 cents, 60 cents, and 90 cents. When I first arrived, I thought the 30-cent Bible was a bargain until I learned that a skilled carpenter made only 26 cents for a ten-hour day. Imagine what would happen to Bible sales in this country if a carpenter, plumber, or electrician had to pay $100 for a copy of the Scriptures.

Why So Many Poor Christians?

To begin with, it must be noted that Christians are not the only poor people in the Third World. The Third World by definition is poor. Some of the countries are so desperately poor that they are now referred to as the Fourth World.[1] At a World Hunger Conference convened in Rome by the United Nations, some countries were regarded as so hopeless from an economic point of view that they were referred to as "bas-

1. The Overseas Development Council lists forty-five countries in this category—countries with less than $300 in annual output per person.

ket cases." Regardless of how much outside help they might receive, the people could not be saved from ultimate starvation.

The poverty of the Fourth World must be seen to be believed. We have poverty here in the United States, but it is a mild form of affluence compared with the poverty in some other countries. Our ghettos are gardens compared with the shantytowns that have grown up around Calcutta, Lima, Mexico City, Nairobi, Cairo, and other metropolitan centers. The poverty level in the United States is between $4,000 and $5,000 a year for a family of four compared with India's $90. Ninety dollars goes much farther in India than it does in the United States; nevertheless, the disparity is enormous.

One of the first things to strike the new missionary when he arrives at his destination is the poverty of the people. He has read about it so it does not come as a complete surprise, but its magnitude is staggering and he wonders if he will ever get used to it. The passage of time inures him to it. This is just as well or he would not be able to stand it.

There is a second reason for the large numbers of poor Christians. The missionaries, by the very nature of their work, attracted the poor. Missionaries were there not simply to save souls, but to minister to the needs of the whole man; and the poor obviously had the greatest needs, both physical and material. Moreover, they had no way of helping themselves. The missionaries, therefore, not only preached the gospel and opened churches; they also opened schools, hospitals, clinics, and other institutions geared to meeting the needs of the people. The poor were naturally attracted to these institutions, especially when they charged little or nothing for their services. Previously no one had cared for their souls or their bodies, and the missionaries seemed like angels from heaven. In India they were the *only* hope of the Untouchables, who had nothing to lose and everything to gain by becoming Christians. Hinduism, of which they were supposed to be a part, offered them absolutely nothing in this life. They did not even have access to the Hindu temple or the village well. They had to live on the outskirts of the village and do the menial tasks that *karma* had assigned to them. Little wonder that they looked upon the missionaries as their sole benefactors and came forward in large numbers to be baptized.

There was still another reason. The missionaries themselves came almost exclusively from the middle class; very few of them were from the aristocracy either of wealth or of culture. They felt more at home with the classes below them than with those above them. They were ill prepared, by practice or profession, to fraternize with the wealthy. Moreover, those who did approach the rich soon found that neither they nor their message was welcome. The rich considered themselves to be self-sufficient and therefore they had no need for religion. The missionaries turned to the poor and they, as always, were willing to listen even if their motives were not always the highest.

How Poverty Affects the Church

Some have maintained that poverty in itself should in no way affect the program of the church. If there are ten families in a church and all are tithers, they ought to be able to support one full-time pastor. In theory this is true, but things seldom work out according to theory. Here in the United States, the most affluent country in the world, not many church members are faithful, consistent tithers. In the mainline denominations the average total giving per member is not more than $150 per year. That is nowhere near a tithe. If we in the United States find it difficult to tithe, how much more do our brothers and sisters overseas! If the Christian family has barely enough to provide one decent meal a day and the children go to bed hungry every night, it is difficult to set aside a tenth of the meager income to support another family.

This grinding poverty is reflected in all aspects of the church's ministry. If they cannot support a pastor, how can they build a church? In a rural area the problem is not so acute. The church does not need money for a building. They can use local materials, primitive though they may be, and donate their time to erect a modest building which will at least shelter them from the elements. In the cities and towns, however, it is a different matter. Materials from elsewhere must be purchased with cash; and the buildings, to be attractive at all, must be fairly substantial. Moreover, the local Christians do not have the skills necessary to erect such a building.

Even where church buildings are available, the furniture and equipment are usually simple, sometimes crude. Lounges, parlors, foyers, Sunday-school rooms, Christian-education equipment, audio-visual aids are all conspicuous by their absence; and chrome kitchens, tiled rest rooms, and other luxury items are unknown.

What is it like to be a Sunday-school superintendent with no printed materials for either students or teachers? The simplest things that we take for granted are not available to many churches in the Third World. About the only thing they have is flannelgraph and that was introduced by, and probably belongs to, the missionary.

Maybe this should not disturb us. Probably we have been too anxious to make churches in our own image. Doubtless we have been too quick to introduce luxury items from the West. We have forgotten that for the first 250 years the early church got along quite nicely without any buildings. At this point it is interesting—and instructive—to learn that the "house churches" that have sprung up in China since the Cultural Revolution of 1966 have neither full-time pastors nor church buildings in which to meet. They are not even organized. They have no set time or place for meetings. They gather in small groups in various homes where the ministry is simple but the fellowship is intimate and precious. Within the past year the government has decided to allow some churches to reopen, but the Christians are by no means certain that they want to return to the churches. Many of them prefer to remain as they are. Is there a lesson here for the Western missionaries? Shall we go on decade after decade saddling the national churches with all the physical and organizational paraphernalia that we consider essential to a good church program? Has the time not come to allow the emerging churches to develop along their own modest lines without all the expensive appurtenances we are accustomed to?

The High Cost of Missionary Support

In the "good old days" a dollar invested in world missions went farther than any other dollar. Both land and labor on the mission field were dirt-cheap. When we set up house in China in the 1930s, we bought a large tree, hired a carpenter at 26 cents a day, gave him a copy of Sears' catalog, and told him to make us a houseful of furniture. When he had finished the job, we called in the painter and he painted the eight pieces of furniture with beautiful black Chinese lacquer. The entire project cost us $15! Later, when our house was destroyed during the Sino-Japanese War, I was able to rebuild it for $20 per room!

Those days are gone forever. Today it costs $20 to buy a decent lock. After World War II, because the price of land was so high, many missions decided to rent instead of building or buying. Now they think they made a mistake, for rents have soared into the stratosphere. In many parts of the world the cost of living is even higher than it is in the United States. In recent years we Americans have been understandably concerned about double-digit inflation. Actually, we are well off compared with other parts of the world. Inflation in Uruguay for the first five months of 1979 was 28 percent. A stripped-down Chevrolet costs $15,000. Gasoline is $4 a gallon in Korea. A head of lettuce sells for $4 in Taiwan. In Ghana a box of corn flakes is $7. A can of shaving cream costs $4 in Thailand. A mission in Brazil paid $2,500 to have a telephone installed. The sum is refundable when the phone is removed.

This unhappy situation has been brought about by two factors: the devaluation of the American dollar and rampant inflation in other countries. Sometimes the American dollar is pegged at a specific figure on the international money market and stays there while the local currency experiences a frightening rate of inflation. Businessmen get around the problem by dealing on the black market. Missionaries, who cannot do this, take a severe beating. The only way to keep their heads above water is for the churches at home to increase their monthly allowance, but the churches themselves are struggling with inflation.

If the Western-based Christian mission is to survive the remainder of the century, the churches at home will have to come to terms with reality and dig deeper into their treasury for the funds needed to support the enterprise. Mission boards on their part will have to cut expenditures to the bone. This means that the missionaries will have to get along on less. In recent years the missionaries have been well cared for by their respective boards, and their quarterly remittances have enabled them to maintain a fairly decent standard of living in the host country. This has been especially true of American missionaries. Those from other countries have not done so well, particularly those from Great Britain.

To outfit a young American missionary couple, who typically take with them as much as they possibly can, may run as high as $5,000. If a car is included—and it usually is—another $5,000 or $6,000 may be required to buy a secondhand car. The time has come for all missionaries to consider seriously the advisability of adopting a simpler lifestyle. There is a great economic disparity between the Western missionary and his counterpart, the national pastor. This is one of the focal points of friction between church and mission today, and something will have to be done if we want to retain the good will of the national church leaders.

Peace Corps volunteers are living in over fifty countries of the world, many of which are among the poorest in what is now called the Fourth World. Peace Corps volunteers are required to live at the level of the people with whom they work, whether in a city, a town, or a village. They are not allowed to own any vehicles, and when they travel they take public transportation. If there is second or third class on the trains, they are expected to take it. In many ways the Peace Corps volunteers have put the missionaries to shame. They have two advantages over the missionaries, however; first, they serve for only twenty-one months; second, only a few of them are married, and fewer still have children. This makes it easier for them to get down to the level of the people. Career missionaries would be endangering their health if they lived at that level for an extended period of time, and their children would be even less likely to survive the ordeal.

Having made that concession, we must acknowledge that many missionaries have had a blind spot at this point and seem to be completely oblivious to the fact that their "affluence" does nothing to ingratiate them with their national co-workers. By adopting a simpler lifestyle they would be walking in the footsteps of Him who was rich but became poor for our sakes that we through His poverty might be rich (2 Cor 8:9). We hear a good deal these days about "incarnational" life, but few who advocate it are prepared to practice it. In all fairness it should be noted that the average missionary lives at a level considerably below that of his friends and relatives in the United States, which means that there are two gaps instead of one: the gap between what the missionary enjoyed at home and what he has on the field; and the gap between his lifestyle on the field and that of the national pastor. The pastors are keenly aware of the second gap; few of them know anything about the first one. In some countries, however, the gap between the missionary and the pastor is rapidly narrowing. The churches in Japan are small but they are wealthy, and their pastors are better paid than the missionaries! It goes without saying that this is the exception, not the rule.

Usually the denominational missionaries are better off than the interdenominational missionaries. The denominational boards have several advantages. They have a "captive" constituency to which they can make direct appeal and expect to get a ready response. The missionaries are "their" missionaries. Moreover, the denominational structure provides a built-in "conveyor belt" on which funds can be sent from the local churches to denominational headquarters in New York, Wheaton, Minneapolis, or Los Angeles. Nobody has to go out to beat the bushes either for funds or for recruits. These boards have a third advantage. They do not require regional offices. All business is transacted from headquarters, so there is no need for them. The faith missions, on the other hand, have a "cultivated" constituency, no conveyor belt, and a need for several regional offices to raise funds and recruit candidates. This is why most denominational missions have much lower administrative costs than the others.

All missions, denominational and undenominational, have some things in common. All find it difficult to raise money for the general fund. It is easier to raise support for candidates going into foreign service than for those going into home missions. It is easier to raise funds for famine relief than for theological education. During the famine in West Africa the Christian and Missionary Alliance appealed for famine relief funds in *The Alliance Witness*. Within three weeks $90,000 had been received at headquarters in New York! If the same appeal had been made for theological education by extension, only a fraction of that amount would have been received, especially in so short a time. The Bangui Evangelical School of Theology in the Central African Republic, sponsored by over one hundred mission boards of the Interdenominational Foreign Mission Association and the Evangelical Foreign Missions Association, has struggled through two years of hand-to-mouth existence with enormous financial needs, whereas one mission of my acquaintance reports that it has more relief funds for Cambodian refugees than it has missionaries to administer them. It is always easier to describe physical need—poverty, disease, malnutrition, hunger—than to depict spiritual need. In fact, it is impossible to portray *spiritual* need in a visual way.

Western mission boards are finding it increasingly difficult to meet their annual budgets. We are facing a major crisis in missionary giving. The mainline denominations faced this a decade ago and were forced to retrench. Now the evangelical missions are having the same problem; they too are facing a financial crisis.

Even the Christian and Missionary Alliance, the most missionary-minded denomination in the country, had difficulty meeting its 1979 budget of over $12 million. President Louis L. King wrote, "Not since the fall of 1975 have we faced a situation as grave as the present one with respect to income for the worldwide ministry of the Christian and Missionary Alliance."[2] To meet the budget they needed an income of almost $2.5 million in the last two months of the year. If the Christian and Missionary Alliance is feeling the financial crunch, it is a safe assumption that other evangelical missions are also feeling it.

The American Bible Society, supported by more denominations than any other Christian organization, had problems in meeting its 1979 budget. As the end of the year approached, it was $500,000 in arrears. As an economy measure it was obliged to close four regional offices in various parts of the country.

The United States and the whole of the Western world are facing an unprecedented financial crisis. In 1979 the price of gold trebled. The energy crisis at home and double-digit inflation, caused in part by the energy crisis and the volatile situation in the Middle East, are eating away at our resources. There is widespread talk of recession. The experts are predicting that sooner or later we Americans must come to terms with reality, pull in our belts, reduce our spending, and curtail our driving in an attempt at conservation. They are even suggesting that unless we can come up with a long-term solution to the energy crisis, the 1980s will see some major changes in the lifestyle of the average American.

Already the churches have begun to feel the pinch. In 1970 it took two hundred members to support one pastor; now it requires three or four hundred members, even though the average salary is only about $15,000 including housing. What does all this mean for the Christian mission? When we remember that the United States provides 66 percent of all Protestant missionaries and contributes almost 75 percent of the total missionary budget, it becomes obvious that what happens here is bound to have a direct bearing on the world mission of the church.

One bright spot is the many missions now emerging in the Third World. Some eight thousand non-Caucasian missionaries are now part of the missionary force, but their countries

2. *The Alliance Witness*, 28 November 1979, p. 32.

are worse off than we are. They too are having horrendous financial and economic problems and cannot be expected to pick up the slack. Their standard of living is already well below ours, so we cannot honestly shift the burden to their shoulders.

If the modern missionary movement is to maintain its momentum, American Christians will have to take their stewardship more seriously. More church members will have to tithe their total income. If that is not enough, we should reduce or eliminate some items in the general budget of the local church in order to increase the missionary budget. In many budgets there are luxury items which could be eliminated or reduced without affecting the total program of the church at all.

One thing we must never do is to reduce our commitment to world missions. We will be greatly assisted in our resolve if we remember—and really believe—the words of Christ: "It is more blessed to give than to receive" (Acts 20:35). If every church member acted on that principle, our financial worries would disappear overnight.

The Political Dimension

The Christian missionary carries with him two important documents, a Bible and a passport. The Bible identifies him as an ambassador for Christ. As such he is a citizen of the world. He is a true internationalist. He represents a universal king, Jesus Christ. He belongs to a universal institution, the Christian church. He carries a universal message, the gospel. In this capacity he would like to think of himself as being above politics, national and international.

The passport, however, links him irrevocably to an earthly kingdom. For better or worse his fortune is bound up with that of his own country. When it performs well, he is happy and proud. When it fails to perform well, he is distressed— sometimes ashamed. Never for a moment can he forget that he is an American, a Canadian, or a Norwegian, as the case may be.

The apostle Paul had no such problem. He was a Roman citizen and ministered within the borders of the Roman Empire. When he got into trouble, he had only to appeal to the local authorities for justice and protection. Modern missionaries have not had it quite so easy. Many of them have been caught in the crossfire of the Sino-Japanese War, the Arab-Israeli War, the Indian-Pakistani War, and civil wars in Nigeria,

121

Zaire, Vietnam, and Burundi, to say nothing of the Cold War, which has a way of heating up from time to time, as recent events in Africa and the Middle East attest.

Political Realities of the New Era

There is no doubt about it; we are living in a new day. The last thirty years have seen more changes in the political configuration of the world than had any previous period. Since the collapse of the colonial system following World War II, the missionary has found himself in a situation greatly different from that of any previous generation. He needs to understand the temper of the times and to recognize certain basic facts, however unpleasant they may be.

1. *The collapse of the colonial system was a good thing even though it brought many problems in its wake.* This is not to say that colonialism was an unmitigated evil, as some militant nationalists would have us believe. It is probably too early to make an ultimate judgment on the colonial system. It had both its good side and its bad side. It must be clearly stated, however, that it was morally wrong and every right-thinking person must applaud its demise. The right of self-determination is one of the inalienable rights of mankind. Every nation wants to be sovereign in the conduct of its own affairs. Good rule is no substitute for home rule. The unholy alliance between the gospel and the gunboat was a millstone around the necks of the missionaries. They can be devoutly thankful that the burden has been lifted. Now they are free to be what they are, ministers of Christ, not agents of Western imperialism.

2. *The collapse of the colonial system has resulted in major changes vis-à-vis the missionary movement.* The role of the missionary has changed. In the past he was the leader; today he is the servant. In most places he is still needed and wanted, but only on condition that he understand his new role. If he is able and willing to fill the servant role, he will find a warm welcome and a fruitful ministry. If not, he might as well remain at home.

The status of the national church has likewise changed. It is no longer under the control of the mission, nor is it part of the "mother" church in the West. It enjoys full autonomy, with its own constitution, organization, and membership. It is in no way subservient to the Western mission that brought it into existence. It has reached maturity; it has declared its independence. Today's missionary must be prepared to work not only *with* the national church, but *under* it.

The image of Christianity has also changed. From the beginning of the modern missionary movement Christianity was identified with colonialism and that fact greatly hindered its acceptance. Now, however, the foreign flags have come down and the gunboats have been withdrawn. Christianity can now chart its own course, develop its own structures, and project its own image without reference to Western missions. Church leaders can now hold their heads high. No longer are they regarded as second-class citizens whose first allegiance is to London, Geneva, or New York.

3. *Very few countries in the Third World are genuine democracies.* Human rights, taken for granted in the West, simply do not exist everywhere. The Third World started out well in this regard; democracy was tried but found wanting. One by one duly elected governments were overthrown, political parties were banned, constitutions were scrapped, and dictatorships were established. Independence, which was supposed to solve all their problems, turned out to be a mirage and the long-suffering people were worse off than before. The white sahibs were replaced by black or brown sahibs. Worse still, economic stagnation and political instability continue to plague the dictatorships. In some parts of the world, governments rise and fall almost with the barometer. The American missionary, with his tradition of an open society with multiparty politics and freedom of speech, press, and assembly, will find life under a dictatorship very irksome.

4. *The American missionary is particularly vulnerable.* There was a time when an American passport was an asset. In some parts of the world today it is more of a liability.

124 TODAY *Global Dimension of Missions*

Since the U.S. emerged as a superpower at the end of World War II, certain conventions of the historical art form—the assault on the U.S. embassy and the U.S.I.A. library, Uncle Sam burning in effigy, YANKEE GO HOME on the compound walls, the vilification of the "paper tiger"—have become so habitual as to represent a rich tradition. Anti-Americanism has grown in direct proportion to American influence in the world.[1]

The United States, as the most powerful country in the world, wields enormous influence; but we have not always used our influence wisely. As a result we sustain a love/hate sort of relationship with the rest of the world. We are at the same time the most loved and the most hated member of the United Nations. We are admired for our open society, our material prosperity, and our advanced technology. We are criticized for our lack of diplomatic finesse, our insensitivity to the feelings and frustrations of weaker states, and our practice of supporting any regime, good or bad, that offers an alternative to Communism.

A nod from our president toppled at least one regime in Asia, that of Ngo Dinh Diem in South Vietnam in 1963. A provocative statement by a United States senator will be carried by satellite to the ends of the earth in a matter of hours. Economic exploitation by our multinational corporations has aroused the ire of the smaller countries, which have no way of competing with what they call "neo-colonialism." The international editions of *Time* and *Newsweek* often carry articles critical of other governments and their leaders. Such articles have been known to lead to anti-American demonstrations in the capitals of the Third World. Between 1945 and 1980 over a hundred of our buildings overseas were burned to the ground, and only the Lord knows how many times our flag has been desecrated by rampaging mobs venting their anti-American feelings. The latest and most violent outburst took place in Iran in 1979-1980.

5. *The Central Intelligence Agency has become the international whipping dog.* The Soviet Union and many Third World gov-

1. *Time*, 14 January 1980, p. 32.

ernments blame the CIA for all the "subversive" activities now going on in various parts of the world. As a result the image of the "ugly American" is uglier than ever. To make matters worse, the CIA has in the past used missionaries in its intelligence-gathering operations, though only a handful were ever on the payroll. In some parts of the world *all* American missionaries are now regarded with suspicion. More than one country has expelled American missionaries, charging that they are CIA agents.

Suggested Strategy for the Future

It is always easier to assess the past than to predict the future. Of one thing we can be sure; the future will be very different from the past. "One age has died; another is striving to be born. We stand in the time of birth-pangs, in which the future still remains obscure."[2] Certain guidelines, however, may help us as we try to chart our course in the years ahead.

1. *The missionary must always remember that he is an ambassador for Jesus Christ, not for Uncle Sam.* His allegiance, therefore, is to a higher power, and one day he will stand before the Judge of all the earth to give account of his stewardship. He is not particularly interested in exporting the American way of life, the capitalist system, or parliamentary democracy, though he may be persuaded that all three are highly desirable. His lodestar is not Robert's *Rules of Order*, or the *Wall Street Journal*, or the *Congressional Record*, but the Holy Scriptures.

The missionary is a world citizen and his chief task is to build the kingdom of God on earth. This being so, he is under no obligation to support, much less defend, all the foreign-policy pronouncements of the United States. Certainly he will abhor the approach which says, "My country, right or wrong." When his country is right, he will in all sincerity try to explain and defend it. When it is wrong, he will have the courage and candor to say so. When his enemies, including the Commu-

2. Stephen Neill, *Colonialism and Christian Missions* (New York: McGraw-Hill, 1966), p. 422.

nists, speak the truth—and they do now and again—he will side with them. Truth does not cease to be truth when it falls from the lips of a Communist.

2. *The missionary must not equate the kingdom of God with any particular political, economic, or social system.* All human systems, including his own, are under the judgment of God and should be evaluated in the light of Holy Scripture. In today's pluralistic world the missionary must be prepared to live and labor under alien systems of various kinds without trying to undermine or overthrow them. He must resist the temptation to jump on every passing bandwagon that promises to solve the political problems of the day.

The nineteenth-century missionaries have been criticized for their failure to distinguish between Christianity and Western civilization and for the naive manner in which they imposed their cultural mores on their converts, making them "little Americans" in the process. Today's critics are in danger of doing in the political realm what the early missionaries did in the cultural realm. One gets the impression from their pronouncements that they are advocating a return to the concept of Manifest Destiny so prevalent in the last century; but instead of the American flag and American commerce, they are advocating the American legal and political systems with their checks and balances, including all the freedoms that have characterized our open society.

3. *The missionary must not assume that Western democracy is for everyone.* Democracy to be effective must be supported by other institutions—a free press, a multiparty system, a universal franchise, and a secret ballot; but what is the use of these things if the majority of the population are illiterate? Moreover, it must be remembered that in many parts of the world the common man has no burning desire to be part of the decision-making process. For centuries he has lived a communal life, with others, usually the tribal chief, making his decisions for him. The same is true of the peasant in his paddy field. He could not care less about free elections and a secret ballot. All he wants is to be left alone with his family and his fields. If his rice bowl is filled twice a day, that is all he asks.

That is one reason why the American forces in South Vietnam did not get more support from the peasantry. They were fighting for something that was not really meaningful to the Vietnamese.

In some countries the social and economic problems are so massive that it is doubtful they can be solved by democratic means. Maybe the best we can hope for in the foreseeable future is a "benign dictatorship." Dictatorship is a dirty word in the North Atlantic community, but not so in other parts of the world. It is simply a matter of fact that many of the developing countries are not ready for democracy. That may come in the future; and when it does, we hope it will be an improvement on our own variety. American democracy, honeycombed with corruption and unable to cope with crime and violence, has little to commend it to the rest of the world. The missionary, then, need not be too greatly disappointed because Western democracy is not sweeping the world.

4. *The missionary in the present situation must be content with whatever freedom is permitted.* He is not likely to be afforded more liberty, religious or civil, than is granted to the nationals. It is both foolish and futile for him to demand what the government is not prepared to grant. It was assumed that the end of the colonial system would bring a full measure of freedom to the oppressed peoples of the Third World, but it has not worked out that way. Of the 161 nations in the world only fifty-one enjoy complete freedom, fifty-five are partially free, and fifty-five have few if any civil rights.[3] Most missionaries are living in the countries in the last two categories.

In Latin America only six countries are genuine democracies, in Asia only five, and in the Middle East only two. India, once the largest democracy in the world, in 1975 outlawed all opposition parties and for some nineteen months jailed many of its leaders. It is feared that Indira Gandhi, returned to power in January, 1980, with an overwhelming majority, may once again assume dictatorial powers. In some countries, Greece and Turkey for example, there is political freedom but

3. *U.S. News and World Report*, 4 February 1980, p. 26.

little religious freedom. In other countries, such as South Korea, Taiwan, the Philippines, and Chile, there is religious freedom but little political freedom. In many countries both forms of freedom are either denied or curtailed. Most Muslim countries and all Communist countries fall into this category.

Today's missionary finds himself in a rapidly changing world as different from the nineteenth century as day is from night. Dictatorships are springing up everywhere. By their very nature they give rise to coups, and coups lead to countercoups. The situation differs from continent to continent and even from country to country. Black Africa, for reasons that are quite understandable, is particularly volatile. Of forty-nine independent states in Africa, forty-three are controlled by dictatorships, military juntas, one-party rule, or a president for life.[4]

Under a repressive regime what is the missionary to do? He has two options: he can mind his own business and continue his work, or he can speak out against the regime and be expelled. Each missionary must make up his own mind what to do in a given situation.

The sympathy of the missionary will most definitely be on the side of the nationals struggling for dignity, liberty, and equality. For a missionary to declare himself in favor of the status quo in a totalitarian state would be disastrous. How and to what extent he should actively aid and abet the cause of freedom is another matter. Before deciding to throw down the gauntlet, he should carefully weigh the immediate as well as the long-range consequences of his action. Should he remain and quietly go about his work, all the while identifying himself with the national aspirations of the oppressed people, or should he publicly oppose the tyrannical regime and bring about his own expulsion?

If he elects to stay, his role will not be an easy one. Like Lot in Sodom, he will feel his righteous soul tormented day after day by the lawless deeds he will have to witness. If he cannot

4. *Chicago Tribune*, 31 May 1977.

remain silent and live with his conscience, he will have to speak out and take the consequences.

If he is expelled, what will happen to the people left behind, Christians and non-Christians, who depend on him for medical and educational facilities? Will the church and the community be better off or worse off without him? If he happens to be the only doctor in a hundred-bed hospital, what will become of his patients when he is gone? It may require more wisdom and courage to remain at his post under difficult and dangerous conditions than to sound off and be expelled from the country.

The Complexity of Third World Politics

The developing countries of the Third World present a confused picture. Their experiment with democracy ended in a fiasco and today they are ruled by dictators who came to power by way of the bullet rather than the ballot. The politicians are in and out of office with all the compulsion and commotion of musical chairs. Governments rise and fall almost overnight, and the traffic moves back and forth between parliament and prison. For the missionary to inject himself into the kaleidoscope of African politics would be an exercise in futility. He has neither the experience nor the expertise to make a worthwhile contribution.

The countries of Latin America gained their independence 160 years ago but are still in the throes of economic, social, and political upheaval. Many Latin American theologians are calling for the overthrow of the unjust power structures and the creation of a new social order. They equate the kingdom of God with socialism; at the same time they denounce capitalism as anti-Christian.[5] They are suggesting that if North American missionaries do not identify with the revolutionary struggles of the oppressed, their days in Latin America are numbered.

5. Gustavo Gutierrez, *A Theology of Liberation*, trans. Caridad Inda, Sr., and John Eagleson (Maryknoll, NY: Orbis Books, 1973), pp. 111-12.

The kind of revolution advocated in Latin America is definitely Marxist. If it succeeds, it will undoubtedly lead to the kind of totalitarian regimes found in China and the Soviet Union. In China the institutional church was completely destroyed during the Cultural Revolution (1966-1969), and in Russia it has been under severe attack for over sixty years. It would be a form of hara-kiri for the American missionary to join the revolutionary forces in Latin America. If the people of Latin America, including the Christian theologians, feel that their only hope is a Marxist revolution, that is their decision and I wish them well; but I have grave fears that the end result will be disastrous for the Christian church. This is not to deny that Latin America has gargantuan problems that may be insoluble by democratic means, but those of us who have lived under a Communist regime can be forgiven if we hesitate to throw in our lot with the Marxists of Latin America.

Several countries of Asia have had a fairly successful history of democracy but in recent years have settled for a modified form of totalitarianism: South Korea, the Philippines, Taiwan, and India. It is a great pity that these countries, which started off with such promise and progress, have found it necessary to resort to dictatorships. In these countries, especially South Korea and the Philippines, there are a large number of American missionaries. Most of them have accepted the status quo with a certain degree of equanimity. A few have spoken out against oppression and have been expelled.

It should be borne in mind that it is the first responsibility of any government to protect its citizens from enemies without and within. When national security is threatened, a government will frequently declare a state of emergency. It may go further and impose martial law, in which case civil rights will be suspended for the duration.

Nobody likes martial law, but we may ask: Is martial law always detrimental to the welfare of the people? Nationals and missionaries coming out of India and the Philippines have testified to the fact that conditions improved after martial law was instituted. The streets were safer, business was better, food was more plentiful, and prices were cheaper. To be sure, certain persons, usually described as "dangerous" or "subversive," went to jail. Opposition parties were outlawed and independent newspapers were banned. At the same time most law-abiding citizens were going about their business with little or no interference. In the case of the Philippines the immediate threat of a Communist takeover was averted. Most Filipinos think that was a good thing. Interestingly enough, in all four countries which have adopted a modified totalitarianism, there has been no curtailment of religious liberty. Some Korean pastors were put in jail, not for carrying on their religious activities, but because they opposed the dictatorial powers of President Park.

In such situations the missionary is likely to find himself on the horns of a dilemma. He may have misgivings about the incumbent regime; on the other hand he may have greater misgivings about a possible successor. He has no guarantee that the rebels, if they come to power, will be less repressive than the regime he finds so offensive.

The words of Malcolm Muggeridge at the Lausanne Congress on World Evangelization in 1974 are appropriate here:

> How many liberations celebrated that led only to servitudes! How many reigns of peace ushered in that only generated new wars! How many liberators installed in power only to become even more ferocious tyrants than those they replaced! The splendid words of the Magnificat go on being fulfilled; the mighty are put down from their seats and the humble and meek exalted, the hungry are filled with good things and the rich sent empty away. Yes, but how soon, how very soon, the humble and meek who have been exalted become mighty, and in their turn fit to be put down! How quickly the poor who have been filled with good things become rich, thereby likewise qualifying to be sent away![6]

A Double Standard

In this respect it is curious to note that some Christian leaders are rightly concerned about the denial of human rights

---

6. Malcolm Muggeridge, "Living Through an Apocalypse," in *Let the Earth Hear His Voice*, ed. J. D. Douglas (Minneapolis: World Wide Publications, 1975), p. 452.

in such countries as Chile, Brazil, South Korea, the Philippines, and others, but manifest little concern for the absence of those same rights in other countries. Delegations have been sent to investigate the fate of political prisoners in the jails in South Korea, but to my knowledge no investigation has been made of political prisoners in China, Cuba, or the Soviet Union.

It has always puzzled me that churchmen in the West can visit China and come home with glowing reports of unprecedented progress and prosperity but say nothing of the fact that basic human rights, civil as well as religious, have been denied in China for more than a quarter of a century. It is common knowledge that during that time there have been no free press, no independent parties, no loyal opposition. A Reuters dispatch from Peking in May, 1977, carried by the *Chicago Tribune*, reported that eight persons had been sentenced to death for starting a new movement called The China Revolutionary Party.[7] All kinds of freedom are guaranteed by the Constitution of the People's Republic of China, including freedom of religion; but in China, as in other Communist countries, there is a considerable gap between the promise on the one hand and the performance on the other.

President Carter in championing the cause of human rights in the Third World was accused of "selective morality" because he withheld foreign aid from some countries on the basis of the human-rights issue, but gave it to others which, though just as guilty, happen to be our allies. I think we have done the same thing in the Christian mission. We have been quick to denounce right-wing regimes for their blatant denial of human rights, but we have been considerably slower to deplore the absence of those same rights in left-wing regimes.

The cry for freedom is heard all over the world, and God knows how much it is needed in some areas. The missionary, however, must be on his guard lest he be tempted to join the chorus, shout the slogans, and wave the banners with all the "freedom fighters" of the world. When it comes to the highly complex and often doubtful issues of politics, the missionary

7. *Chicago Tribune*, 31 May 1977.

does well to recognize the limitations of his own calling, knowledge, and expertise; he should not rush in where angels fear to tread. He need not assume that his allegiance to Jesus Christ requires him to join the picket line every time an opposition newspaper is banned or a local politician goes to jail. The jails of the Third World are filled with political prisoners, some of the right and others of the left. There is little that the well-meaning missionary can do about it. To identify with one group is to alienate the members of the other groups. The missionary's aim is to become all things to all men that by all means he might win some (1 Cor 9:22).

Stephen Neill sounds a word of caution: "Nothing would be gained if the Church were to identify itself uncritically with 'the forces of revolution.' For revolution nearly always incorporates itself in one political party, and a Church which has become the Church of one political party has ceased to be the Church of all other political parties."[8] No one has expressed it better than Gonzalo Castillo Cardenas: "The Church has no right to deny her own nature, her own message, by identifying herself with any human program of social transformation."[9]

The missionary's chief task is to preach the gospel to every creature and to make disciples of all nations. He should think twice before allowing any cause, however worthy, to jeopardize his high calling as an ambassador for Jesus Christ.

8. Neill, *Colonialism*, p. 424.
9. Quoted in C. Peter Wagner, *Latin American Theology: Radical or Evangelical* (Grand Rapids: Eerdmans, 1970), p. 26.

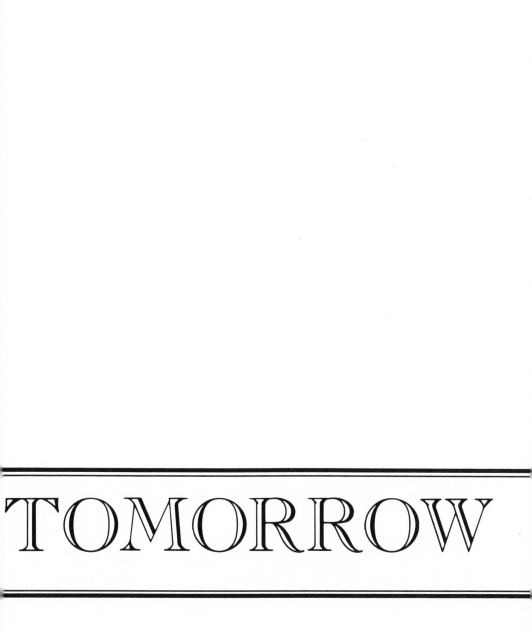

TOMORROW

PART I

Crucial Issues

CHAPTER 10

Definition
of Mission

The Christian mission is rooted first of all in the character of God. It is validated by the command of Christ to His followers to go into all the world and preach the gospel to every creature. It is designed to meet the needs of mankind.

The Christian mission is almost always based on the Great Commission recorded in the closing verses of Matthew's Gospel, but that is not all there is to it. Some attention must be given to the words of Christ in John 20:21: "As my Father hath sent me, even so send I you."

There is a real sense in which our mission is the continuation of His mission. Several times in the Gospel of John Jesus tells His hearers that when He came into the world He did not act on His own. He was sent by the Father on a threefold mission: to reveal the Father (John 1:14, 18); to destroy the works of the devil (1 John 3:8); and to save the world (John 3:17).

The word *missionary* comes from the Latin word *mitto*, which means "to send." In the New Testament the Greek word is *apostello*, which means the same thing. Peter, James, and John were not the first apostles in the strict sense of the word. John the Baptist was an apostle, for it was said of him: "There was a man sent from God, whose name was John" (John 1:6). Jesus Christ was also an apostle; He is actually referred to as the "Apostle and High Priest of our profession" (Heb 3:1).

As He drew near to the end of His ministry, Jesus began speaking of His return to the Father. In His high-priestly prayer He said: "I have finished the work which thou gavest me to do" (John 17:4). Consequently He gave advance notice to His disciples. He said: "I came forth from the Father, and am come into the world; again, I leave the world, and go to the Father" (John 16:28). Doubtless He spent much of the forty days between the resurrection and the ascension elaborating on this theme, preparing the disciples to become apostles.

In effect Jesus said to the disciples: "My mission is finished; yours is about to begin. As the Father was incarnate in me [John 14:11], so I will be incarnate in you [John 17:23]. Your mission is to be an extension of my mission. The church is to be an extension of the incarnation. Those who received me, received my Father; those who receive you will be receiving me [Mt 10:40]. Without the Father I could do nothing [John 5:19], and without me you will be able to do nothing [John 15:5]. As the Father invested me with all authority in heaven and in earth [Mt 28:18], so have I invested you with authority [Mt 16:19]. 'Whose soever sins ye remit, they are remitted unto them; and whose soever sins ye retain, they are retained' " (John 20:23).

Since the church's mission was to be an extension of Jesus' mission, our mission should parallel His in power, purpose, and program.

The Power

Evangelicals have emphasized the deity of Christ almost to the point of totally overlooking His humanity. We assume that in His capacity as the Son of God He had access to unlimited supernatural power, and it was that power which He employed in performing His ministry. Not so. His humanity was as genuine as His deity, and He glorified God on earth by living a life characterized by dependence and obedience. Because of this He is now said to be the "author and finisher of our faith" (Heb 12:2). It was said of Him that He "learned . . . obedience by the things which he suffered" (Heb 5:8). Only so can He be our example. It is a mistake to attribute His miracles to His unique role as the all-powerful Son of God. He was also the Son of Man, and it was in that role that He went about His earthly ministry.

One of Jesus' first acts at the beginning of His ministry was to teach in the synagogue in His hometown of Nazareth. The Scripture for the day was Isaiah 61:1: "The Spirit of the Lord is upon me, because he hath anointed me to preach the gospel to the poor. . . ." After the reading of the lesson He said: "This day is this scripture fulfilled in your ears" (Lk 4:16-21).

Peter, preaching the gospel to Cornelius, summed up the entire life and ministry of Jesus by saying: "God anointed Jesus of Nazareth with the Holy Ghost and with power: who went about doing good, and healing all that were oppressed of the devil; for God was with him" (Acts 10:38).

It is clear from these two passages that Jesus needed a special anointing with the Holy Spirit in order to accomplish His earthly ministry. Not only did He need and receive that kind of anointing; He told His disciples that they also would need the same kind of anointing. It was for this reason that He told them to tarry in Jerusalem until they were anointed with the Holy Spirit (Lk 24:49), just as He had been at the beginning of His ministry. Again on the day of the ascension He reminded them of their need of spiritual power: "Ye shall receive power, after that the Holy Ghost is come upon you; and ye shall be witnesses unto me both in Jerusalem, and in all Judea, and in Samaria, and unto the uttermost part of the earth" (Acts 1:8).

If Jesus needed a special anointing of the Holy Spirit for His mission, the church could hardly expect to get along without a similar anointing. It is instructive to note that when Jesus gave the Great Commission as recorded in John's Gospel, He added the words: "Receive ye the Holy Ghost" (John 20:22).

The Purpose

Christ's mission had a definite twofold purpose: to save and to serve. "The Son of man," He said, "is come to seek and to save that which was lost" (Lk 19:10). Paul said: "This is a faithful saying, and worthy of all acceptation, that Christ Jesus came into the world to save sinners" (1 Tim 1:15). He came to save them, not simply from the hands of their enemies, as many expected (Lk 1:71), but from the penalty and power of their sins (Mt 1:21).

Jesus' mission was to provide the gospel; His apostles' mission was to proclaim it. By proclaiming the gospel they would be cooperating with Him in His mission of redemption. The apostles could not in any ultimate sense "save" others, but in a relative sense they could engage in a saving ministry. Paul spoke of his "power" in the gospel (1 Cor 9:18) and went on to say: "Unto the Jews I became as a Jew, that I might gain the Jews. . . . To the weak became I as weak, that I might gain the weak; I am made all things to all men, that I might by all means save some" (1 Cor 9:20-22). There was a sense, then, in which Paul could "save" others.

There was another purpose to Christ's mission: to serve. He said: "The Son of man came not to be ministered unto, but to minister" (Mt 20:28). He demonstrated this fact by the life He lived. He was the Servant of God, as prophesied by Isaiah, but He was also the servant of men, which is far harder. To His disciples He said: "I am among you as he that serveth" (Lk 22:27). In the upper room, just before His passion, He gave the disciples a dramatic demonstration of His servanthood by washing their feet. This was not a token gesture; it was intended to teach them once and for all that the best way to serve God is to serve men. No man can be a true servant of God if he is unwilling to be a servant of men.

This is contrary to accepted practice in the world. Jesus warned His disciples not to follow the world in this regard. He said: "The kings of the Gentiles exercise lordship over them; and they that exercise authority upon them are called benefactors. But ye shall not be so: but he that is greatest among you, let him be as the younger; and he that is chief, as he that doth serve" (Lk 22:25-26). Jesus went on to ask the question: "Whether is greater, he that sitteth at meat, or he that serveth? is not he that sitteth at meat? but I am among you as he that serveth." All of this was in answer to a quarrel among the disciples as to who of them should be accounted the greatest.

Missionaries, like other Christians, have not taken kindly to the servant role. In the early days they were masters and were so regarded by their converts. Later on, as the converts grew in strength and numbers, the missionaries became partners. Now the time has come for them to assume the servant role, following in the footsteps of the One who said: "Ye call me Master and Lord: and ye say well; for so I am. If I then, your Lord and Master, have washed your feet; ye also ought to wash one another's feet" (John 13:13-14).

The Program

If our mission is an extension of Christ's, our program should square with His program. What did His program involve? The clearest statement is found in Luke 4:16-19. His mission included, besides the preaching of the gospel, healing the brokenhearted, preaching deliverance to the captives, recovering of sight to the blind, and setting at liberty those that are bruised.

As one studies the four Gospels it becomes clear that the gospel as preached by Jesus was intended to be holistic—to meet the needs of the whole man. In Matthew 4:23 we read: "Jesus went about all Galilee, teaching in their synagogues, and preaching the gospel of the kingdom, and healing all manner of sickness and all manner of disease among the people." Teaching, preaching, healing—this threefold ministry corresponded roughly to the three parts of man: mind, soul, and body.

There is today an ongoing debate in mission circles regarding the true nature of the Christian mission. What exactly does it involve? Should we concentrate on soul saving, or should we engage in other pursuits as well—nation building, community health, social service, political activity? The camp is well divided. Conservatives tend to equate mission with evangelism and do an excellent job of saving souls, but they are loath to get involved in some of the other activities. Liberals, on the other hand, do a good job in the area of social service but show little interest in saving souls. In fact, some of them reject the idea of personal salvation as being too self-centered and individualistic.

It may be that the two camps are not as far apart as they seem. The gospel as preached by Jesus is both personal and social. He said: "Thou shalt love the Lord thy God with all thy heart, and with all thy soul, and with all thy strength, and with all thy mind; and thy neighbor as thyself" (Lk 10:27). The first is personal, the second social. The conservatives are right when they emphasize the personal aspect of the gospel; the liberals are right when they emphasize the social aspects. Both are right in what they include but wrong in what they omit. The true gospel is first personal and then social. To preach only one aspect is to preach an emasculated gospel, and that would certainly have been repudiated by Jesus.

Repeatedly Jesus asked the question: "Wilt thou be made whole?" The word *whole* comes from an old Anglo-Saxon root, *hal*, from which we get our words *health* and *holiness*. In order to be "whole" man needs both. In his mundane existence man needs a body, preferably a sound body. No religion places more honor on the body than does Christianity. We find Jesus cleansing the leper, healing the sick, feeding the hungry, even raising the dead. Sickness, pain, weakness, and death are all part of the kingdom of Satan which Jesus came to destroy. When He sent out the Twelve, He gave them instructions to heal the sick and cleanse the leper.

Most of the Oriental religions, particularly Hinduism and Buddhism, are world-renouncing. To them the body is a highly undesirable thing, something that stands in the way of man's quest for spirituality. To cultivate his soul he must neglect, if not abuse, his body. Salvation does not include the body; that is something to be sloughed off when the soul enters Nirvana.

In contrast to all this is Christianity, which is a world-affirming religion. Jesus taught that man's most precious possession is his soul, and warned that if that is lost *all* is lost. But nowhere did Jesus denigrate either the body or its needs. He said: "Man shall not live by bread *alone*" (Mt 4:4), but he does need bread. In short, man has physical needs which are God-given. Jesus went so far as to sanction the act of David and his warriors when they ate the shewbread, which was to be eaten only by the priests (Mt 12:4). So essential are the life and health of the body that in dire circumstances the elemental needs of human nature take precedence over religious ritual.

The New Testament writers refused to settle for a dichotomy between body and soul. In Paul's Epistles faith and love are frequently mentioned in the same verse (Col 1:4; 1 Thess 1:3). John brings the two together in his First Epistle (3:23). James insists that faith and works belong together and goes so far as to say that without works faith is dead (James 2:14-26). Genuine faith in Christ always leads to love for the brethren, and love does not stop with the brethren; it goes on to embrace the world in all its varied needs—physical, mental, material, and social, as well as spiritual. When the question is asked: "Am I my brother's keeper?" the Christian's answer must be yes. He cannot, like the priest and Levite, pass by on the other side (Lk 10:31-32). The love of Christ will compel him to share his resources, however meager, with those around him.

The Example of Jesus

When Jesus saw the multitudes, He was moved with compassion, not only because they were like sheep without a shepherd, but also because they were sick and needed to be healed (Mt 14:14). When they were hungry He fed them, five thousand on one occasion (Mk 6:34-44) and four thousand on another (Mk 8:1-9). He knew that their motives were not always pure, that many of them were interested only in the loaves and fishes, not in the miracle itself (John 6:26) nor in the doctrine.

Jesus never attached any strings to His beneficence. He healed people because they needed healing. He offered healing for body, mind, and soul, and they were free to accept one, two, or all three. On one occasion he cleansed ten lepers, only one of whom returned to give thanks to God (Lk 17:11-19). Jesus was disappointed, as evidenced by the fact that the writer makes mention of the ingratitude. Jesus did not respond in kind, however. He did not pronounce a curse on them, nor did He revoke the healing. He allowed it to stand because it was a good thing in and of itself. Wherever He found oppression, He did His best to alleviate the situation and set the victims free. If they decided to follow Him and become His disciples, well and good; if not, He continued to act mercifully anyway. He would do good whether or not others responded to His goodness. Goodness is its own reward. Never once did He say to anyone: "I have healed your body; now you should follow me."

There are those who object to this point of view, saying that because Jesus was the unique Son of God, the Messiah of Israel, His mission was messianic and should not be regarded as a model for ours. There is an element of truth in this contention. He was a unique person, and in some respects His mission was unique. His atoning death and His victorious resurrection were unique events. His offer of the kingdom was made first to the Jews as part of their national heritage, and His miracles were a demonstration that the kingdom of God had indeed already come in power. In that sense His messianic mission was geared particularly to the Jews. When the Jews turned down the offer and He began to speak in wider terms of "other sheep which are not of this fold," He did not terminate, or even modify, the so-called messianic activities listed in Luke 4:18-19. They continued to the end.

The Practice of the Early Church

It is clear from His teaching that Jesus meant these "messianic" activities to continue into the church age, for He told His disciples: "He that believeth on me, the works that I do shall he do also; and greater works than these shall he do; because I go unto my Father" (John 14:12).

Some have argued that the "greater works" are spiritual and include the miracle of conversion brought about by the preaching of the gospel. If we grant that interpretation to be correct, what do we do about the clause: "The works that I do shall he do also"? Any Bible scholar will tell us that the "works" in John's Gospel are always miracles. If this is so, Jesus must have intended His church to perform the same miracles that He performed; otherwise, the statement does not make sense. When we turn to the Acts of the Apostles, we find that this is exactly what happened.

Church historians generally agree that miracles played a large part in the evangelization of the Roman Empire. Latourette, Gibbon, and Durant all list miracles among the factors which promoted the spread of the faith in the first few centuries.

Even a cursory glance at the New Testament will convince the reader that the early Christians had a high degree of social concern, which was undoubtedly a carry-over from the example of Christ. In the opening chapters of the Acts of the Apostles the believers shared not only their income but also their capital, thereby practicing a Christian form of communism. "All that believed were together, and had all things common; and sold their possessions and goods, and parted them to all men, as every man had need" (Acts 2:44-45). So patent was their love for the brethren that the non-Christians said of them: "Behold how they love one another."

Their love was expressed in concrete social action. The apostle John asks: "Whoso hath this world's good, and seeth his brother have need, and shutteth up his bowels of compassion from him, how dwelleth the love of God in him?" (1 John 3:17). He goes on to say: "My little children, let us not love in word, neither in tongue; but in deed and in truth."

In the Pauline Epistles the early Christians were encouraged not only to love one another but to bear one another's burdens as well, thus fulfilling the law of Christ (Gal 6:2). They were exhorted not to be weary in well doing but to do good unto all men, especially to them of the household of faith (Gal 6:9-10). Several times in the pastoral Epistles Paul tells his readers to engage in good works as part of their Christian profession (2 Tim 3:17; Titus 2:7, 14; 3:1, 8, 14). Only by so doing could they adorn the doctrine of God their Savior in all things (Titus 2:10).

It is clear that the early Christians regarded good works— or social service—as an integral part of their Christian life and testimony, and they probably did a better job than did any succeeding generation.

Adolf von Harnack, in a chapter entitled "The Gospel of Love and Charity," lists ten eleemosynary activities of the early church: alms in general, and their connection with the cultus and officials of the church; the support of teachers and officials; the support of widows and orphans; the support of the sick, the infirm, and the disabled; the care of prisoners and people languishing in the mines; the care of poor people needing burial and of the dead in general; the care of slaves; the care of those visited by great calamities; the churches' furnishing work, and insisting upon work; the care of brethren on a journey (hospitality), and of churches in poverty or any peril.[1]

The Meaning of Mission

It is in connection with the meaning of mission that we encounter the greatest misunderstanding. Two extreme views are espoused, one by the evangelicals and the other by the liberals.

Many evangelicals take a very narrow view and equate mission with evangelism. According to them our only obligation is to preach the gospel, to save souls, and in this way to assist Christ in building His church on earth.

There are others who take the opposite view and believe that mission includes all that God is doing in the world today.

1. Adolf von Harnack, *The Mission and Expansion of Christianity in the First Three Centuries* (New York: Harper & Row, 1962), p. 153.

They are convinced that He is working out His purposes in and through the revolutionary ferment of the times; and they insist that when the church joins the ferment, she is engaging in mission. According to this view, God is working primarily in the world, not the church; and if the church wants a piece of the action, she had better join the revolutionary forces. To do this the church should adopt the agenda of the world. In fact, some go so far as to suggest that the best thing the church can do is to close its doors, or—and they quote the words of Jesus to support their contention—to fall into the ground like a grain of wheat and die (John 12:24).

The truth lies somewhere between these two extremes. The word *mission* includes evangelism, to be sure, but it is by no means restricted to evangelism. On the other hand, it is not so broad as to include everything that God is doing or permitting in the world. John Stott defines mission as "everything that God sent the church into the world to do."[2]

The word *mission* necessarily has a wide connotation. It includes the total obligation of the church to the world. Jesus told His disciples that they were to be salt and light in the world, that they were responsible to do good unto all men, friend and foe alike. They were to love their enemies, bless them that cursed them, do good to them that hated them, and pray for them that despitefully used them and persecuted them (Mt 5:44).

As followers of Christ they were expected to share both the gospel and their goods with the world. James says: "If a brother or sister be naked, and destitute of daily food, and one of you say unto them, Depart in peace, be ye warmed and filled; notwithstanding ye give them not those things which are needful to the body; what doth it profit?" (James 2:15-16). E. Stanley Jones used to say: "If I have something which my brother needs more than I need it, I am duty bound as a Christian to let him have it." That is Christian social concern carried to its ultimate length.

2. John R. W. Stott, *Christian Mission in the Modern World* (Downers Grove, IL: Inter-Varsity, 1975), p. 30.

When the early-nineteenth-century missionaries went to the field, they engaged in a full-orbed program that included not only evangelism and church planting, but also medical, educational, and agricultural work. All of this they regarded as part of the mission of the church. Doctors, teachers, and technicians were all referred to as missionaries, and no one quarreled with the designation.

The Meaning of Evangelism

It is absolutely necessary to make a clear distinction between mission and evangelism. To equate the one with the other is to make a grave mistake. They are not the same.

What, in simple terms, is evangelism? Evangelism is the proclamation of the evangel—nothing more and certainly nothing less. What is the evangel? It is the Good News that God loved the world, that Christ died for all, that God was in Christ reconciling the world to Himself, that all men everywhere, regardless of class, color, culture, or any other consideration, can be saved if they will repent of their sins and believe the gospel. The word *evangel* was not coined by the sacred writers, any more than were the words *church* and *grace*. All three were taken from the common parlance of the day, enriched, elevated to a higher plane, and invested with a Christian content quite unknown in the Greco-Roman world. For the Christian the evangel is not *any* good news, but the specific Good News that Paul called the "truth of the gospel" (Gal 2:5). It is called the "gospel of God" (Rom 1:2) in the sense that it originated with God, not man. It is called the "gospel of Christ" (Rom 1:16) because it pertains to the person and work of Christ, more particularly to His death, by which He paid the full penalty for our sins, and to His resurrection, by which He conquered all the demonic powers of death and hell and ushered in the kingdom age with its promise of life, power, justice, peace, and hope.

To suggest that social service, community development, and nation building are all an integral part of evangelism is to prostitute the meaning of the term. These activities are right and good and have their proper place; under certain conditions they can be a nonverbal form of Christian witness; but *do not refer to them as evangelism*. Evangelism is a special term reserved for a special activity: the proclamation of the gospel.

Evangelistic work has sometimes been used as a catchall phrase to include everything that the general missionary does in contrast to the well-defined and highly specialized activities of medical and educational missionaries. One evangelistic missionary in China spent much of his time organizing fly-swatting campaigns. Swatting flies was indeed a highly desirable occupation, as any missionary to China could testify; but it would be a great mistake to refer to the undertaking as evangelistic work.

This is not to suggest that all missionaries should be engaged in evangelistic work. Mission work is vast and varied. Evangelistic work is narrow and restricted and includes only one thing—the proclamation of the gospel.

The Matter of Priority

The real issue revolves around the question of priority. If mission includes evangelism in addition to all these other activities, which is most important? Is one activity more important than the others, or are they all equally important?

There are some who hold that mission is mission, and all the activities connected with it are equally important. They are not happy with current terminology. Orlando Costas, for example, refuses to use the term *prime* mission of the church. He prefers to speak of the *total* mission of the church.[3]

That is begging the question. There is no doubt that the New Testament attaches supreme importance to the evangelistic work of the church. Nothing is quite as important as the proclamation of the gospel. John the Baptist came preaching. Jesus also came preaching. Paul said: "Woe is unto me, if I preach not the gospel" (1 Cor 9:16). He never ceased to won-

3. Orlando E. Costas, *The Church and Its Mission: A Shattering Critique from the Third World* (Wheaton, IL: Tyndale House, 1975), p. 11.

der at the grace of God that changed him from a persecutor of the church to a preacher of the gospel. To his dying day he marveled at the manifold grace that conferred on him the high privilege of preaching "among the Gentiles the unsearchable riches of Christ" (Eph 3:8). He saw to it that the men he gathered around him also became preachers of the gospel. His final instructions to his most faithful coworker, Timothy, were: "Preach the word; be instant in season, out of season. . . . do the work of an evangelist, make full proof of thy ministry" (2 Tim 4:2, 5).

The church's mission does not take place in a social or spiritual vacuum, but in the world of men. The church is always the church for others. Indeed, the church is the only institution in the world that exists for the sake of others. Its supreme mission is to meet the world's greatest need.

Whether we believe that man's greatest need is physical, material, or spiritual is determined largely by what we believe concerning the lostness of man. If one accepts the idea of universalism in any form, then he believes that man's spiritual needs are basically met, for all men are in Christ and on their way to heaven. They do not need the gospel; they are already "saved." That being so, we should forget the gospel and get on with the job of improving man's lot here and now in a cruel, hostile world controlled by oppressive structures and demonic forces.

If, on the other hand, one believes that man is made in the image of God and possesses an immortal soul that will live as long as God lives, either in fellowship with Him or alienated from Him, then he believes that man's greatest need is to be saved, not only for time but also for eternity. To improve his lot here and now but permit him to end up in hell is to fail in our mission. This was the teaching of Christ when He asked: "What shall it profit a man, if he gain the whole world, and lose his own soul? Or what shall a man give in exchange for his soul?" (Mk 8:36-37). The most profound question any man can ask during his life on earth is: "What must I do to be saved?" On the answer to that question depends his happiness here and hereafter.

The Scriptures clearly teach that the sinner's only hope is to turn from his wicked way and embrace the gospel. There is no other hope held out to him. He has no other option. It is, therefore, imperative for him to hear and believe the gospel. The missionary's first concern, then, is to preach the gospel, to be instant in season and out of season, to seize on every opportunity to press home the claims of Christ. The fact that most men are not conscious of their spiritual needs and cry out for help only in other areas of need serves to underscore the gravity of the situation. The most perilous aspect of man's lostness is the fact that he does not know he is lost (2 Cor 4:4).

Vernon Mortenson, former general director of The Evangelical Alliance Mission (TEAM), defended the primacy of evangelism in the following analogy:

A hospital is a lot of things. It is a hotel where people must be housed in comfort. It is a restaurant where hundreds of meals are served daily. It is a communications center where the switchboard handles dozens of calls an hour. It is a business office where records, accounts, flow charts, and job descriptions are kept. It is a training center where doctors, nurses, and other medical personnel increase their skills.

But above all else the hospital is a place where people are healed. The purpose for its existence is the healing of the body. Therefore, central to all its varied activities is the work of the surgeon and other medical specialists. All the other activities would be pointless and futile if they did not further the skill of the medical practitioner.

Missionary work is also a lot of things. It is a combination of the skills of many trades and professions. It is a building, because houses, churches, schools and hospitals must be built. It is linguistics, because languages must be reduced to writing, grammars and dictionaries compiled, and translations undertaken. It is medical work, because people are afflicted with a great variety of diseases which sap their strength and carry them to an early grave.

It is business administration, because finances must be cared for, personnel assigned and directed, and the work evaluated. It is relief work, because famines plague the world and natural calamities befall great numbers of people. It is education, because millions have no other opportunity of breaking out of ignorance and poverty.

But above all, its indispensable purpose is the preaching of salvation through Jesus Christ so that man's dire spiritual need may be met. It is the discipling of converts so they in turn will be able to minister to souls around them. It is the establishing of believers in spiritually effective congregations according to the New Testament pattern so there will be a living and expanding permanent witness in the community.

CHAPTER 11

Humanization
or Salvation?

Humanization or salvation? This is one of the most crucial issues for Christian missions. The discussion used to revolve around principles, programs, and policies, but now the very foundation of the missionary movement is called in question. We are no longer sure what the Christian mission is or what it is supposed to accomplish.

In a series of lectures at Scarritt College in 1966, Tracey K. Jones said: "Fifty years ago the missionary's understanding of his vocation was clear." But the former concept of the missionary "has been shattered. It cannot be pasted back together."[1]

David J. Hesselgrave wrote: "Evidence could be marshalled to demonstrate that the missionary of today suffers from a very real identity crisis. Furthermore, there is every indication that this crisis will become more accentuated in the future."[2] Others agree with him. Walter Freytag said: "Formerly mission had problems; today it has itself become a problem."[3] William B. Frazier was even more emphatic:

1. Tracey K. Jones, *The Missionary Intruder* (Nashville: Scarritt College for Christian Workers, 1966), p. 49.
2. David J. Hesselgrave, "The Missionary of Tomorrow—Identity Crisis Extraordinary," *Missiology*, April 1975, p. 226.
3. Ronald K. Orchard, ed. *The Ghana Assembly of the International Missionary Council, 28th December, 1957, to 8th January, 1958.* London: Edinburgh House Press, 1958, p. 138.

155

No longer are [missionaries] preoccupied with problems of personnel and finance; no longer is their thinking dominated by the difficulties of mission method and maintenance. . . . Today missionaries sense that the missionary enterprise itself may be in danger of foundering. What troubles them is not so much the manifold hardship of doing their job, but the far more debilitating uneasiness of wondering if they really have a job to do.[4]

There are many factors which help to explain this distressing phenomenon: personal, psychological, social, cultural, and semantic; but the most important is theological. In recent years we have witnessed the emergence of the new morality, the new evangelism, and the new theology. Not the least of these is the new theology.

In the nineteenth century the missionary body, almost without exception, believed that all men are lost and need to be saved; that there is only one way of salvation—through faith in Jesus Christ, who is the way, the truth, and the life; and that in order to be saved one must hear and believe the gospel. The greatest of all questions was: "What must I do to be saved?" To that question there was only one answer: "Believe on the Lord Jesus Christ, and thou shalt be saved" (Acts 16:31).

Times have changed, however, and theologians have changed with them. The theological confusion in the West has spread to the Third World and even missionaries have been infected.

That modern man, especially in the Western world, has become dehumanized no one would wish to deny. On every hand there is ample evidence that the times are out of joint.

Industrial production and scientific advancement have led to unprecedented affluence, but the human heart can never be content with material possessions. Man is working harder and living longer, but he is enjoying life less. Western civilization, based on Christian principles, has already begun to decline. We are living, so we are told, in a post-Christian era.

4. William B. Frazier, "Guidelines for a New Theology of Mission," in *Mission Trends No. 1: Crucial Issues in Missions Today*, ed. Gerald H. Anderson and Thomas F. Stransky (Grand Rapids: Eerdmans, 1974), p. 27.

Western man with his penchant for progress has created a mammoth industrial-military-political machine which he can no longer control. Moreover, he has produced nuclear weapons capable of reducing the planet to cinders in a matter of minutes. In the face of such potentially dangerous powers man has lost his moral courage and doubts that he can survive the remainder of the century. Life has lost its meaning and purpose. In a word, he has become dehumanized.

Factors Contributing to Dehumanization

1. *Urbanization.* The Western world is leading the way in urbanization. In the United States 70 percent of the population lives in the urban areas. The Third World is not far behind. Calcutta, Cairo, and Caracas are huge metropolitan centers with slums that defy description. Only China has solved the problem of overcrowded cities with their high unemployment. There the traffic moves in one direction only—from the city to the countryside—not by choice but by order of a totalitarian government.

The cities offer many of the amenities of technological civilization, but they have a way of devouring their inhabitants. People live in high-rise apartments where doors are secured by two or three locks. In the inner cities it is not safe to walk alone after dark. There are crowds everywhere—in the streets, in the subways, in the department stores, in the office buildings. There are many people but few friends. Neighbors are neighbors only in the sense that they live next door. No one knows their names. No one even bids them the time of day in the elevator. If they get into trouble, the others run for shelter or look the other way. Everyone looks out for Number One, while the "lonely crowd" proceeds on its lonely way.

2. *Industrialization.* In former times farmers in the rural areas produced their own food, made their own clothes, built their own houses, and fashioned their own furniture. They were self-sufficient. Almost everything they possessed came from the "good earth," which belonged to them. Everybody

was a friend to everybody else, and people lived together, worked together, played together.

Not so in today's cities, where a large plant may employ fifty thousand persons on the assembly line. The individual employee is lost in the crowd. His only consolation is the paycheck he gets at the end of the week, and that barely keeps him and his family going until the following Friday. He is a mere cog in the wheel of a gigantic machine. Moreover, he does only one insignificant thing on the assembly line; he never has the satisfaction of seeing the finished product. It is difficult for him to take any interest, much less pride, in his work. This is in stark contrast to former days when 80 percent of the people lived on the farm and everyone derived a certain amount of satisfaction from his own creative work. Then everyone lived close to nature and had a feeling of being in touch with God.

3. *Alienation.* When one moves to the city, he finds it difficult to make friends. The people he works with go their own way when it is quitting time, and he does not see them again until the following morning. He returns home only to find his "neighbors" as busy and tired as himself. He spends his evening with his eyes glued to the television. Church would be a good place to make friends, but he cannot find a church of his denomination nearby so he soon loses contact with the church. In no time at all he begins to feel rootless and homeless even though he is surrounded by thousands of people, none of whom can help him because they are in the same predicament. He ends up with a few acquaintances and no friends. Unable to find satisfaction in life or work he soon develops a sense of alienation. Little wonder that he complains of dehumanization.

Rationales Behind the Plea for Humanization

1. *The Ideological Argument: The Marxist view of society.* Politically the United States has rejected Communism. During the 1976 elections the Communist Party garnered only sixty thousand votes. In academic circles, however, socialism as advo-

cated by Karl Marx is by no means dead. My son teaches philosophy in a Midwestern university. He tells me that he is the only non-Marxist in the department. I have been told on good authority that there are more committed Marxists in the West than in the Soviet Union. Intellectuals in the Soviet Union may be party members but they have no illusions about life in a totalitarian society. Marxists in the West are familiar only with Marxist theory, not with life in a Communist country.

A former student of mine, now a missionary in West Germany, attended a crash course in German at a local university. Imagine his surprise when he discovered that he was the only non-Marxist in a class of thirty-two! The other students regarded him as something of a curiosity. They did not think a non-Marxist would attend university in West Germany.

Here in the United States large corporations, such as AT&T, IBM, and Exxon are in danger of being broken up by Congress. Capitalism is blamed for inflation on the one hand and unemployment on the other. As for profit, it has become a dirty word. College students absorb these ideas almost by a process of osmosis. In time they come to believe that socialism is the wave of the future and the only hope of the oppressed worker on the assembly line or the deprived youth in the ghetto.

Marxists have consistently drawn attention to the inequities of modern society, especially in the Third World. Man, they say, has become completely dehumanized by the social and economic power structures of our day. The only way to free himself is to smash the structures and build again on an entirely different foundation, socialism.

2. *The Sociological Argument: The secularization of Western life.* There was a time when Western civilization was basically religious in its orientation. For hundreds of years Chistianity provided both the matrix and the motif of Western civilization, including art, music, sculpture, literature, philosophy, and theology. Today Western civilization is in danger of coming apart at the seams because its underlying strength, grounded in religious convictions, is fast ebbing away. Little by little God has been pushed from the center to the circum-

ference; and man, with his modern techniques and massive achievements in science and technology, has moved into the center of the scene. The whole world revolves around a new center of gravity called man. Man is indeed the measure of all things.

In such a world man does not need to be "saved" in the biblical sense. All he needs is to be set free from the demonic influences that have dehumanized him. He needs freedom to find himself, to be his own man, to go his own way, to do his own thing, to be the master of his fate, the captain of his soul. In the 1960s some theologians went so far as to say that God is dead. This makes it possible to be a Christian and an atheist at the same time.

3. *The Theological Argument: The Old Testament teaching of Shalom.* Not only have scientists and sociologists settled for a secular view of life; theologians have done the same. They have returned to the Old Testament and have come up with the Jewish concept of *Shalom*. The word means peace, but it also includes the idea of well-being and material prosperity. It was God's intention that man should be happy and enjoy life free from poverty, sorrow, injustice, anxiety, and oppression. Time and again the people of Israel were told that if they would obey God and keep His covenant they would enjoy His full blessing: flocks, herds, children, peace of mind, health of body, material prosperity, and all the other things that make up the good life. In a word, they would enjoy the fulness of human life ordained of God. Salvation in this sense has no vertical dimension. It is social, not individual; material, not spiritual; temporal, not eternal. It has nothing to do with forgiveness of sins, reconciliation with God, or life everlasting.

Placed side by side these three arguments make a strong plea for humanization as opposed to the biblical doctrine of salvation, and in ecumenical circles the emphasis is on humanization. The vertical dimension of salvation, which figures so prominently in the preaching of Jesus and the apostles, is acknowledged in theory but all but denied in practice. The opening paragraph in the *Uppsala Report* on "Renewal in Mission" says:

> We belong to a humanity that cries passionately and articulately for a fully human life. Yet the very humanity of man and of his societies is threatened by a greater variety of destructive forces than ever. And the acutest moral problems all hinge on the question: "What is man?"[5]

Years before, Dietrich Bonhoeffer made a similar statement:

> To be a Christian does not mean to be religious in a particular way . . . but to be a man. It is not some religious acts that makes a Christian what he is but a participation in the suffering of God in the life of the world.[6]

Certain Distinctions That Have Been Lost

In the new theology certain fundamental distinctions have been lost. As a result Western theology is in a shambles and the Christian missionary has an identity crisis.

1. *Between the secular and the sacred.* For centuries the Judeo-Christian revelation has taught that some things are sacred: the priesthood, the sabbath, marriage, the church, and so forth. Today we are being told that this is a mistake. God is the God of creation as well as redemption, and as such He has established His claim over the whole world and over all of life. Nothing is profane. "Unto the pure all things are pure" (Titus 1:15). For the Christian all things are sacred: family, employment, business, pleasure; nothing is to be regarded as secular or profane. Gustavo Gutierrez summed it up in a sentence: "Since God has become man, humanity, every man, history, is the living temple of God."[7]

5. Norman Goodall, *The Uppsala '68 Report* (Geneva: World Council of Churches, 1968), pp. 27-28.
6. Dietrich Bonhoeffer, *Letters and Papers from Prison*, 2d ed. (London: SCM Press, 1956), p. 166.
7. Gustavo Gutierrez, *A Theology of Liberation* (Maryknoll, NY: Orbis Books, 1973), p. 194.

This kind of thinking has invaded mission circles:

> Thinking about mission is being profoundly influenced by the church's openness toward the world, that is, the phenomenon of secularization. The human and worldly are being taken more seriously than ever before. . . . Rigid barriers between sacred and secular realities are breaking down.[8]

2. *Between the church and the world.* The loss of the second distinction grows out of the loss of the first. If everything is sacred, it becomes rather difficult to maintain that there is an essential difference between the church and the world. For a long time we have believed that there is. The church is *in* the world but not *of* the world. The church includes only those who have been united with Christ by faith in His unique person and work; the world includes the entire human race regardless of faith or morals. In the New Testament Satan is referred to as the god and prince of this world, which is alienated from the life of God (Eph 4:18), opposed to the law of God (Rom 8:7), and exposed to the wrath of God (John 3:36).

Now we are told that it is a mistake to make these distinctions. God has no favorites. The world as well as the church belongs to God. Indeed, He is working today primarily through the world, not through the church. For all practical purposes there is no distinction between the church and the world.

This kind of thinking has a direct bearing on the Christian mission. Three quotations from *Mission Trends* will suffice:

> The church is sent to the nations, not only to enrich, but to be enriched. The world has a mission to the church as well as the church to the world. . . . Only by clothing itself with the cultures of the world is the church able to recognize the depths of its own catholicity.[9]

> The failure of the Christian mission today is not a failure to convert the world to the church, but a failure to convert the church to the world.[10]

8. Frazier, "Guidelines," p. 25.
9. Ibid., p. 31.
10. Ibid., p. 33.

If the church is to emerge successfully from the crisis of irrelevancy . . . it will be through a gradual awakening to the fact that the world, and not the church, is the focal point of God's saving action, and that the Christian mission is a joining in that activity in the world.[11]

3. *Between the saved and the lost.* The Bible clearly teaches, and evangelicals have always believed, that some men are saved and others are lost. Those who are "in Adam" are lost; those who are "in Christ" are saved; and the difference between the two is of supreme importance.

We are now asked to give up this old-fashioned idea. *All* men are saved by virtue of Christ's work on the cross. The favorite proof text is 2 Corinthians 5:19: "God was in Christ, reconciling the world unto himself." As a result all men, believers and unbelievers, atheists and apostates, are part of the "new humanity" of which Christ is the Head. If man is lost it is simply "because he does not know who he is."[12]

Has this new theology affected the Christian mission? It certainly has. Consider, for example, this quote from *Mission Trends*: "The missionary aim of the church is not to bring men the gift of salvation, but to acclaim . . . the saving mystery already at work in them."[13]

4. *Between witness and service.* John Stott has said that the Christian mission equals witness plus service, but he retains the distinction between the two. There is a sense in which Christian service is a valid form of Christian witness. Without the service the witness would be greatly weakened, but that is not to suggest that they are one and the same.

This is what many of our ecumenical friends are saying, however. The only form of evangelism in which they believe is "presence" evangelism. They minimize the place of "proclamation" evangelism. "Witness," they say, "is not for the sake of conversions, but conversions for the sake of witness."[14]

11. Ibid., pp. 33-34.
12. Goodall, *Uppsala '68*, p. 5.
13. Frazier, "Guidelines," p. 29.
14. Ibid., p. 30.

5. *Between Christianity and the non-Christian religions.* Christians have always believed that there is something unique about the Judeo-Christian revelation; that while other religions may and do contain many high ethical concepts, their major doctrines of God, man, sin, and salvation are basically, if not entirely, false.

Now this, too, is being called in question. Christianity has no monopoly on truth. To present Jesus Christ as *the* way, *the* truth, and *the* life is to engage in cultural imperialism. Such an approach only offends the sensibilities of our non-Christian friends and leads not to conversion but to confrontation. So we are informed that "the aim of the missionary message is to free people for a saving contact with the best in their own religious traditions."[15]

Under such an arrangement proclamation is replaced by dialogue, which does not focus on conversion to Christ but on a common concern for humanity. "In dialogue we share our common humanity, its dignity and fallenness, and express our common concern for that humanity."[16]

6. *Between the missionary and the nonmissionary.* The term *missionary*, we are told, smacks of nineteenth-century imperialism and should be dropped from our vocabulary. Besides, every Christian is a missionary just as long as he lets his light shine. A missionary "is anyone who increases by participation the concretization of the love of God in history."[17]

If these distinctions are done away with, what do we have left? Very little of what might be described as conventional missionary ministry or message. Salvation is defined almost entirely in human terms and involves social justice, liberation, and human development. This comes out clearly in the Introduction to the *Uppsala Report*:

15. Gregory Baum, "Is There a Missionary Message?" in *Mission Trends No. 1: Crucial Issues in Missions Today*, ed. Gerald H. Anderson and Thomas F. Stransky (Grand Rapids: Eerdmans, 1974), p. 81.

16. Goodall, *Uppsala '68*, p. 29.

17. Kosuke Koyama, "What Makes a Missionary?" in *Mission Trends No. 1: Crucial Issues in Missions Today*, ed. Gerald H. Anderson and Thomas F. Stransky (Grand Rapids: Eerdmans, 1974), p. 128.

The most obvious and widely acknowledged feature of the Assembly was its preoccupation—at times, almost, its obsession—with the revolutionary ferment of our time, with questions of social and international responsibility, of war, and peace, and economic justice, with the pressing, agonizing physical needs of men, with the plight of the underprivileged, the homeless, the starving, and with the most radical contemporary rebellions against all 'establishments', civil and religious.[18]

So impressed were some China experts with the massive social experiment in that country that at one time they compared Mao Tse-tung to Jesus Christ.[19] One visitor to China in 1975 said that if the kingdom of God has appeared anywhere on earth it is in Communist China.

Evangelical Response to Humanization

1. All forms of exploitation are to be condemned for three good reasons. Inasmuch as all men are made in the image of God, to sin against man is to sin against God. When David confessed his sin of adultery and murder, he said: "Against thee, and thee only, have I sinned" (Ps 51:4); and when the prodigal son returned from the far country, he said to his father: "I have sinned against heaven, and in thy sight" (Lk 15:21).

Inasmuch as all men are brothers by virtue of their common humanity, to sin against man is to sin against humanity. Paul said that no man lives to himself (Rom 14:7). We can also say that no man sins to himself. Whenever he sins, he involves others in his sin. Sin is social as well as personal and very often the innocent suffer along with the guilty.

Since all moral behavior has a reflex action, one cannot sin against others without at the same time degrading oneself. Sin dehumanizes the sinner who commits the sin; it also dehumanizes the society in which the sinner lives and moves.

18. Goodall, *Uppsala '68*, p. xvii.
19. Donald E. MacInnis, "Implications of China's Revolution," in *Mission Trends No. 1: Crucial Issues in Missions Today*, ed. Gerald H. Anderson and Thomas F. Stransky (Grand Rapids: Eerdmans, 1974), p. 274.

2. Today's emphasis on humanization is unbiblical because it is completely, or almost completely, preoccupied with the material side of man's nature. Man as created by God is preeminently a spiritual being. In the Bible man is always identified with his soul, not with his body. Man *is* a soul; he *has* a body. "In the day that thou eatest thereof *thou* shalt surely die," was God's warning to Adam (Gen 2:17); but it was not until 930 years later that his body finally succumbed to death.

There are two parts to man's nature: the physical (the body) and the spiritual (the soul). Both were created by God and therefore both are important. Man cannot live by bread alone, said Jesus. He has a body and for that he needs bread, but he is more than body. He is a spirit as well and for that he needs freedom. To feed a man's body and educate his mind but do nothing for his soul is not the biblical view of salvation. Jesus made this quite plain when He said: "What shall it profit a man, if he shall gain the whole world, and lose his own soul?" (Mk 8:36).

John Stott is absolutely right when he asks: "Is anything so destructive of human dignity as alienation from God? How can we seriously maintain that political and economic liberation is just as important as eternal salvation?"[20]

3. The root cause of dehumanization is not found in the social, economic, and political structures of the world, but in the sinful nature of man himself. Man has always had a tendency to blame his misery on someone or something else—the system, the environment, heredity, misfortune, or even the machinations of his enemies. Rare is the man who has the honesty to blame his misery on himself. Nations do the same. The Soviet Union in December, 1979, sent a hundred thousand armed troops into Afghanistan to prop up the Communist regime and blamed the situation on American imperialists.

20. John R. W. Stott, *Christian Mission in the Modern World* (Downers Grove, IL: Inter-Varsity, 1975), p. 35.

Before man can improve his lot, he must be willing to face reality and acknowledge his responsibility for the predicament in which he finds himself. It is true that man has lost his authentic humanity. *He lost it not in a ghetto but in a garden.* Having lost his humanity, he proceeded to turn the garden into a ghetto. Now he blames all his ills on the ghetto!

We need constantly to bear in mind the biblical description of the fall and the results that flowed from it. With his eyes wide open and with the full knowledge of the awful consequences of his act, Adam put forth his hand and partook of the forbidden fruit. Instantly something happened; sin came into his life and God went out. From that day to this, man has wandered to and fro as a spiritual vagabond on the face of the earth that God intended him to subdue. He has sailed the seven seas; he has traveled to the ends of the earth; he has even visited the moon; he has conquered the wilderness and made the desert to blossom like the rose; he has founded empires and dynasties; he has built cities and castles; he has heaped up for himself riches and honor. But for all that his *soul* is an orphan still. In his heart there is what H. G. Wells called a "God-shaped blank" that nothing on earth can ever fill. His spirit, like Noah's dove, flits back and forth between "rough seas and stormy skies."

The Bible describes man as being dead in trespasses and sins (Eph 2:1). He has plenty of physical, intellectual, and social life, but he is completely devoid of spiritual life. He is alienated from the life of God (Eph 4:18), ignorant of the truth of God (Rom 1:25), hostile to the law of God (Rom 8:7), disobedient to the will of God (Titus 3:3), and exposed to the wrath of God (John 3:36). He has been separated from God for so long that he has become naturalized in the unnatural and actually loves darkness rather than light (John 3:19).

The virus of sin has penetrated into every part of man's constitution. His mind has been darkened (Eph 4:18), his emotions have been vitiated (Rom 1:26-27), and his will has been enslaved (John 8:31-36). In theological terms, he is "totally depraved." Even his body has been affected by the fall, so that now it is subject to weakness, sickness, pain, and finally death

(Gen 3:19). To sum it all up, he is now subhuman—less, far less, than God intended him to be. In a word, he has been dehumanized, and he has no one to blame but himself.

4. The demonic structures of oppression under which man is now suffering did not evolve of their own accord. They were created by man himself, sinful man, whose two outstanding characteristics are selfishness and pride.

It is fair to ask: If we succeed in overthrowing these demonic structures, have we any reason to believe that they will be replaced by better structures? After they have been demolished, will man have more freedom or less? If the Communist world is any criterion, the answer is less.

The Communists more than anyone else have fought to destroy these demonic structures. In some twenty countries of the world they have succeeded, but in every instance oppressive regimes continue in the form of a "dictatorship of the proletariat." Millions of oppressed persons have risked their lives and the lives of their dear ones to escape from the "paradise" established by the Communists—and the mass exodus continues. In Cambodia the Communist regime of Pol Pot committed genocide on its own people. Hitler is universally regarded as the greatest tyrant of the twentieth century for killing six million Jews in the gas chambers of Germany. Mao Tse-tung killed at least six million Chinese in his lifetime, but he has been regarded by many as a benefactor. The only difference between Hitler and Mao is that Hitler selected his victims on the basis of race whereas Mao chose his on the basis of class; otherwise there is little to choose between the two. The modern world seems to have had a double standard of morality.

5. The worst form of alienation is man's alienation from God, not his alienation from himself or his fellowmen. Karl Marx spoke of three kinds of alienation and blamed all three on the wicked capitalist system, but all of them are on the horizontal level. These are, indeed, very real forms of alienation and something should be done about them; but man's basic problem is that the vertical relationship between him and God has been severed, and with that connection gone all

other connections are at loose ends. That is the *root* cause of all forms of alienation.

6. Jesus Christ is God's idea of "authentic humanity." Jesus was both God and man, and in His humanity He showed us what God intended man to be. There was nothing counterfeit about His humanity. He was *genuine* man. Three characteristics made His humanity authentic in the eyes of God: His complete trust in the goodness of God (Mt 11:25-26); His complete dependence on the guidance of God for His words (John 12:49) and His deeds (John 5:19); and His complete obedience to the will of God (Phil 2:5-11; Heb 5:8).

Because of His authentic humanity Jesus could say: "In the world ye shall have tribulation: but be of good cheer; I have overcome the world" (John 16:33). His conflict with the powers of darkness led Him ultimately to the cross—the most glaring example of injustice in the history of the world. It was on the cross that He destroyed principalities and powers, making a cosmic spectacle of them and triumphing over them through it (Col 2:14-15).

7. Man can never achieve authentic humanity until he returns to God his creator. Augustine was expressing a profound principle, not a pious platitude, when he said: "Thou hast made us for Thyself and our hearts are restless till they rest in Thee."

Man was made in the beginning *by* God and *for* God. God intended man to find his highest happiness, not in himself or his achievements or his possessions, but in fellowship with God. God is still calling: "Adam, where art thou?" and "What hast thou done?" Man's only hope is to return to God. That is the true meaning of the incarnation. Jesus said it in a single sentence: "Come unto me, all ye that labour and are heavy laden, and I will give you rest" (Mt 11:28). He also said: "If the Son therefore shall make you free, ye shall be free indeed" (John 8:36).

8. There is only one way back to God—through Jesus Christ. There are many paths but only one way; many prophets but only one Savior; many religions but only one gospel. If this smacks of cultural imperialism, so be it. Jesus claimed to be

the way, the truth, and the life. He went on to say that no man can come to the Father but by Him (John 14:6). As followers of Christ we have no choice. Jesus Christ was the unique Son of God and the unique Son of Man. We accept both His deity and His humanity. He taught the truth; He lived the truth; He was the truth. For us He is the King of truth and we take our stand with Him. If the world does not understand us, so what? It did not understand Him either.

9. This being so, the greatest benefit we can confer on any human being is to introduce him to Jesus Christ. Man's allotted time on earth is seventy years. This ephemeral life is only a preparation for the life to come. Man's eternal destiny is settled here, and it depends entirely on what he does with Jesus Christ. He can accept Him and be saved forever, or he can reject Him and be lost forever. It is appointed unto men once to die, and after death the judgment (Heb 9:27). Little wonder that Paul said: "Woe is unto me, if I preach not the gospel!" (1 Cor 9:16). He added: "I am made all things to all men, that I might by all means save some" (v. 22). It was his highest ambition and his greatest privilege to "preach among the Gentiles the unsearchable riches of Christ" (Eph 3:8).

Stephen Neill, dean of the missiologists, who gave a lifetime of service to the cause of Christ in India, wrote:

> In India missionaries found themselves faced by the challenge of the scheduled communities [Untouchables]. Desperately poor, illiterate, sunk in habits which made it almost impossible for them to lift themselves up out of misery, these people did not seem to be exactly the material out of which flourishing churches could be built up. There were in fact two views as to the way in which they could be approached. One group held that social reform must precede evangelism; first improve social conditions and then the preaching of the gospel can follow. Others held that from the start the gospel of salvation must be preached. How can humanization be effected except by the direct and loving approach of a human being, in whom the oppressed can see the likeness of the Man Jesus Christ, the One in whom the true nature of human life is seen? How can a man become conscious of his own true being except through

acquaintance with the living Christ, the true liberator from everything that mars and distorts the existence of God's children?

The working out of these two views is interesting. Those who started out with the idea of social reform were singularly ineffective in bringing it about, and never got on to the preaching of the gospel. Those who started with a gospel of conversion, perhaps without intending it brought about a social revolution, as believers became liberated from harmful habits and became aware with new self-respect that even under the yoke of oppression many things in their situation could be changed. It is a simple fact that two members of these oppressed communities are now bishops of the Christian Church.[21]

21. Stephen Neill, *Salvation Tomorrow* (Nashville: Abingdon, 1976), p. 84.

CHAPTER 12

Demand for Moratorium

The idea of a moratorium is not altogether new. For many years we have seen the slogan, "Yankee, Go Home," scribbled across the billboards of the world. More recently the wording has been changed to read, "Missionary, Go Home." Indeed, James Scherer has written a book with that title.

The person most often identified with the demand for moratorium is the Reverend John Gatu, general secretary of the Presbyterian Church in East Africa. He first introduced the idea in 1971. In essence moratorium involves three proposals: (1) that we discontinue sending missionaries to the Third World and that missionaries now on the field not be replaced when they come home on furlough; (2) that Western funds likewise be withdrawn; (3) that there be a five-year cooling-off period which would allow both church and mission a time for review, reflection, and reassessment regarding the situation.

In expressing these views certain leaders have made rather harsh statements. Canon Burgess Carr, former general secretary of the All Africa Conference of Churches (AACC), said: "The moratorium is a debate about the structures of exploitation, spiritual exploitation at that. Why should someone save his soul at the expense of emasculating my humanity? Why should I be portrayed as a perpetually helpless nobody in order to reinforce the racial and spiritual arrogance of people in Europe and America?"[1] The Lusaka Assembly of the AACC (1974) made the following statement: "Should the moratorium cause missionary sending agencies to crumble, the African church would have performed a service in redeeming God's people in the Northern Hemisphere from a distorted view of the mission of the church in the world."[2] Emerito Nacpil, dean of Union Theological Seminary (Manila), spoke of the "death of the present missionary system" and went on to say: "The most *missionary* service a missionary under the present system can do today in Asia is to go home."[3]

Observations

1. The demand for moratorium is by no means unreasonable, given the situation as it has existed in some parts of the world for well over a hundred years. Missionaries, like everyone else, have their blind spots; one of them has been to hold on to power too long.

2. The demand for moratorium originated in Africa and the most strident voices have come from that part of the world. There are valid reasons for this. The impact of Christianity on culture has been considerably greater in Africa than in other parts of the world, and it has been over a much shorter time span. The Asian churches had several hundred years to adjust; those in Africa did not. There the changes have been much greater and have come much faster.

3. To date, the demand for moratorium has been largely confined to the ecumenical wing of the Third World churches. There has been little support from the more conservative church leaders. Will this continue indefinitely? When the conservative churches are as old and well organized as the ecumenical churches are now, will they too begin to talk about

1. Burgess Carr, "Internationalizing the Mission," mimeographed paper, p. 4.
2. *Ecumenical Press Service*, 20 June 1974, p. 11.
3. Emerito P. Nacpil, "Mission but not Missionaries," paper presented at a Consultation of Methodist Missionaries and Churches in Asia, Kuala Lumpur, Malaysia, February 1971, p. 4.

moratorium? They have not yet used the term, but some of them have already made other demands.

4. The loudest cries for moratorium have been made at ecumenical gatherings. When these leaders return to their home churches, however, they find little support at the grass-roots for their point of view.

5. The demand for moratorium has been given a mixed reception. It has been rather well received by the mainline denominations, for it fits in with their declared policy of planned retreat in recent years. Conversely, it has been viewed with a jaundiced eye by the more conservative mission leaders, but they did come to grips with the problem at the Lausanne Congress in 1974. Article 9 of the Lausanne Covenant has a guarded statement:

> A reduction of foreign missionaries and money in an evangel-ized country may sometimes be necessary to facilitate the na-tional church's growth in self-reliance and to release resources for unevangelized areas. Missionaries should flow even more freely from and to all six continents in a spirit of humble service.

6. The demand for moratorium is said to include money as well as personnel, but the demand has a hollow ring as long as the All Africa Conference of Churches and similar ecu-menical bodies accept huge subsidies from Western sources. One gets the impression that the churches would not be averse to accepting the funds now used to support missionaries.

7. Whether or not we agree with the demand for morato-rium, it would be unwise to turn a completely deaf ear to the proposition. Obviously some leaders in the "younger" churches feel very strongly about the matter or they would not have expressed themselves in such abrasive terms. Where there is so much smoke, there is bound to be some fire. It would be an act of folly to brush the whole thing aside. It merits careful and honest appraisal. Regardless of who is right and who is wrong, we should search our hearts and examine our methods to make sure that we are free from all forms of paternalism,

which, after all, is the root cause and prime target of the demand.

What Lies Behind the Demand?

It is not without reason that the churches have called for a moratorium. Rightly or wrongly, they feel that as long as the missionaries remain, the problems will continue. The only way to solve the problems, therefore, is for the missionaries to withdraw, at least for the time being.

1. Third World churches have a natural, God-given desire for autonomy. In the political realm we hear a great deal about self-determination. It was part of Woodrow Wilson's Fourteen Points. It was reaffirmed by Roosevelt and Churchill in the Atlantic Charter. It has been applied across the board politically, but it has yet to be applied with equal force in church and mission circles. Missionaries have been in the driver's seat so long that it is almost impossible to get them out, and few are willing to relinquish power voluntarily. The churches not only want to cooperate with the missions; they also want to be part of the decision-making process.

2. Third World churches have a legitimate desire to contextualize the gospel, making it meaningful to Christians and non-Christians alike. Evangelism, worship, and theological education—all have been much too Western in orientation and content. Worship must be "in spirit and in truth" (John 4:24), but it does not have to be Western in style. On the whole, missionaries have been slow to recognize this fact; consequently, the churches feel that the only way to effect change is for the missionary to withdraw to give them an opportunity to find themselves.

3. Prior to World War II the peoples of the East looked to the West for inspiration and leadership. Western civilization appeared to be superior to any other kind. Since the war the situation has changed drastically. Not only is the Christian element in Western civilization on the decline; Western civilization itself is in jeopardy. If we cannot solve our own problems, how can we solve those of the Third World? Christians

and non-Christians in the Third World are sadly disillusioned with the West, and who can blame them? In country after country the attempt is being made to revive and promote the indigenous culture, which was often plowed under by the colonial administrators. It used to be an asset to have a white man on the mission compound. That is no longer true.

4. It is by no means certain that the overseas churches want to get rid of the missionaries permanently. They do not want to go it alone even if they could. They recognize the universal character of the Christian church and are keen to maintain contacts with churches around the world. What they want is mutuality. They have something to give as well as something to receive, and they would like this fact to be recognized. For much too long they have been on the receiving end of everything, not only money; the time has come for them to be regarded as equal partners in the church and its mission.

Objectionable Features in Western Missions

It is always easier to spot the mote in our brother's eye than to discover the beam in our own. Western missionaries have often been guilty of such shortsightedness. They have, in most instances, been blissfully unaware of those features of their life and work which have been so offensive to the national churches and their leaders.

1. The charter of the famous London Missionary Society (1795) warned its early workers not to take any form of denominationalism to the mission field. They were to take only "the glorious gospel of the blessed God" (1 Tim 1:11). The emerging churches were to be free to decide on their own brand of church polity. This was a good idea, but few missionaries paid any attention to it and proceeded to reproduce their own denominations in all parts of the world.

In some cases denominational loyalty led to competition, even rivalry. To help solve this problem the practice of comity was introduced. In some fields, such as the Philippines, it worked well. In Japan it was all but ignored.

The churches in the Third World want the right to determine their own affiliation. They prefer cooperation with other churches in their own countries to affiliation with the "mother" denominations in the West. It is widely recognized that denominationalism does not mean nearly as much to Christians in the Third World as it does to church members here at home. It is noteworthy that the churches in Communist China have long since renounced denominationalism and are content to be known simply as Christian churches. The move in the beginning was inspired by the Three Self Movement at the instigation of the government. It will be interesting to see what develops along this line now that the government has revived both the Three Self Movement and the Religious Affairs Bureau. If the "house churches" are permitted to continue, they will, I believe, prefer to remain without denominational labels.

2. Compared with other overseas enterprises the missionary movement has operated on a shoestring budget, but the missionaries are rich by comparison with the national workers. Western funds have not always been used wisely. Sometimes there has been waste of money and effort. The national churches are aware of this and think that, given the opportunity, they could make a wiser and more economical use of available funds. This they cannot do as long as the missionaries are on hand to pull the purse strings. Under these circumstances the church leaders are understandably restive.

3. Along with waste of money there was duplication of effort. Instead of pooling their resources in men and money, each mission went its own way and did its own thing. The net result was an enormous amount of duplication, particularly in the area of theological education. Each mission had its own Bible school or seminary to be sure that the graduates were not only sound in doctrine but also loyal to the denomination. In Taiwan alone there are over thirty theological schools, and in South Korea the number is much higher.

The national leaders can hardly be expected to wax enthusiastic over this sort of thing. They would prefer to have half a dozen good, strong schools rather than thirty or forty weak ones; but as long as the missionaries are in charge, the situation will not change.

4. The last feature is probably the most offensive: holding on to leadership too long. No man wants to preside over the liquidation of his own empire, and missionaries are no exception. They have done what the colonial administrators did; they have held on to power too long. This is not universally true; in some instances the churches were given their independence long before the governments received theirs. As a rule, however, it is correct to say that the missions dragged their feet in this matter. Bong Ro, executive secretary of the Asian Theological Association, reported as recently as 1973 that 60 percent of the Bible colleges and seminaries in Asia still had missionaries as presidents. Obviously this is not acceptable to the church leaders in Asia. How can the situation be altered? By asking the missionaries to leave. At least that is what the advocates of moratorium believe.

Why Western Missions Object to Moratorium

The idea of moratorium has not been well received in conservative circles, and in every case the missions believe they have legitimate reasons.

1. The missions object to moratorium on theological grounds. Many of them fear that if the missionaries pull out and the church leaders are left on their own, there will be nothing to keep them from being sucked into the ecumenical stream. Others fear that, without the missionaries on hand to guide them, the church leaders may accept the findings of higher criticism and not be able to withstand the inroads of liberal theology. Still others fear that the church leaders will go too far in the matter of contextualization and end up with syncretism. These are matters of great concern to conservative mission leaders.

2. Conservative missions also object on administrative grounds. If the missionaries withdraw, what is to become of all the property and buildings they acquired through the years? Who will move into the missionary residences? And if the

missionaries return later, will they get these houses back? And what about the schools and hospitals with all their valuable equipment? Will they become bones of contention for the church leaders, whose responsibility it will be to decide what to do with them? More than one national church has been split over the disposition of mission property. It is only good stewardship to see that these institutions continue to be used for the purpose for which they were built in the beginning.

3. Others object on financial grounds. They are not at all sure that the moratorium includes both men *and* money. They have a suspicion that what the church leaders are after is the financial gain they can achieve by a moratorium. If they agree to withdraw the missionaries, will the churches be able and willing to foot the bill for all the programs formerly maintained by the missions? There is reason to doubt that the churches have the financial strength to carry on some of the activities without subsidies from the West. If that is the case, will the churches demand Western money? Some missions would be willing to continue their subsidies even after the missionaries are withdrawn; but most of them feel that if the churches are to get along without men, they should also get along without money.

4. There are also pragmatic grounds. These relate to the home constituency. The faith missions are hard pressed at this point; they are not entirely free to act on their own. They depend for their support on a very conservative constituency that may object to moratorium in any or all of its forms. These churches give liberally when they know the missions and missionaries they support, but they are not enthusiastic about supporting national churches or their leaders. If the missions, with their superior knowledge and expertise, are willing to go along with the demand for moratorium, they may find themselves in deep water with the churches which support them. Churches have been known to discontinue a mission's support upon learning that its missionaries use the Revised Standard Version, cooperate on the field with Billy Graham Crusades, or even with Evangelism-in-Depth. There is a sense in which

the leaders of the faith missions are walking a tightrope. One false step and down they go.

Various Kinds of Moratorium

Up to this point we have been discussing moratorium as enunciated by such leaders as Gatu, Carr, Nacpil, and others; there are other forms of moratorium and these should be recognized. There are at least four, two voluntary and two involuntary.

1. The first is voluntary withdrawal for political reasons. This is not very common but it has occurred. The White Fathers voluntarily withdrew from Mozambique in the 1970s when the Portuguese colonial administration opposed liberation and took repressive measures against political activists. The United Church of Christ did the same in Angola, and for the same reason.

2. A second form of voluntary withdrawal is for administrative reasons. Some missions, when their objectives had been achieved, decided that no further purpose would be served by prolonging their stay; so they withdrew their missionaries, either bringing them home or sending them elsewhere. The United Presbyterians did this in Mexico and the United Methodists in Uruguay.

3. Then there is involuntary withdrawal for financial reasons. A classic example is the widespread retreat during the Depression of the 1930s. Mission after mission had to recall its workers for lack of financial support. With the soaring cost of missionary support in our day this may happen again. Already there are high-cost areas of the world, such as Tokyo, to which missions are reluctant to send their workers. Even the gigantic, affluent IBM corporation has replaced American employees in Tokyo with Japanese personnel.

4. By far the most common form is involuntary withdrawal for political reasons. Mass evacuation has been the bugbear of Christian missions for a long time, but in the past thirty years the problem has become almost pandemic. First it was China in the early 1950s. That was followed by the Sudan, Cuba,

and Burma in the 1960s. In the 1970s it was Somalia, Iraq, Yemen, and Ethiopia, and, most recently, Iran. Wycliffe Bible Translators has been expelled from five countries, and the end is not yet.

Justification for Moratorium

C. Peter Wagner has listed four reasons why, in his view, the concept of moratorium is valid.

1. *Western cultural chauvinism.* This is expressed in a variety of ways: economics, politics, technology, communications. Missionaries, immersed as they are in their own culture, have a tendency to export Western culture along with the Christian gospel. Some of this is unavoidable. It is quite impossible for the missionary to divest himself of all cultural hangovers; but he could, and should, do a better job than he has in the past. "Missionaries must keep in mind that they go into other cultures to spread the Gospel, not to 'civilize' people different from themselves."[4]

2. *Theological and ethical imperialism.* Leaders in the Third World churches are no longer content to read Barth, Brunner, and Bultmann, or even Calvin and Luther. They have special needs that systematic theology as we know it has never addressed. Even our biblical theology has not come to grips with the moral and spiritual problems confronting Christians in the Third World. The time has come for Third World leaders to be given the freedom to develop their own ethnotheologies. Missionaries who are unable or unwilling to make this concession are guilty of theological imperialism.

3. *Paternalistic interchurch aid.* One of the greatest mistakes of missionaries of the past was the unwise use of Western funds, which led to dependence on the part of the emerging churches. Even after the missionaries had relinquished their positions of power, they continued to wield considerable influence by virtue of the financial aid they were in a position

4. C. Peter Wagner, "Colour the Moratorium Gray," *International Review of Mission*, April 1975, p. 171.

to give—and financial power is even greater than political power. The fact that the "younger" churches of the Third World are poor by Western standards makes them all the more vulnerable. Wagner refers to interchurch aid as the "syndrome of church development...which has all too often reduced the evangelistic effectiveness of evangelical and ecumenical missions alike."[5]

4. *Nonproductive missionaries.* There was a time when *any* white missionary was welcome, for by his very presence in the community he lent a certain degree of prestige to the church, to say nothing of the fact that he usually had money to dispense. That day is gone forever. Nowadays he must have something to offer. In a word, he must have some gift or skill that will enable him to make a solid contribution to the cause of Christ in the host country. Missionaries who cannot produce should be recalled by their boards, but this has seldom been done. The churches have therefore been forced to take drastic action and issue a call for moratorium.

Some Pertinent Questions

In closing this discussion certain questions should be asked. Is the moratorium to be partial or complete? Is it to be temporary or permanent? Does it involve men or money or both? Is it to be voluntary or involuntary? Is the decision to be unilateral by the church, or is it to be a bilateral decision? Is the concept essentially good or bad? Is the demand right or wrong? Is moratorium likely to help or hinder the cause of Christ? Does moratorium mean the end of world missions as we have understood the term? Is the motive behind moratorium right or wrong? Does moratorium apply to Third World missionaries, or only to Western missionaries? Are there parts of the world from which missionaries could be withdrawn with good effect for all concerned? Does the concept of catholicity require the presence of Western missionaries in the Third World churches?

5. Ibid., p. 173.

Moratorium in and of itself is neither good nor bad, right nor wrong. Much depends on the purposes and motives involved. Two extremes should be avoided. Western missions should not assume that the evangelization of the world is the "white man's burden" and on that account rush in where angels fear to tread. On the other hand the "younger" churches of the world should think twice before giving the missionaries their walking ticket when less than 2 or 3 percent of the population in a given country is Christian. The task is unfinished. None of us—Western mission leaders or national church leaders—can afford to rest on our laurels.

CHAPTER 13

Contextualization of Theology

Ever since the middle of the nineteenth century missionaries have accepted Henry Venn's definition of an indigenous church as one that is "self-supporting, self-governing, and self-propagating." The Madras Conference of the International Missionary Council in 1938 came up with a better definition: "An indigenous church, young or old, in the East or in the West, is a church which, rooted in obedience to Christ, spontaneously uses forms of thought and modes of action natural and familiar in its own environment."

In recent years a new word has appeared: *contextualize*. Arthur F. Glasser, former dean of Fuller's School of World Mission, said: "The latest 'in' word is *contextualization*. Overnight it has won many friends, provoked much lively debate and even spawned a first-class journal (*Gospel in Context*)."[1] Like every other new theological concept, the word has made as many enemies as friends. The battle lines are drawn and there are plenty of proponents on both sides. It is not my intention to join the controversy. Rather I wish to discuss certain issues concerning theological education in the Third World which,

1. Arthur F. Glasser, "Help from an Unexpected Quarter or, the Old Testament and Contextualization," *Missiology*, October 1979, p. 403.

in spite of all the fine talk about indigenization and/or contextualization, have not yet been resolved. If the reader does not like my use of *contextualization*, he may substitute the word *indigenization*. The difference between them is not great enough to quarrel about. Contextualization goes beyond indigenization, but the latter is certainly included in the former.

In the parable of the mustard seed in Matthew 13 Jesus portrays the external expansion of the kingdom. The small seed ultimately grew into a large tree in which the birds of the air built their nests. Made of straw, string, twigs, mud, and other materials, the nests were not an integral part of the tree. The tree of Christianity was first cultivated in the soil of Asia. From there it was transplanted by Paul to Europe, where it flourished for fifteen hundred years, growing into a huge tree. In the last two or three centuries the tree has been transplanted back into the soil of Asia. Unfortunately, the missionaries took the nests along with the tree, and as a result Christianity has not really taken root in overseas soil. Because of this the national churches now emerging in the Third World are calling—some of them rather loudly—for an indigenous form of Christianity.

Reasons for the Call for Contextualization

There are at least four reasons why the Third World churches are calling for the contextualization of theology.

1. *The stigma of the colonial image.* It is simply a matter of record that the modern missionary movement, through no fault of its own, was part and parcel of the political, economic, and cultural thrust of the West into the East during the heyday of colonialism. In China the alliance between Christianity and imperialism was extremely close. After the Opium War (1839-1842) two groups of foreigners pressed into China: the merchants with their opium and the missionaries with their Bibles. The Chinese can be forgiven if they have difficulty in understanding why the same "Christian" country—Great Britain—should have insisted on importing into China two such diverse commodities as opium and religion.

2. *Western elements in Christian worship.* Our Roman Catholic friends were the worst offenders in this area. They went so far as to insist that the mass be recited in Latin to the natives of the New World. We Protestants were not much better. An Episcopal service in Patagonia differs little from one in Pittsburgh. A Baptist church in Burma has all the earmarks of one in Boston. The Third World churches are calling for change. They want their own modes of worship which will more closely reflect their own divergent cultures.

3. *The desperate need for a theology that speaks directly to the Third World Christian.* The national Christians want Christian theology to speak to *their* situation, to answer *their* questions, and to meet *their* needs. As any missionary will acknowledge, this has not been the case. Too long the Western missionary has been content to teach a Western theology—all the way from Augustine to Paul Tillich.

4. *The foreignness of Christianity.* The national Christians want to make the gospel as attractive and meaningful as possible to their own people. The foreignness of Christianity has been the greatest single obstacle to its acceptance in many parts of the world. In Asia, where fewer than 3 percent of the people have become Christians, Christianity is known as a "foreign religion." In Africa it is regarded as the "white man's religion." If the believers in the Third World are ever to win their friends and neighbors to Christ, they must present Him in Asian, African, or Latin American dress.

Factors Which Prompted the Call for Contextualization

1. *The rise and spread of nationalism.* Under the colonial system the national cultures were almost plowed under. English, French, or Spanish became the official language. Western history and science were taught in the schools. Western political institutions were established. Now the governments of the newly independent countries are doing their best to correct the situation. They want to recover and preserve their own culture. The churches want to do the same. They do not want

to be the only institution in the country out of step with the times.

2. *The resurgence of the non-Christian religions.* During the colonial period Christianity was accorded preferential treatment by the colonial administrators, and the indigenous religions had to take a back seat, especially among the intellectuals, many of whom were educated in Western-style schools. Now the non-Christian religions are on the move, engaging for the first time in missionary activities of their own and winning converts in the process. Not a few former Untouchables in India have left the Christian church and returned to the Hindu fold in order to qualify for government aid. The churches naturally want Christianity to be able to hold its own under these conditions, which have heightened their realization of the need for contextualization.

3. *A desire for authentic selfhood.* Caught up in the modern milieu, many churches have an identity crisis. They do not quite know how to fit into the new situation in which they find themselves. Church members want to be good Christians and patriotic citizens as well. This is sometimes difficult to achieve in the eyes of non-Christians; hence the crisis.

Mistakes Made in Theological Education

The missionaries made a number of mistakes in educating theological students, mistakes which should be corrected as soon as possible.

1. *Failure to determine whether the students had spiritual gifts.* We accepted students without inquiring whether or not they had spiritual gifts to be cultivated. Schools were often small and enrollment was low, so the missionaries could not afford to be too selective. Moreover, many of the students were young people who had had little or no opportunity to discover their gifts. That was something they hoped to find out as they went along. One needs more than a "call" to full-time Christian ministry. There should also be the gifts needed to make the call effective. Without them the student may become a dropout.

The Pentecostal churches in Latin America adopted an altogether different approach, with gratifying results as we all know.

> In the Chilean Pentecostal Church for a man to graduate as a "worker," he must have won many people to Christ; to graduate as a "pastor," he must have led people to Christ, brought them together and formed a missionary church; to graduate as "reverend," he must have planted five or six churches.[2]

2. *Failure to make sure the students maintained their cultural contacts.* In many instances the student was removed from his natural environment and kept in a "hothouse" for three or four years. By the time he graduated he was so accustomed to a semi-Western lifestyle that he was virtually incapacitated for the very work to which he was originally called. He often found it difficult, even impossible, to return to his own town where life was simple and the people unsophisticated. He was much more at home in a bigger town or city where he could have access to the amenities of modern civilization.

3. *Failure to encourage self-reliance.* The mission often subsidized education to the point where the graduate expected to be supported by mission funds later on. Some missions waived all board, room, and tuition charges on the understanding that after graduation the worker would remain in the employ of the mission for a stipulated number of years.

4. *Failure to emphasize discipleship.* In many Bible schools the emphasis was on the training of leaders rather than the making of disciples. The apostle Peter speaks of two kinds of growth: growth in knowledge and growth in grace (2 Pet 3:18). Most seminaries, at home as well as overseas, find it easier to produce the first than the second. It is certainly easier to measure growth in knowledge than growth in grace. As a result most theological schools have failed to use adequate means to ensure a balance between the two. It is therefore possible for the student to make good marks and graduate with honors

2. Peter Savage, "Four Crises in Third World Theological Education," *Evangelical Missions Quarterly*, Fall 1972, p. 32.

but not be able to cultivate his own spiritual life. He may have a head full of knowledge but his life may be devoid of the fruit of the Spirit.

5. *Failure to maintain a proper balance.* In theological education it has been difficult to maintain a good balance between classroom instruction and field education. A certain amount of Christian service is often required but it is not commensurate with the theoretical knowledge received in the classroom. David Yang, an outstanding Chinese evangelist, organized a *Ling Kung T'uan* (Spiritual Work Team). The team members spent half of their time in the classroom and the other half engaging in evangelistic work and ministering in the churches. The combination of learning and doing was a good mix. Classroom instruction is much more relevant and helpful if the student is required immediately to put it into practice.

6. *Failure to enlist the cooperation of the churches.* Theological education for the most part was under the control of the missionaries. Very few Bible schools were the responsibility of the church. Most of the teachers and all of the administrators were missionaries, a fact which gave the whole operation a foreign flavor. Nowhere was this more prominent than in the area of curriculum.

> The classic curriculum found in most seminaries and Bible colleges has followed the patterns that have existed for the last two hundred years, where emphasis has been placed on the digestion of packets of knowledge rather than on bringing each student to spiritual maturity and effective ministry.[3]

Little wonder that a group of Asian leaders expressed concern over the growing crisis in theological education: "Many of our seminaries and Bible schools," they stated, "are stereotypes of Western models and are curriculum-examination oriented rather than training men practically for pastoral ministry in Asia."[4]

3. Ibid., p. 31.
4. Ibid., p. 28.

What the Missionaries Gave Theological Students

The curriculum exported to the mission field was a carbon copy of courses taught in seminaries at home: Greek, Hebrew, apologetics, homiletics, church history, New Testament, Old Testament, systematic theology, church music, Christian education, personal evangelism, and so on.

The average seminarian in the Third World has no need of Greek and Hebrew. Apologetics is based on Aristotelian logic and the theology of Thomas Aquinas. It is helpful to Western students but does nothing to prepare the Asian pastor to defend his faith against the claims of Hinduism, Buddhism, Confucianism, or Islam. Church history is really Western church history. Little or nothing is said about the origin and development of the churches in the Third World. I have in my library a five-volume *History of the Christian Church.* Seventy-seven pages are devoted to Martin Luther, 65 to John Wesley. William Carey, on the other hand, rates only a page-and-a-half, while David Livingstone's name simply appears in a list of "great missionaries." Hudson Taylor is not even included in the list! The author gives 227 pages to the church in the United States, but only 12 to one hundred years of missionary work in Africa, Asia, Latin America, and Oceania! In the West we speak of *The* Reformation and have courses on the subject. We even offer courses on Luther, Calvin, Wesley, and others. Our brethren overseas look upon *The* Reformation as just another episode in the history of the Western church; as for special courses on Luther, they would prefer to know something about what K. S. Latourette called "The Great Century" of Christian missions, and thus become acquainted with the origin and history of the churches in the non-Western world.

What Theological Students Needed

The Third World churches got the theology we gave them, not the theology they needed. They needed a theology that would help relate Christianity to the cultural and religious climate in which they live. Doctrines and practices taken for granted here are burning issues with them. Contrariwise, important issues here are of little interest to them. Systematic theology as taught in the West has much to say about verbal inspiration and inerrancy of the Scriptures, and seminarians are taught to defend these great doctrines with all the ability they can muster. In the Third World these are nonissues, taken for granted by all pastors and teachers. Of far greater importance is the uniqueness of the Christian faith and the finality of Jesus Christ, and how these fit into a pluralistic situation in Asia, the home of the great ethnic religions of Hinduism, Buddhism, Confucianism, and Islam, not to mention Communism.

Every seminary in India should have a course on Hinduism, designed to enable the student to understand that great religious system and how to deal with such concepts as *avatara* (incarnation), *samsara* (transmigration), *karma* (moral law of cause and effect), *Brahman* (universal soul), *atman* (individual soul), and *maya* (illusion). The supreme social problem in India is the caste system. What does Christianity have to say about caste?

In China there is another set of problems dealing with *yin-yang*, *feng-shui*, and *t'ien-ming*. The cardinal virtue in Confucian culture is filial piety, the ultimate expression of which is ancestor worship. In Japan there has been emperor worship in addition to ancestor worship. Throughout East Asia there is Buddhism with its sacred writings and major doctrines and religious rites.

What about the Muslim countries of the world, with a total population of 700 million? Islam has more in common with Christianity than the other religions. In spite of the fact that the Koran borrows heavily from the Old Testament and the Gospels, there are some major doctrinal differences to be overcome.

In Latin America the big issue is liberation. The majority of intellectuals are convinced Marxists and the seminarian must be taught how to deal with Marxists on their own ground. It is not enough to quote Scripture to them. Does Christianity have any hope to offer to the downtrodden, oppressed peoples of the world, or is it all "pie in the sky by and by"?

In Africa the churches have altogether different social and religious problems: polygamy, the purchase of brides, circumcision, witchcraft, and so on. Are these dealt with anywhere in theological education?

In the West we have been accustomed to individual conversion and tend to look upon anything else with suspicion. What about group conversion? Is it possible? Desirable? What about miracles, myths, visions, and dreams? In the West dreams and visions have no place in Christian experience. Miracles fare a little better, but not much, depending on the group. They are found in the Bible, to be sure; but are they valid for today? Some say yes; others no. What about demon possession and exorcism, mentioned so often in the New Testament but of little interest to the Western theologian?

In the West meditation is largely a lost art. As for mysticism, only the saints go in for that. In the East, however, meditation, mysticism, fasting, and other forms of asceticism are common practices; yet they have almost no place in theological education.

Personal evangelism, as conducted in the Third World, reflects the course taught in the West. Few missionaries have been creative enough to come up with a new approach tailored to the needs and cultural outlook of the national population. E. Stanley Jones blazed a trail with his round-table conferences and his *ashrams*, but few ever took their cue from him. In fact, he was regarded by many as a maverick whose brand of evangelism was to be avoided rather than adopted.

It is true that Western missionaries have been insensitive to the needs and desires of the churches in the Third World. They made almost no effort to adapt Christianity to the needs of their converts, still less to the needs of the non-Christian population. Evangelism, education, liturgy, music, and architecture—all were dressed in Western garb. Little wonder that converts to the faith were accused of "eating the foreign religion." They stood out, not as "pilgrims and strangers" in the biblical sense, but as traitors and apostates.

A Model School

The Discipleship Training Centre (DTC) in Singapore, founded by David Adeney in 1968, is one of the few theological schools making a sincere effort to cope with these problems. At DTC they emphasize six important things: community life, application, discipleship, holiness, family ethics, and endurance.

Teachers and students live together in the same dormitory, thus making possible an intimacy of fellowship in which the students get to know the teachers as persons rather than as professors. Teaching and preaching, important as they are, are only a means to an end. Life as well as mind must be changed. There must be growth in grace as well as growth in knowledge. The Word must be applied to the life. Theological students must be doers of the Word; hence the emphasis on application.

For the best modern-day example of discipleship we must go to India, where the disciple chooses a particular guru and attaches himself to his person, living under his roof, sitting at his feet, eating at his table, listening to his words, walking and talking with him in the marketplace, even helping with the household chores. In a word, he shares the total life of the guru. In the give-and-take of this intimate fellowship the disciple gradually takes on the character of his guru. Before long he finds himself thinking, talking, acting like him. When he gets through, he is a carbon copy of the guru. That is discipleship.

Holiness of life and character is also important. God's word to Israel was: "Be ye holy, for I am holy." In the New Testament we read: "Holiness, without which no man shall see the Lord" (Heb 12:14). That is true for the saint as well as the sinner. It is important for the seminarian to know what holiness is and what it is not. Some, with a legalistic turn of mind, equate it with a long list of don'ts. For others it has a mystical connotation. Still others identify it with the Keswick message or the charismatic movement.

Family ethics is of immense importance, especially in Asia, where rigid family structure is often inimical to the Christian faith. First-generation Christians are torn between filial piety and loyalty to Christ. Marriage in the Orient is a family affair, arranged by the parents. What if non-Christian parents insist on giving their believing daughter in marriage to a non-Christian? What about baptism, regarded by non-Christian parents as an irrevocable break with family tradition? The believing son or daughter may attend church and read the Bible, but he or she must stop short of public confession of Christ in baptism. Phil Parshall, a veteran missionary in the Muslim world, said this about baptism:

> The implications of this ceremony reverberate throughout nearby villages and towns. Abdul Mohammad has openly declared himself a traitor to Islamic social structures, political and legal systems, economic patterns. Worst of all, the religion of his fathers has been profaned and desecrated. He has now become a worshiper of three gods, a follower of a corrupted religious book, an eater of pork, a drinker of wine, and a member of an alien society of warmongers and adulterers.[5]

Idolatry is another tradition observed by the family in cases of sickness and death, and in connection with funeral rites. The Christian is expected to take part; but, of course, idolatry is roundly condemned in the Bible. What should he do? Yet little attention is given to the practical implications of idolatry in a non-Christian culture.

Endurance may sound like a strange emphasis in a seminary; but in the non-Christian countries of the world believers find themselves facing the same problems as did the early Christians: hatred, discrimination, ostracism, pain, persecution, in some places even death. In such circumstances it is necessary for Christian leaders to develop a theology of suffering which will enable much-tried believers to endure hardness as good soldiers of Jesus Christ (2 Tim 2:3), remembering

5. Phil Parshall, "Contextualized Baptism for Muslim Converts," *Missiology*, October 1979, pp. 501-02.

the words of our Lord: "He that endureth to the end shall be saved" (Mt 10:22). The Christians in China were probably not prepared for the sufferings they have endured during the last thirty years under a Communist regime.

Guidelines for Contextualization

Contextualization, like many other things, is easier said than done. If it is to be done effectively and constructively, it should follow certain well-defined guidelines.

1. Some elements in Christianity are absolute and cannot be changed. If Christianity is to remain true to its own genius, it must be exclusive. If that is offensive to some, we cannot do anything about it; that is the way it is. There are in Christianity certain doctrines which are absolutely essential and therefore cannot be contextualized. The tendency is to make the list too long by including denominational distinctives. This we must try to avoid. The Scriptures must be allowed to speak for themselves. Such a list should certainly include the inspiration and authority of the Scriptures. The doctrine of the Trinity should cover the holiness and love of God the Father; the virgin birth, atoning death, bodily resurrection, ascension into heaven, and second coming of Christ; and the regenerating and sanctifying power of the Holy Spirit. The doctrine of salvation should set forth the nature of sin, the lostness of man, and salvation by grace through faith alone. These, it would seem to me, are absolutely vital to what Paul called "the truth of the gospel." To tamper with them is to trifle with the truth.

2. Some elements are relative and may be changed. In Galatians 1 Paul makes a ringing statement concerning the *truth* of the gospel and pronounces a curse on anyone, man or angel, who comes with "another gospel" (v. 8). In Philippians 1, however, when he is speaking of the *preaching* of the gospel, he rejoices even when those who do the preaching desire only to add affliction to his bonds (vv. 15-18). It was enough that Christ was preached, even though both method and motive were wrong. We should not lose sight of the dif-

ference between these two chapters. When it comes to non-essentials there should be liberty to contextualize the Christian faith, thus making it attractive and intelligible to the non-Western world.

There is nothing sacrosanct about various kinds of liturgy, modes of worship, methods of evangelism, or styles of architecture.

Let us begin with architecture. Must church buildings conform to any particular style? Do we really *need* church buildings? The early church got along without them for 250 years! Must they have pews, crosses, pulpits, spires, stained-glass windows? Would an inquirer not feel more at home in a building that resembles one of his own?

What about church music? Should the hymns all be Western hymns translated into the vernacular, or should the Christians be encouraged to write their own hymns and use their own tunes? As for musical instruments, are pianos and organs the only "Christian" instruments? Would the worshipers not enjoy the music more if they used their own instruments?

Must the main service of the week be on Sunday? Could it not be on Friday in Bangladesh, or on Saturday in Nepal, or on Poya Day in Sri Lanka? If Jesus said in John 4 that worship can be conducted anywhere, can it not also be conducted any time? Must the form of service be identical with that in the West? Must every service begin with the invocation and end with the benediction? Must one man always be in charge of the entire service? If the congregation wants to participate in audible simultaneous prayer, is that not in good form? Must the congregation sit in pews if at home they sit on the floor? Why should the *outward* form of worship not conform as far as possible to what they have been accustomed to in their own religions?

3. All cultures have both good and bad elements. The early missionaries tended to reject everything that was strange to them. Christianity was equated with civilization. The Roman Catholic missionaries in the New World were of the opinion that the Indians had to be civilized before they could become Christians. In South America they established mission settle-

ments, known as reductions, to facilitate the Christianization of the Indians. The residents of these reductions were converted to the Christian faith and to Spanish culture. Protestants did not go that far, but they did tend to reject the indigenous cultures along with the "pagan" religions.

Fortunately today's missionaries, with a little help from the anthropologists, are much less iconoclastic than their forerunners. It is now generally agreed that all that is inherently good should be retained. Only that which is contrary to the clear teaching of Scripture is to be rejected.

4. Who is to decide what is good and what is bad—the missionaries, the nationals, or both? The missionaries have a better understanding of Scripture but they are not likely to appreciate the nuances of the indigenous culture—certainly not in their earlier years on the field. The nationals, on the other hand, are thoroughly acquainted with their own culture, but they may lack an adequate understanding of the Scriptures. The best way to handle this delicate matter is to have the nationals and the missionaries pool their knowledge and experience and try to arrive at a consensus that will preserve the integrity of the Christian faith and at the same time retain the wholesome elements in the indigenous culture.

5. The Holy Scriptures stand in judgment on all cultures. They alone are the final court of appeal. All cultures and religions, Christian and non-Christian alike, stand under the judgment of the Word of God. Any rite or custom that is clearly contrary to the explicit teaching of the Bible must be eliminated. If this works a hardship on the converts, so be it. That is the price they will have to pay for their allegiance to Jesus Christ. Patience is required, however, while first-generation Christians are coming to grips with these momentous problems.

6. When a bad custom must be abandoned, every effort should be made to provide a functional substitute. It is not enough to denounce a "pagan" practice; something must be put in its place. A glaring example of failure in this regard was that of the missionaries in China to provide any kind of substitute for ancestral worship, which, being the ultimate

expression of filial piety, was exceedingly dear to the hearts of the Chinese. If the missionaries could have solved this problem, their evangelistic efforts would undoubtedly have been much more successful than they were. After a hundred years of missionary effort the Chinese Christians, Roman Catholic and Protestant, never numbered more than 1 percent of the population.

The Danger of Syncretism

In our efforts to contextualize theology, we may carry the process too far and run the risk of ending up with a watered-down version of Christianity totally foreign to the New Testament. What may pass for "indigenous Christianity" may turn out to be nothing but "Christopaganism." Once that point is reached, it is exceedingly difficult to correct the situation.

The danger of syncretism is all the greater when a "people movement" is involved. When people enter the Christian church one by one and there is ample time for counsel and instruction, the moral and doctrinal standards of the New Testament are likely to be preserved intact. But when a large group of people decide en masse to accept the Christian faith, there is no guarantee that the individual members have had a personal conversion experience, without which they will never be anything more than nominal Christians. They may be simply following the orders of the tribal chief or the village elder without any change of heart on their part. When a significant number of these persons enter the church without sufficient instruction, they may very well bring their paganism with them. Once they have been baptized and have been admitted into the fellowship of the church, it is almost impossible to persuade them that a vital link is missing.

This is especially true of people who come from an animistic background. Animism has been such an integral part of their everyday life that it is very difficult to separate their old religion from life. When they are illiterate, and many of them are, the problem is compounded many times. It is much harder to impart Christian instruction in oral form only and usually not very satisfactory.

Many of these factors are present in Black Africa, where twenty thousand persons are reported to be embracing Christianity every day. There is no way to give such large numbers of people the biblical instruction they need to make them into strong, intelligent believers.

It was this that caused George Peters to identify Christopaganism as the greatest problem facing the church in Black Africa. Byang Kato shared this point of view and labored hard to correct the situation.[6]

6. See Byang Kato, *Theological Pitfalls in Africa* (Kisumu, Kenya: Evangelical Publishing House, 1975).

CHAPTER 14

The Dynamics of Church Growth

During the last decade a great deal has been written about church growth. This is understandable, since it has been the most dynamic movement in mission circles in recent years. Evangelicals owe a debt of gratitude to Donald McGavran, father of the Church Growth Movement, and to the Fuller School of World Mission, which has majored in church growth.

McGavran has his supporters and his detractors. In ecumenical circles church growth has not been given a warm welcome. It has drawn considerable criticism from evangelicals in the United Kingdom. North American evangelicals, with some exceptions, have looked with favor on the movement. The Interdenominational Foreign Mission Association and the Evangelical Foreign Missions Association, representing almost eighteen thousand missionaries, have welcomed the emphasis on church growth and have benefited greatly by the insights it provides. Church-growth workshops and seminars have been held in all parts of the mission field with great profit to church leaders and missionaries alike.

More recently the church-growth emphasis has spread among the churches here at home. Many churches, when they came to realize that much of their growth was biological or by transfer and therefore not real growth at all, began to show an interest. They reckoned that if the principles of church growth can work on the mission field, there is no reason why they should not be applied here at home too. So, in one way and another, at home and abroad, the movement continues.

Church growth does not "just happen." There are certain definite factors which enter into the picture. These factors can be divided into two categories, natural and supernatural.

Natural Factors

1. *The quality of the seed.* In Matthew 13 Jesus gives us seven parables of the kingdom. In the first two parables He speaks of the "seed." In 13:19 the seed is the *word* of the kingdom. In 13:38 the seed is said to be the *children* of the kingdom. Both ideas are important. We have long since been accustomed to the idea that the seed is the Word, but it may come as a surprise to some that the children of the kingdom are also referred to as the seed.

Pope Paul III ordered that the Indians of the New World should be converted by the "preaching of the evangelic gospel and by the good life." The seed is sown in the hearts of men by the preaching of the gospel. It is also sown in a community by the presence of Christians who exhibit the "good life." If there is to be genuine, lasting fruit both kinds of seed must be present.

There is no problem with the gospel as the seed. Whenever it is preached in sincerity and truth, there is bound to be fruit. What about the children of the kingdom as the seed? That may be a different matter. The children of the kingdom are not always a good advertisement for the gospel of the kingdom. When that happens, the gospel loses its attraction, often its power.

That is one reason why we should be careful not to attach undue importance to numerical growth. Growth in grace and character is more important. One of the great stumbling blocks to the acceptance of the gospel is the failure of Christians to live up to their profession. All of us profess more religion than we are able to practice, and in that sense we are all hypocrites. When people turn their backs on the church because it is "full of hypocrites," there is some truth in the accusation.

The German philosopher Friedrich Nietzsche remarked on one occasion: "I could more readily believe in your Savior if I could find more people who had been saved by Him." How many Christians know what it means to be saved—truly saved? Saved, not from the "big" sins they were never tempted to commit; but saved from the "little" sins—the sharp tongue, the haughty look, the quick temper, and a hundred-and-one other sins—which they commit every day.

When Jesus stood before Annas the high priest, He was asked about His disciples and His doctrine. I do not think He had any trouble defending His doctrine. Not so with His disciples. One of them sold Him for thirty pieces of silver. Another denied Him three times with oaths and curses. Two of them—the Sons of Thunder—wanted to call down fire from heaven to destroy a whole village when they were refused hospitality. I wonder how Jesus "defended" the disciples. If Annas had inquired into these actions (and he might well have done so), I wonder how Jesus would have responded. He could not deny that which was true. He could not defend that which was wrong. He probably would have said nothing.

The world is still inquiring about Jesus' disciples and His doctrine, and Jesus is still having difficulty defending the disciples. All the while the world in its cynicism is shouting, "The doctrine, yes; the disciples, no."

Dr. B. R. Ambedkar was for many years the leader of the sixty million Untouchables in India. Realizing that Hinduism had nothing to offer, he studied Christianity under Bishop J. Waskom Pickett in Bombay. After six months of study he said to the bishop: "When I am studying the life of Christ with you I feel that we Untouchables should become Christians; but when I examine the lives of the Christians here in Bombay, I say to myself: 'No, that is not what we want!' " In October, 1956, Dr. Ambedkar and seventy-five thousand of his followers, in a public ceremony before three hundred thousand spectators in Nagpur, renounced Hinduism and embraced Buddhism.

It is difficult to exaggerate the influence of a changed life. The ultimate apologetic for Christianity is not found in books but in boots. If our life betrays our faith, nobody is going to take the gospel seriously. Jesus was right when He declared that the seed is the children of the kingdom.

2. *The condition of the soil.* The first of the seven parables in Matthew 13 is the parable of the sower. In that parable the fruit—or the harvest—depends, not on the seed nor on the sower, but on the soil. There are four kinds of soil, resulting in four kinds of harvest. The sower and the seed were the same in all four instances; the deciding factor was the soil.

The four kinds of soil can be compared to the various kinds of response found in the human heart. They may also have a wider connotation and refer to the different kinds of cultural and religious soil found in various parts of the world.

The soil that brought forth almost no fruit is like the soil we find in the Muslim world, where missionaries have labored for many years without seeing any lasting fruit. The second type of soil is like the soil in Asia, the home of the great ethnic religions of the world. It is better than the first kind, but the results have been very meager. After five hundred years of missionary work not quite 3 percent of Asia's people are Christian. The third kind of soil is like that found in Latin America, which, from a missionary point of view, has proved to be much more fruitful than that of Asia. The soil which produced an abundant harvest, thirty-, sixty-, or even a hundredfold, can be compared only to Black Africa, where twenty thousand persons are embracing the Christian faith every day.

How are we to account for the enormous disparity in results between Black Africa and the Muslim world? Did all the "good" missionaries go to Africa and all the "poor" ones to the Middle East? Of course not. The deciding factor was the cultural and religious soil into which the seed of the gospel fell.

3. *The vagaries of the weather.* By "weather" is meant the political, social, and economic climate of a given place or time. It is simply a matter of record that when peace and prosperity

prevail religious interest declines. It is when things go wrong, when life breaks down, when bills pile up, when health is shattered, or when death invades the family circle that people give serious consideration to spiritual things. As long as they are self-sufficient—or think they are—they go their happy-go-lucky way without a thought of God.

This is true not only of individuals at the personal level, but also of large groups on a tribal or even a national level. It was when the Roman Empire was going into decline that large numbers of citizens joined the church. Will Durant wrote: "In the chaos and terror of the third century men fled from the weakened state to the consolations of religion; and found them more abundantly in Christianity than in its rivals."[1]

In the last months before Phnom Penh fell to the Communists in 1975, hundreds of Cambodians, many of them devout Buddhists, professed conversion. In 1979 thousands of Vietnamese "boat people" found Christ in the refugee camps in Thailand. Having lost all their earthly possessions and in some cases their loved ones too, they wanted something that offers them hope beyond this life.

It disturbs some people that so many come to Christ only after everything else has failed. Their motives, they say, are wrong; such converts cheapen the gospel and weaken the church. Those who work in the refugee camps are warned against the danger of a "utilitarian approach" to the gospel. Sinners should be confronted with the majesty and sovereignty of God, His wrath against sin, and His demand that all men everywhere repent. They should believe the gospel, not for what they can get out of it, but for the glory of God and for the praise of His grace. Those who present the gospel are criticized for making it man-centered and need-oriented.

But we need make no apology for our presentation of the gospel. That is precisely what the gospel is supposed to be— man-centered and need-oriented. Jesus said: "They that be whole need not a physician, but they that are sick" (Mt 9:12).

---

1. Will Durant, *Story of Civilization*, vol. 3, *Caesar and Christ* (New York: Simon and Schuster, 1944), p. 650.

Most people came to Jesus from a sense of need, not from a sense of sin, but He did not turn them away on that account. Rather, He encouraged them by saying, "Come unto me, all ye that labour and are heavy laden, and I will give you rest" (Mt 11:28). That is the glory of the gospel. It helps man where he hurts. In the words of John Newton, "It soothes his sorrows, heals his wounds, and drives away his fear." In the more picturesque words of Isaiah, it gives him "beauty for ashes, the oil of joy for mourning, the garment of praise for the spirit of heaviness" (Is 61:3). If it fails to do that, it is not the gospel at all.

Supernatural Factors

It is a good idea to examine the natural factors in church growth, but we must not stop there. There are supernatural factors as well, and in the final analysis these are more important than the natural factors.

1. *The sovereignty of God.* Paul was the greatest missionary of all time, and he realized that missionary work is a divine/human enterprise. He said, "I have planted, Apollos watered; but God gave the increase" (1 Cor 3:6). Again he said: "We are labourers together with God" (1 Cor 3:9). God in His sovereignty has ordained that He will work through the church for the salvation of the world. He could save the world on His own without any help from us, but He has chosen not to do it that way. Paul and Apollos will do their part and God will do His. They cannot do His part; He will not do theirs; but working together they will get the job done.

The workers do not choose their role in the harvest field. Some are called by God to be sowers and others are called to be reapers (John 4:37-38). Given our choice we would all want to be among the reapers; but if all were reapers, there would be no sowers, and without sowers there would be no harvest to reap.

The sovereignty of God relates to persons, places, and times. Paul was a "chosen vessel"—chosen by the sovereign act of God. Luther, Edwards, Wesley, Finney, and Moody were all "chosen vessels." So are Billy Graham and Oswald Hoffman. These men were not holier than other men of their time. Some of them, like Moody, were hardly intellectual giants; but God used them in a remarkable way to achieve His purpose for the church and for the world in their day and generation.

The sovereignty of God relates to places. How are we to account for the fact that revival will break out in one city and not in another, in one church and not in another, in one school and not in another? After World War II some missionaries in Japan banded together to pray for revival. They knew there was no other way to make a lasting impression on the nation of Japan. They vowed that they would continue to pray until the revival came. They fasted; they prayed; they confessed their sins; they called on God to bare His mighty arm. Revival never came.

How different it was in Indonesia in the 1960s. The fire fell; revival came; souls were saved; churches were renewed; and membership doubled and trebled in a few years. All we can say is that "God moves in a mysterious way His wonders to perform."

The sovereignty of God also relates to time. Jesus' last word to His disciples was: "It is not for you to know the times or the seasons, which the Father hath put in his own power" (Acts 1:7). God works in one way in one century and in an entirely different way in another. His ways are past finding out. While we do not understand all the factors that enter into His thinking and planning, we can be certain that He knows the end from the beginning (Is 46:10) and is working all things after the counsel of His own will (Eph 1:11).

During my days in China I worked in the northern part of the province of Anhwei in central China. North of the Yangtze River church growth was so great that we could not cope with the influx of converts. New churches (called outstations) grew up almost overnight, and the city church had to draw up guidelines to restrict the mushroom growth of such churches. The southern half of the province, on the other hand, was as barren as the north was fruitful. There were more converts each year in the one county of Fowyang than in all the counties of South Anhwei together. How can we account for the difference? The natural factors were the same in both areas; we can only fall back on the sovereignty of God to explain it. It pleased Him to work in the north, not in the south.

2. *The power of the Spirit.* The most important event in the Acts of the Apostles is the coming of the Holy Spirit at Pentecost. That event explains all the other events. Some fifty-five times the Holy Spirit is mentioned in the Acts. The book should really be called the Acts of the Holy Spirit.

In any discussion of church growth there is always the temptation to lose sight of the ultimate factor, the Holy Spirit. This is particularly true of Americans who, with our pragmatic approach to the problems of life, think that with the proper tools and techniques we by our own strength can accomplish anything.

After the resurrection Jesus gave two commands to His disciples. One was to "go." The other was to "tarry"—until they were endued with the Holy Spirit. On the day of the ascension He again made reference to Pentecost, saying: "Ye shall receive power, after that the Holy Ghost is come upon you" (Acts 1:8). Only then could they be successful witnesses.

John E. Skoglund in his book, *To the Whole Creation*, refers to the Holy Spirit as "the missing person." That is exactly what He is in many churches today. Someone has said that if the Holy Spirit were to be withdrawn from the world, He would not be missed. Ninety percent of the church's programs would go on as usual. Small wonder that we see so little church growth here in the West.

Robert H. Glover, missionary statesman during the first half of the century, wrote: "Christian missions are no human undertaking, but a supernatural and divine enterprise for which God has provided supernatural power and leadership."[2] Referring to the Holy Spirit he said: "He came as the divine Commander-in-chief of the forces and the campaign, and was at once recognized and acknowledged as such. His coming

2. Robert Hall Glover, *The Bible Basis of Missions* (Chicago: Moody, 1964), p. 70.

imparted the divine character to every aspect of the enterprise."[3] John R. Mott said virtually the same thing: "Missionaries . . . are absolutely united in the conviction that world evangelization is a divine enterprise, that the Spirit of God is the great missioner, and that only as He dominates the work and workers can we hope for success in the undertaking to carry the knowledge of Christ to all people."[4]

Wherever the power of the Holy Spirit has been manifest, church growth has always resulted. A recent example is the revival that broke out in the early 1970s in Western Canada. It began in the Ebenezer Baptist Church in Saskatoon and from there spread to the Circle Drive Alliance Church, which has witnessed eight hundred conversions in the intervening years. During this time the church spawned four "daughter" churches. After each "exodus" the church continued to grow until today it is the largest Christian and Missionary Alliance church in the world.[5]

The two men who did most for church growth in China were Jonathan Goforth and John Sung. Both were revivalists of the first order. Wherever they went, backsliders were restored, souls were saved, and churches were revived. The result in every case was unprecedented growth. It has never failed.[6]

Behind every outburst of real mission in the life of the church, we find a company or companies of believing men and women who have waited and prayed until the Spirit of God has come upon them; then in the Spirit's power they have gone out to witness to the mighty acts of God. In every instance the new movement to mission parallels the waiting, praying group of disciples in the Jerusalem upper room at Pentecost. The church can find its mission in no other way than through earnest men

3. Ibid., p. 63.
4. John R. Mott, *The Decisive Hour of Christian Missions* (New York: Student Volunteer Movement, 1910), p. 103.
5. See *The Alliance Witness*, 9 January 1980.
6. For details concerning the life and ministry of these two men see Jonathan Goforth, *By My Spirit* (Grand Rapids: Zondervan, 1942), and Leslie Lyall, *John Sung, Flame for God in the Far East* (Chicago: Moody Press, 1956).

and women in small companies praying and waiting until the
Holy Spirit comes upon them in power.[7]

Martyn Lloyd-Jones, former preacher at Westminster
Chapel, London, takes a rather dim view of modern evangelistic campaigns in contrast to the enduring growth that
results from revival. This is what he said in a recent interview
with Carl Henry:

> I have always believed that nothing but a revival—a visitation
> of the Holy Spirit, in distinction from an evangelistic cam-
> paign—can deal with the situation of the church and of the
> world. The Welsh Presbyterian Church had roots in the great
> eighteenth-century evangelical revival, when the power of the
> Spirit of God came upon preachers and churches, and large
> numbers were converted. I have never been happy about or-
> ganized campaigns.
>
> I just can't subscribe to the idea that either congresses or
> campaigns really deal with the situation. The facts, I feel, sub-
> stantiate my point of view; in spite of all that has been done in
> the last 20 or 25 years, the spiritual situation has deteriorated
> rather than improved. I am convinced that nothing can avail
> but churches and ministers on their knees in total dependence
> on God. As long as you go on organizing, people will not fall
> on their knees and implore God to come and heal them. It
> seems to me that the campaign approach trusts ultimately in
> techniques rather than in the power of the Spirit.[8]

3. *The role of miracles.* No one can read the four Gospels or
the Acts of the Apostles and not be impressed with the role
of miracles in the ministry of Christ and the life of the early
church. In the Gospels thirty-five separate miracles are described in some detail. These were designed to demonstrate
Christ's power over man, nature, and demons. The fourfold
purpose was to authenticate His messianic claim (John

---

7. John E. Skoglund, *To the Whole Creation* (Valley Forge, PA: Judson Press,
1962), p. 88.
8. "Martyn Lloyd-Jones: From Buckingham to Westminster: An Interview by
Carl F. H. Henry," *Christianity Today*, 8 February 1980, p. 29.

10:24-25), to inculcate faith in Him (John 20:31), to induce national repentance (Mt 11:20-24), and to alleviate human suffering (Acts 10:38).

These miracles were not restricted to the ministry of Christ. According to Jesus they were to be repeated in the witness of the early church (John 14:12). That is exactly what we find when we turn to the Acts of the Apostles. Miracles in the early church served much the same purpose as they did in the ministry of Jesus—the inculcation of faith. In almost every instance the miracle is followed by a statement to the effect that "many believed" (Acts 5:14; 9:42).

It is doubtful that Christianity would have survived, much less succeeded, in the Roman Empire without the miracles.

In the New Testament, the strongest impressions seem to have been made by miracles. . . . Again and again it was a miracle which brought interest and conviction. The visions which preceded the conversion of Cornelius, the blinding of Elymas the sorcerer which convinced the Proconsul Sergius Paulus that Paul and Barnabas could invoke a mightier spirit than he could, the earthquake followed by the magnanimous conduct of the prisoners which led to the baptism of the Philippian jailer and his household, are only some of the many which come immediately to mind.[9]

In twelve to fifteen short years Paul planted churches in four of the most populous provinces of the empire. To what did he ascribe his success? His ability as a preacher? His knowledge as a theologian? His tried-and-true methods as a veteran missionary? Definitely not! It was to the mighty signs and wonders which were an integral part of his ministry. Writing to the believers in Rome he made it quite clear: "I will not dare to speak of any of those things which Christ hath not wrought by me, to make the Gentiles obedient, by word and deed, *through mighty signs and wonders*, by the power of the Spirit of

9. Kenneth Scott Latourette, *The First Five Centuries* (New York: Harper & Brothers, 1937), p. 119.

God; so that from Jerusalem, and round about unto Illyricum, I have fully preached the gospel of Christ" (Rom 15:18-19).

The Pentecostal Church is the fastest growing denomination in the world. They have achieved church growth where others have failed. In Latin America they represent two-thirds of all evangelicals; and in some countries, notably Chile, they account for 90 percent. All kinds of studies have been made of Pentecostal work in Latin America. Their success has been attributed to various human factors—social, cultural, and economic; but not enough attention has been paid to the divine factor, the power of the Holy Spirit manifested in mighty signs and wonders. While others have been busy *analyzing* church growth, the Pentecostals have gone quietly about the business of *producing* church growth. If they were asked for the secret of their success, they would undoubtedly ascribe it to the power of the Holy Spirit, doing His own thing, in His own way, for His own glory.

The proponents of church growth, with few exceptions, have emphasized the human factors and all but overlooked the divine factor. We need constantly to remember that except the Lord build the house they labor in vain that build it (Ps 127:1); or, in the words of Zechariah, it is not by might nor by power but by the Spirit of the Lord (4:6).

Continuing Problems

CHAPTER 15

The Decline
of the West

The rise of the West coincided with the Vasco da Gama era, which began around 1500. The massive impact of the West on the East during that period is without parallel in the history of the world. William H. McNeill in his book, *The Rise of the West*, says: "From the perspective of the mid-twentieth century, the career of Western civilization since 1500 appears as a vast explosion, far greater than any comparable phenomenon of the past both in geographic range and in social depth."[1]

Our generation has witnessed the end of that era, which coincided with World War II. Since then the great European powers have been in rapid retreat from their colonial empires, first Britain, then France and Holland, and finally Spain and Portugal. Small pockets of colonialism remain, but the system has been progressively, if reluctantly, dismantled. The United Nations, which began with 51 members in 1945, now has 153 members. Most of the new members are ex-colonies of the European powers. Great Britain, once the proud mistress of the seas, is no longer great. Thirty-five years after the close of

1. William H. McNeill, *The Rise of the West* (Chicago: University of Chicago, 1963), p. 567.

the war she is still trying to adjust to the social, economic, and political realities of the new era. Neither the Socialists nor the Conservatives have been able to solve her problems.

Not without reason the United States is regarded as the most powerful nation in the world. She is the undisputed leader of the free world; only the Soviet Union, the other super power, poses any real threat to her. No other country, or combination of countries, can match the military might of Uncle Sam. This being so, I shall in this chapter confine myself largely to the deteriorating situation here in the United States, recognizing that what is true of the United States is also true to a large extent of Western Europe.

In the Political Sphere

We Americans can be proud of the stability of our political institutions. Congressional elections every two years and presidential elections every four years come and go without a shot being fired or a drop of blood being shed. Compared with other parts of the world this is a rare achievement.

When we begin to scrutinize American politics, however, we soon discover that under the surface all is not well. We glory in our free elections, but hardly more than 50 percent of the electorate bother to vote in a presidential election. Fewer than 30 percent of our youth between the ages of eighteen and twenty-five, who demanded a voice in the decision-making process in the turbulent sixties, ever go to the polls.

To get into office the politicians have to make all kinds of glowing promises. Once in office they forget or ignore all the promises that got them there. Their chief concern seems to be to ensure reelection the next time around. In fact, politicians have acted in such a cynical manner that they are very near the bottom of the list as far as the confidence of the populace is concerned. They express great solicitude for the "interests of the people," but this is simply part of the campaign rhetoric.

There is probably more corruption in politics than in any other profession. Nicholas von Hoffman, in his syndicated column in the *Chicago Tribune* (February 16, 1980), referred to Congress as "America's most corrupt organization." His opening statement read: "There are only 535 members of Congress. . . . In no other office of the same size does such a high percentage of the employees so regularly disgrace themselves and dishonor the organization they work for." It was Congress that drove President Nixon from the White House when he was accused of "obstructing justice," but when its own members are involved in shady dealings, the Ethics Committee looks the other way.

In 1979 Jane Byrne became Chicago's first woman mayor. She promised to do away with graft, corruption, and nepotism, but things remain the same. The "city that works" no longer works. In her first year in office policemen, firemen, schoolteachers, and transportation workers all went out on strike. It is common knowledge that muncipal politics is honeycombed with corruption and that many of our big cities are really controlled by organized crime.

Last year over nine hundred murders were committed in Chicago. Murder with handguns has reached alarming proportions. From 1966 to 1972, forty-four thousand American servicemen were killed in Vietnam. During the same period fifty-two thousand Americans were killed in the United States with handguns. Still Congress refuses to pass a gun-control law. In Japan, where they have such a law, deaths by handguns are 191 *times* lower than in the United States! Who would have thought that three outstanding leaders, John and Bobby Kennedy and Martin Luther King, would be gunned down in cold blood? It is nothing short of a national disgrace that all presidential candidates must now have secret-service protection, even before they reach the White House.

In the Social Sphere

The deterioration of American society since World War II is shocking in the extreme. President Carter in a televised speech in the fall of 1979 said that America is suffering from what he called a "general malaise." It has infected all segments of society—the homes, the schools, the courts, the prisons, and the military.

Nowhere is the breakdown more conspicuous than in our home life. In recent years there has been a huge increase in the number of divorces. In some parts of the country the divorce rate is overtaking the marriage rate. Broken homes result in broken hearts and broken lives, and invariably it is the children who suffer most. It used to be that divorce was a last resort after all attempts at reconciliation had failed. Now the persons concerned are often not interested in reconciliation. They have made up their minds; they want divorce, not counsel. Divorce used to be granted only for adultery, then for mental cruelty, and later for incompatibility. Now, with no-fault divorce, husbands are walking out on their wives for no other reason than that they have decided to marry their secretary. Couples who have lived together happily for twenty years are now breaking up.

Along with the broken home go juvenile delinquency, drugs, alcoholism, premarital sex, and a host of other evils that are sapping the vitality of our youth. The drug problem first gained widespread attention with the college dropouts—known as hippies—in the 1960s. Since then the problem has filtered down first into the high schools and now into the junior high schools, and it is by no means confined to the ghettos. It is now common in the schools of suburbia, where money to buy drugs is more available. As a result the overall quality of public education is rapidly deteriorating, so much so that colleges and universities have to offer courses in remedial English to incoming freshmen. In some school systems the teachers themselves cannot spell correctly. All of this leads to cheating to get into college and then to cheating to pass exams in college. In Boston there are two firms that sell term papers for a fixed fee. They will guarantee an A, a B, or a C on the paper, depending on the price!

In recent years prison riots have become common in all parts of the country. The main reason is overcrowding. Prisons erected at the turn of the century to accommodate twelve hundred inmates now house twice that number. In February,

1980, a prison riot in New Mexico took the lives of over thirty inmates, many of them hacked to pieces by their fellow prisoners. And if the judicial system worked better, the prisons would have many more inmates than they now have. Many criminals are never caught. Of those who are, only a small percentage are ever convicted; and of those an even smaller percentage ever go to prison.

Alcoholism is now a major medical health problem in America. It is estimated that one out of ten persons is an alcoholic, and one alcoholic directly affects three other persons. This means that sixty million persons in the United States are directly affected by alcoholism. Some large corporations, General Motors among them, have an alcoholic-rehabilitation program for their employees. It used to be that only adults had a problem with alcohol. Now teen-agers are also involved. The government and hundreds of private corporations and foundations are spending tens of millions of dollars every year in an effort to help alcoholics. Nobody seems to think it would be a good idea to get rid of the root cause of alcoholism—alcohol. We had prohibition once and it did not work, so they say it cannot be done. If India, with a population three times as large as ours, can enforce prohibition, it is rather strange that we cannot do the same. How shall we explain the many Muslim countries in the world? They all have prohibition and apparently they can enforce it. I lived in China for fifteen years and never once saw a drunken man. Let us face it; alcoholism in the United States is a national disaster. We may ask: Can a country that spends more money on liquor than on books be regarded as civilized?

In the Moral Sphere

In spite of what the First Amendment says about the danger of establishing a religion, our Founding Fathers were men with deep moral and religious convictions who believed that they were setting up on this continent a Christian nation. They wholeheartedly believed in the Ten Commandments and the Sermon on the Mount and were deeply conscious of their dependence on almighty God, and for almost two hundred years the value system they espoused was maintained intact.

In this postwar period there has been a marked erosion of ethical and moral standards. The floodgates opened in the turbulent sixties with the "sex revolution." Since then American society has been floundering like a ship without either chart or compass. Prostitution, the "oldest profession in the world," has always been with us; but with more and more business and professional men "on the road," the trade has picked up considerably. Men otherwise considered respectable now cheat on their wives with impunity, and almost as many wives cheat on their husbands. Adultery used to be frowned on; today it is not only accepted, it is flaunted. "Wife-swapping" is an increasingly popular weekend pastime, especially in the suburbs.

Television as a scientific invention is one of the marvelous breakthroughs of the twentieth century. It has fallen into the hands of the wrong people, however—the entertainers. The three large networks are interested only in profit, and the fate of every show is determined by the Nielsen ratings.

As an educational tool television has no end of possibilities. Now and again, in times of national emergency, the electronic media do a superb job, for which we are all genuinely grateful. When the emergency is over, it is back to business as usual, and the business is entertainment-geared to the lowest common denominator. Most shows at best are a waste of time. They do nothing for the mind, still less for the soul. Culturally, television is a wasteland. Morally it is fast becoming a cesspool. Little by little the entertainment is getting more "daring," and the viewing public, gradually drugged into a state of stupefaction, does not have the moral backbone to object. Love plots used to be content with a triangular affair with two women after one man or vice versa; but today love has turned to lust and the scenes include premarital sex, adultery, homosexuality, and incest, all of which is unadulterated garbage.

As if that were not enough, violence is thrown in for good measure. If all the shows involving sex or violence were removed from the screen, there would not be much left. That, however, would be no great loss. *Moody Monthly* had a point when a couple of years ago it carried an article titled: "No TV Is the Best TV." I do not watch the shows which feature violence, but I cannot help seeing the spot commercials promoting them; and in every case there are kicking, punching, screaming, mugging, shooting. Seldom does a fifteen-second commercial fail to mention the word *kill* or *murder*. This is absolutely nauseating to any clean-minded, self-respecting citizen.

Worse than all of this is the widespread use of abortion, sanctioned in 1973 by the Supreme Court. How any woman can persuade herself that aborting a three-month-old fetus is not an act of murder is difficult to understand. We used to think of abortion as one of the more despicable features of a pagan civilization in the last stages of decay, but it has now become commonplace in the United States. For the first time in history a civilization based on Christian principles has sanctioned this form of murder. The Oath of Hippocrates declares: "I will not give to a woman an instrument to produce abortion." Now pregnant women, married and unmarried, can have an abortion on demand, and the practice is more widespread than the public realizes.

According to the Alan Guttmacher Institute of New York City, nearly one out of every three pregnancies ends in abortion. Three out of four abortions involve unmarried women. This indicates that abortion is closely linked to premarital sex, which has become so common. In 1978 the estimated number of abortions was 1,374,000. The actual figure could have been as high as 1,456,000. If this kind of mass murder continues, it is difficult to see how the United States will escape the judgment of God.

In the Economic Sphere

For many decades the United States has been the industrial colossus of the world. Had it not been for our enormous industrial capacity, the Allies would not have been able to win

World War II. In more recent years we have begun to slip. Other countries, notably West Germany and Japan, threaten to overtake us.

Something has happened to the old-fashioned work ethic which is part of our religious heritage that goes back through the Puritans to the Reformation. The labor unions, which did so much for the workingman in the first half of the century, now threaten the American economy by their ever-increasing demands for higher wages, shorter hours, and additional fringe benefits. They are now aiming for a four-day week—with five-day pay.

If productivity went up with wages, the situation would not be so bad, for the one increase would balance the other; but this does not happen. As wages go up, productivity goes down, affecting both the quantity and the quality of the goods produced. Every year millions of cars have to be recalled by the manufacturers in Detroit; as a result, German and Japanese cars, better and more fuel-efficient than ours, are claiming an ever larger segment of the market.

The economic situation in the United States continues to deteriorate. In spite of President Carter's pledge to reduce the size of the bureaucracy and balance the budget, nothing changed. Only twice in the last twenty years has the federal budget been balanced. The interest on the national debt is $73 billion per year—$330 for every man, woman, and child in the United States. Inflation is running into double digits. With the prime rate soaring even beyond 20 percent at times, mortgages are difficult to get. Home financing has almost come to a halt and the housing industry is in a slump. The New York Stock Exchange has held up fairly well; but the bond market, traditionally the strongest of all the financial markets, is in chaos.

With decreasing productivity at home it is more and more difficult to compete abroad. In 1978 the trade deficit of the United States was $39.5 billion. The same year Japan had a *surplus* of $19.7 billion! The reason is not hard to find. Japan's industrial base turns over once every ten years, ours once every thirty years. In recent years twenty-two new blast furnaces have been built in various parts of the world, fourteen of them in Japan, none in the United States. Is it any wonder that United States Steel, the largest steel corporation in the world, closed thirteen plants in December, 1979? This, they said, was due to "lagging productivity and foreign competition." The Ford Motor Company lost 1.5 billion dollars in 1980, the largest deficit in the history of the United States.

The energy crisis, sparked by the sudden increase in the price of oil by the Organization of Petroleum Exporting Countries (OPEC) in 1973, is still with us, in spite of the fact that a Department of Energy was created by President Carter several years ago to deal with it. The department has not done anything to solve the problem and neither has the Congress. Our leaders in Washington have neither the wisdom nor the will to impose gas rationing or to introduce wage-and-price controls. While they have been doing nothing, the price of gold tripled in one year, and the value of the American dollar dropped drastically in Europe and Japan.

Instead of providing the country with bold and decisive leadership in these difficult times, Congress is dragging its feet, hoping that the problem will go away or that the American people will have enough self-discipline to solve the problem on their own. The simple fact is that Americans are not known for their self-discipline, especially in peacetime, and cannot be expected to take effective action without outside pressure.

We have been accustomed to thinking of the United States as one of the "have" nations of the world. When it comes to oil and certain strategic minerals, however, we are a "have-not" country, and our dependence on Third World countries is increasing with every passing year. If these countries in time of war were to join our enemies, we would be in trouble. In this respect we are far more vulnerable than we like to admit.

In the Military Sphere

We emerged from World War II as the undisputed leader of the free world, and for more than two decades we remained the most powerful military force in the world, far ahead of our closest rival, the Soviet Union. In the last decade the scales have been tipping slowly but surely in favor of the Soviet Union. In 1964 our lead in nuclear warheads was seventeen to one. Today it has shrunk to three to two. The Soviet Union has surpassed the United States in intercontinental and submarine-launched ballistic missiles. In conventional arms the Soviet Union is outproducing the United States in tanks, combat planes, helicopters, attack submarines, and other combat vehicles. That is why we are pinning our hopes on SALT II. It will stop some aspects of the arms race, which we obviously are losing.

Equally disturbing is the condition of our armed forces. In 1979 all four branches of the service had difficulty in meeting recruitment targets.

> Even more worrisome than the numbers is the exodus from the services of experienced officers and non-commissioned officers on a scale that already is forcing a cutback in normal activities. The Navy alone has 20,000 fewer petty officers than it needs. Planes are grounded for lack of experienced crews and critical jobs in other areas are assigned to personnel with inadequate experience or training.[2]

A more fundamental question involves the mood of the American people. We did very poorly in Vietnam and since that time have been exceedingly wary of getting militarily embroiled in other parts of the world.

Our failure to do anything about Castro's military adventures in Angola and Ethiopia has led the leaders in the Kremlin to believe that we have lost our will to fight. This perception on their part, right or wrong, undoubtedly led to the invasion of Afghanistan by the Soviets in December, 1979. Following that invasion President Carter announced the resumption of registration for the draft, only to find that college students from California to Massachusetts protested, chanting: "Hell, no; we won't go."

2. *U.S. News and World Report*, 11 February 1980, p. 22.

In spite of our vast military might, we are virtually helpless in the face of growing anti-Americanism throughout the world. Our flag is desecrated, our embassies are burned to the ground, our diplomatic personnel are held hostage, our businessmen are kidnapped and held for ransom—and we appear to be impotent. International terrorism, including assassinations, kidnappings, bombings, and personal assaults, is increasing at an alarming rate. Incidents of this type were up from 206 in 1972 to 2,662 in the first nine months of 1979. Of Americans abroad, businessmen provided 55 percent of all the targets for terrorists, followed by 28 percent for diplomats, 8 percent for police and soldiers, and 4 percent for newsmen. Experts agree that advanced societies are increasingly vulnerable to terrorist activity, and our society is getting more vulnerable all the time. It is clear that the peoples of the Third World no longer fear Uncle Sam, John Bull, or anybody else.

Zbigniew Brzezinski, national security advisor to President Carter, summed it up in a paragraph:

> During the last decade and a half, our geostrategic position has been challenged—in part, because our rivals have improved their position and have been acquiring a global reach. The political transformation of mankind—the most profound that history has witnessed—involves the sudden appearance on the world scene of Asian, African, and Latin American countries, whose cumulative impact on the international system means the end of the Eurocentric era in world affairs.[3]

In the Religious Sphere

So drastic has been the decline of religious influence in recent years that the experts are now agreed that we have entered a post-Christian era. This is particularly true in Western Europe, where the Roman Catholic Church is in the throes of an authority crisis and where the state churches, Anglican and Lutheran, are at their lowest ebb since the Reformation.

3. *U.S. News and World Report*, 31 December 1979/7 January 1980, p. 36.

Humanism, materialism, and Marxism dominate the scene. There are so few committed Christians that their influence is practically nil. Interestingly enough, the most vibrant churches in Europe are behind the Iron Curtain. In Western Europe religion is no longer a force to be reckoned with.

We can be grateful that the situation in the United States is much better, at least on the surface. Church attendance continues high, many churches having two or three services on Sunday morning. Church giving still outpaces inflation. Church construction is booming. The Bible continues to be a best seller, and religious publications and broadcasts are breaking all previous records.

For all of this we should be profoundly thankful, but a closer look will reveal the fact that all is not well. It is embarrassing to admit that while we are enjoying a religious boom, we are at the same time facing an ethical and moral breakdown unprecedented in our history. Much of our religion is only a façade behind which the decay is eating at our vitals. According to George Gallup there are forty million "born again" evangelicals in the United States, but the influence they wield in business, politics, education, and law is negligible. They go to church on Sunday, but during the rest of the week they travel incognito. They think like the world, talk like the world, act like the world. Their overall lifestyle differs little from that of their next-door neighbor.

Instead of being the salt of the earth and the light of the world, the American church is for the most part only a reflection of American society. When it comes to political theories, economic aspirations, business practices, social mores, and professional ethics, there is not much to choose between them. Mark O. Hatfield, senator from Oregon, made an astute observation along this line:

> Some churches judge the success of their ministry by growth of the number of members or by the size of their new buildings. Some evangelistic campaigns are judged purely on the numbers of dollars contributed or decisions made, rather than on the qualitative basis of relationships and incarnational love.

Within the church, we have too frequently allowed the style of the culture to take over, with its belief in success, growth, abundance, and fame.[4]

The Effect on Christian Missions

What has all this to do with the world mission of the Christian church? The answer is: Plenty.

During the early part of the modern missionary period the West knew little of the East and the East knew less of the West. The missionary, more than anyone else, formed a bridge between East and West. He introduced Western culture to the East and interpreted Eastern culture to the West, and in both instances he did a good job.

Now everything is changed. The missionary, once our main spokesman, is greatly outnumbered by businessmen, diplomatic and military personnel, and tourists, who are not always the best advertisement for the American way of life, much less the Christian religion. Our multinational corporations have been guilty of bribery on a massive scale. Wherever American servicemen have settled in large numbers, prostitution has burgeoned and brothels have multiplied. In Vietnam servicemen sired thousands of children who now, abandoned by their fathers and despised by their mothers, and unable to hide their parentage, are probably the most pitiable of all the war victims.

What about the American tourists, now numbering in the millions every year? They are welcomed largely for the dollars they bring with them. Their uncouth manners, their flagrant wealth, their scanty clothing, their consumption of alcohol, their exploitation of sex, their failure to understand and observe the social amenities of a different culture, do little to enhance the image of the "ugly American." The so-called Hippie Trail that stretched from Amsterdam to Kathmandu is strewn with the dropouts of American society. The presence

4. Mark O. Hatfield, "Finding the Energy to Continue," *Christianity Today*, 8 February 1980, p. 22.

of dirty, disheveled American hippies, basking like beggars in the bazaar in Kathmandu, is indeed a strange sight and one that does not make life for the Christian missionary any easier.[5] Diplomatic "incidents" have been created in Turkey, Mexico, and other countries when American hippies on their way home tried to smuggle drugs. Hundreds of them ended up in prison. Some of them are still there.

The influence of American culture is so enormous that it has penetrated every nook and cranny of the world. Our movies, our magazines, our television shows, our music, even our clothes are in great demand even in Communist countries. Unfortunately it is usually the least desirable of these productions that find their way abroad.

The leaders of the Third World countries are beginning to realize that their cultures are in danger of being swamped by American culture, which, apart from science and technology, is inferior to their own. Not only is it inferior; it is actually degrading. Several countries have expelled the Peace Corps—whose members are certainly among our best representatives in the Third World—accusing the volunteers of undermining the morals of their youth. What happened in Iran in 1979 is an example of what has been going on. The American public had considerable difficulty understanding the "irrational" behavior of the Ayatollah Khomeini or the blind passion of the "students" holding the American hostages. The Iranians were against the American government for its support of the Shah, but deeper than that was their pathological animosity towards the decadent Western culture introduced by forty thousand Americans working in Iran. Finally their rage reached the boiling point and resulted in the capture of the American embassy in Tehran.

With access to worldwide satellite communications, every person in the world with a radio or a television set had a blow-by-blow account of the melancholy events in Iran during 1979-1980. American culture was denounced before the eyes

5. For an account of one missionary's attempt to reach these hippies with the love of Christ, see Floyd McClung, Jr., *Just off Chicken Street* (Old Tappan, NJ: Fleming H. Revell, 1975).

of a watching world, and the American government was made to look like a helpless giant being tormented by the intransigence of a small country one-sixth its size.

The American image is damaged by the Americans who go abroad. At home it suffers in the eyes of those who come here from the Third World. There are at present in the United States about 250,000 students from countries all around the world, including some from Communist China. These students, the cream of their societies, will be the leaders of tomorrow, and their impressions of the United States will be exceedingly important in the days to come.

Foreign students are usually here for three or four years, during which time they have ample opportunity to see all aspects of American civilization. They sample our cuisine, including hot dogs, hamburgers, and Coke; they listen to our music, examine our art, visit our museums, and attend our sporting events; they read our newspapers and magazines—including *Playboy* and *Cosmopolitan*; they watch the six-o'clock news, the soap operas, and the late-night movies. They read about street gangs in the ghettos, crime in the streets, drugs and vandalism in the schools, corruption in politics, shoplifting, juvenile delinquency, and other features of daily life in our big cities. If they listen to our morning news, they are served up a long litany of murders, rapes, muggings, arson, drug-related incidents, thefts, and a host of other undesirable things that have taken place overnight.

More damaging still is the shabby treatment African students, often mistaken for American Blacks, receive while in the United States. Mengistu Haile Mariam, Marxist leader of Ethiopia, came twice to the United States for military training. Today he has no love for Uncle Sam and has turned for help to the Soviet Union. Part of the reason is the racial prejudice he encountered while here. Such unfortunate experiences are difficult to forget and more difficult to forgive.

There was a time when only pessimistic preachers spoke of impending doom. Now scientists, sociologists, and politicians have all joined the chorus and are predicting judgment to come. Alexander Solzhenitsyn in his address at Harvard

University spoke some plain words about the decadence of American culture and solemnly warned that unless we change our course we are heading for destruction. Some people thought he, a visitor in our midst, should have been more polite in his remarks. After all, we gave him asylum. Instead of being criticized, Solzhenitsyn should be congratulated for having the courage and the honesty to speak out as he did.

Solzhenitsyn is not the only one to sound the death knell of Western civilization. Others are saying the same thing. Martyn Lloyd-Jones, when asked what he foresees for the next twenty years, replied:

> I'm afraid I see nothing but collapse. I think that democracy is the ultimate position politically; we've passed through all other forms of government. But beyond democracy there now looms either dictatorship or complete chaos. . . . I'm not sure at all that we have 20 years. Several factors are present that have never been present before. In the past, great civilizations in various parts of the world would collapse but would not devastate the rest of the world. Today the world is one vast whole. What happens in one place happens everywhere. I think we are witnessing the breakdown of politics. I think even the world is seeing that. Civilization is collapsing.[6]

Bong Rin Ro, executive secretary of the Asian Theological Association, is deeply concerned regarding the future of Christian missions in Asia:

> Changes in the West have great repercussions in Asia and other continents. Moral decadence, lack of discipline, the breakdown of law and order, and economic instability in the West have serious effects in Asia. Asians formerly looked up to the West in admiration for their way of government and the ethical, moral principles provided by Christianity. When I was in high school in Korea, I was taught that Western civilization epitomized democracy, law and order, and high moral principles influenced by the Christian Church. However, now the situa-

6. "Martyn Lloyd-Jones: From Buckingham to Westminster: An Interview by Carl F. H. Henry," *Christianity Today*, 8 February 1980, p. 34.

tion is different. Asians see American tourists walking on their streets almost naked in their backless and braless dresses. Muslims and Hindus who practically cover their bodies from head to foot look at the barefoot, unkempt American hippie with his long, uncombed hair and wonder if Christianity which they equate with Western culture has any decent ethics.[7]

Someone may say: "So what? Missionaries are ambassadors for Jesus Christ, not for Uncle Sam. They are supposed to preach the gospel of Christ, not the American way of life." That is quite true, but the two cannot be completely divorced—at least, not in the thinking of the Third World. Whether we like it or not, there is such a thing as guilt by association. We may deny that the United States is a Christian country, and hope thereby to refute the link which the Third World sees between the American way of life and Christianity. But they will not buy that. As far as they are concerned, we *are* a Christian country and no amount of cheap talk about the separation of church and state will make any difference.

Citizens of the Third World know that Christianity has been a force in the Western world for centuries. During the Middle Ages European history was church history, and the Roman Catholic Church was the strongest and wealthiest institution on the Continent. Citizens of the Third World know that the Pilgrims came to this land primarily to gain religious freedom. They know—as some of us seem to have forgotten—that in spite of our doctrine of the separation of church and state, the United States has from the beginning regarded itself as a Christian country. Only in very recent years have we repudiated our religious heritage.

This being so, citizens of the Third World have every right to judge Christianity by its influence on Western culture. If the gospel has not done any more for us, why should they expect that it will do more for them? Surely they can be forgiven if they say to us, "Physician, heal thyself."

7. Bong Rin Ro, "Building the National Leadership," an unpublished paper presented to a group of mission leaders in Wheaton, Illinois, in 1976.

CHAPTER 16

The Rise and Spread of Nationalism

The missionary has only himself to blame for the rise and spread of nationalism, for it was he who sowed the seeds of nationalism. By reducing hundreds of languages to writing, translating books, especially the Bible, and conducting tens of thousands of schools in all parts of the world, he did more than anyone else to create within the minds of the people a desire for the freedom and dignity that go with self-rule.

Nationalism is not directed exclusively against the white man, though he, for understandable reasons, has had to bear the brunt of its negative effects. The Chinese in Southeast Asia, who formerly enjoyed the confidence and cooperation of the colonial administrators, are now the victims of all kinds of discrimination, sometimes outright persecution. The Indians in East Africa have shared the same fate. During Idi Amin's regime forty thousand of them were summarily expelled from Uganda, leaving their household goods and their bank accounts behind. In the 1970s Japanese businessmen in Indonesia and other countries were attacked in the streets by mobs of agitators who were tired of the "neo-colonialism" practiced by the Japanese.

Let no one imagine that nationalism is a phenomenon confined to the Third World. The Indians and Pakistanis have been the victims of racial prejudice in the United Kingdom, where they have migrated in large numbers and are now competing for jobs in the textile and other industries. Canada faces a constitutional crisis with the growing demand for secession by the province of Quebec. The reasons for this are not all economic. They are cultural as well. The future of the English-speaking Canadians in Quebec is bleak indeed, even though Quebec voted not to secede. What is this but a form of nationalism?

Nationalism and Politics

1. If colonialism was the greatest force in the world in the nineteenth century, nationalism has been the most powerful force in the twentieth century, stronger even than Communism. It was nationalism that led to the collapse of the vast colonial system. The Christian missionary now finds himself in a political situation very different from that of any previous generation.

2. So powerful has this force been that it has actually changed the face of Communism. Before the rise of Communist China the Communist world, with the single exception of Yugoslavia, was united under the leadership of the Soviet Union. With the passing of time this unity has been seriously eroded and today there are several brands of Communism, among them the Soviet brand and the Chinese brand. The Chinese accuse the Russians of "revisionism" and the Russians castigate the Chinese for following the United States down the road to capitalism. There are other brands of Communism in Cuba, Angola, Ethiopia, and Albania. The most bizarre kind is found in Cambodia, where the government is trying to establish a new society without currency, education, or cities. In Europe there is developing still another kind of Communism, Eurocommunism. How and to what extent it differs from orthodox Marxism is still unknown.

The leaders in all of these countries profess allegiance to Marxism-Leninism, but they reserve the right to go their own way without blindly following the guidelines laid down by Moscow or Peking. They want to develop their own national brand of Communism which will be more responsive to the needs of their own people. This trend is totally unacceptable to the Soviets, who would like to be regarded as the undisputed leader of the Communist world.

3. Nationalism is at the bottom of much of the unrest in many parts of the world today. The colonies have received their independence from the European powers, but in many countries there are sizable ethnic groups which are demanding their independence from the central government. In some cases whole provinces have tried to break away. The civil wars in Nigeria, Zaire, Sudan, Indonesia, and the Philippines all came under this category.

In other parts of the world ethnic minorities are demanding that they be permitted to form their own state, or at least be given local autonomy within the country. The Somalis in Ethiopia and Kenya want to be a part of Somalia. The Kurds in Iran and Turkey want their own state, as do the Baluchis in Iran, Afghanistan, and Pakistan. In many instances the boundaries were drawn up by the colonial administrators, who thought in terms of their own convenience rather than the needs and aspirations of the peoples involved. Burma got its independence from the British in 1948. Now the tribespeople in the northeast want their independence. The same is true of the Naga tribespeople in northeast India.

4. Nationalism has not always lived up to its own expectations. It was assumed that the demise of the colonial system would bring full freedom to the oppressed peoples of the world, but it has not worked out that way. The newly independent countries started out with high hopes and great expectations. Democratic regimes were duly installed, only to give way in a year or two to military dictatorships, usually of the right. One by one the freedoms associated with democracy disappeared, and today the people actually have less freedom than they had under the colonial system.

The situation in Africa is complicated by the presence of over eight hundred tribes, each with its own language and culture. The large, powerful tribes almost always impose their will on the smaller and weaker tribes. All the best jobs in government are reserved for members of the dominant tribe; and as soon as it has consolidated its hold on the country, all other political parties, which are drawn along tribal lines, are outlawed.

Of particular interest to the Christian is the erosion of religious freedom. Governments in various parts of Africa have cracked down on Christians, accusing them of undermining the indigenous culture. In some countries the Christians have been forced to revert to "pagan" rites and practices to prove their patriotism. Chad in the 1970s is an example of this.

5. Nationalism is a potent force in international affairs. This comes to focus in the United Nations, where the newly independent countries now form a formidable voting bloc, independent of the United States and its allies and of the Soviet Union and its allies. So fierce is their nationalism that over ninety countries—Yugoslavia and Cuba among them—have banded together to form a group known as the Non-Aligned Nations. With the death of Marshall Tito, Fidel Castro became the leader of this group. The fact that each of these nations, many of them small, has one vote in the General Assembly of the United Nations gives them an unrealistic sense of power, and they take great pride in exercising their independence in the United Nations. About the only thing they have in common is their opposition to all forms of colonialism, including what they call "neo-colonialism." It is not surprising that they wish to remain neutral and do not want to be drawn into the Cold War between East and West.

Nationalism and the Indigenous Churches

Under the colonial umbrella the Christians felt a sense of security. They could depend on the colonial administration to pursue an evenhanded policy with regard to the various ethnic groups within a given country. In many instances the nationals had more faith in the colonial administrators than in their own politicians. This was true in India at the time of partition in 1947. As long as the British were in charge, Hindus and Muslims lived together in a condition of peaceful coexistence. When independence was about to be granted to the subcontinent, the Muslims, under Mohammed Ali Jinnah, demanded that they be given their own separate state. Outnumbered by the Hindus almost ten to one, they refused to be part of a Hindu state, fearing they would be second-class citizens. They did not trust the Hindus to be as fair as the British had been. They got their own independent state, Pakistan.

Now that the colonial umbrella has been removed, the Christians in Asia are a small, weak minority with little or no power. Not only have they been deprived of the protection afforded by the colonial system, they have also suffered other setbacks. The non-Christian religions, dormant for a long time, are now demanding and receiving special concessions from their governments. Some of them have been declared the state religion and given all the power and prestige that go along with such patronage. Islam is the state religion in Malaysia; consequently Malays are off bounds as far as evangelistic efforts are concerned, though the gospel may be preached to the Chinese, who are Buddhists. Moreover, the government recently decreed that all literature must be in the official Malay language. The churches, made up almost exclusively of Chinese, have had all their literature in that language. Now they must produce hymnbooks, Bibles, and all other forms of Christian literature in the Malay tongue. The Nationalist government in Taiwan made Mandarin the official language of the entire island, and went so far as to confiscate Bibles and other literature in the tribal languages. These are just two examples of the kind of discrimination suffered by Christian churches in the newly emerging countries of the Third World.

Nowhere is nationalism running higher than in Iran, where Ayatollah Khomeini has called for an Islamic Revolution. The Christian church, representing less than 1 percent of the population, is concerned for its survival. One pastor was stabbed to death. Another barely escaped with his life, thanks to the timely intervention of his wife. It takes great courage for pastors and other church leaders to remain at their posts in the face of such danger, especially when they could avoid it by leaving the country.

In former days the churches enjoyed a good deal of prestige because of the schools and hospitals connected with them. Now all that is changed. Most of these countries prefer socialism to capitalism, so they have introduced socialized medicine. It is becoming increasingly difficult for church or mission to compete with government-supported institutions with the latest equipment. Nearly all church schools have been incorporated into the national school systems supported with tax revenues. Both moves are good and legitimate; nevertheless, they have robbed the churches of two avenues of social outreach.

Nationalism and Western Missions

Western missions because of their very nature have been harder hit than the indigenous churches. With nationalism in the saddle, mission agencies are more and more on the defensive. It will require much wisdom and patience for missions to continue to function under modern conditions. Not only is it a brand new ball game; the rules of the game have been drastically changed as well.

In order to place the problem in proper perspective it is necessary to make some general observations.

1. Every sovereign state has the right to exclude or expel any alien it considers undesirable. This is in contrast to the nineteenth century, when missionaries came and went without so much as a passport or a visa. Missionaries from the United Kingdom, Canada, Australia, and New Zealand find it easier than others to get into such Commonwealth countries as Nigeria, Kenya, Ghana, Uganda, India, and Pakistan, but even they cannot take anything for granted. They, too, must have passports and visas; and when they get there, they must be careful not to offend the authorities.

Some countries have decided to curtail missionary activity by setting a quota on the number of persons who will be admitted each year. Thailand is an example. Two hundred residence permits are allotted to each foreign nation. When the quota is filled, others may enter only on a visitor's visa, good for one year.

Other countries allow missionaries to enter on a nonquota basis, but they are permitted to remain for only a certain length of time. It is not particularly difficult to get into Malaysia, but the missionary may remain only ten years. After that he must leave and never return. Such an arrangement is costly and disruptive. The average missionary is just coming into his own after ten years; but as he reaches the peak of efficiency, he is forced to leave.

In order to gain entrance to some countries it is necessary to prove that there are no qualified nationals to fill the role the missionary plans to fill. India is sometimes referred to as a closed country. It is not closed, simply difficult to enter. Anyone going to India today, missionary or not, must prove to the Immigration Office that among 650 million Indians there is not one who can do the job he is going to do. This is not always easy to do!

The reason for India's position is clear. Unemployment in India is high, especially among well-trained intellectuals. Industrial development is not keeping up with educational development, with the result that the market is glutted with intellectuals who cannot find work. Under these conditions it is not surprising that the Indian government has taken the steps it has to resolve the problem of unemployment among the white-collar class. It is right and proper that the top jobs in industry, education, business, and the church be filled by Indians, not foreigners.

2. Nationalism has affected the social status of the missionary. In colonial days the missionary enjoyed enormous prestige and was given rights and privileges denied to the nationals. He seldom had to wait in line for anything. He went to the head of the line while the local people waited until he was served. In many instances he took advantage of his exalted

status. The missionary was never as arrogant as the other expatriates, but he accepted happily the deference paid to him as a member of the ruling race.

Now all that is gone. The missionary, instead of being at the head of the immigration line, may find himself at the end. It may take him three days and ten visits to various offices to get his personal belongings through customs. One missionary in Bolivia waited two years to get his driver's license. Another had to pay $3,000 duty on his secondhand car.

It is not uncommon for missions to have to pay duty on medical and other supplies intended for hospitals and clinics. Even disaster-relief supplies have been held up in customs until the matter of duty could be cleared with some high government official. When Mother Teresa of Calcutta was granted the Nobel Peace Prize in 1979, there was talk in India of obliging her to pay income tax on the award of $190,000.

3. The missionary is a guest in the host country. As such he has no rights, only privileges, and he had better not abuse them. The nineteenth-century missionary needed courage to face the difficulties and dangers of those days. The twentieth-century missionary requires patience to cope graciously with the endless red tape involved in his dealings with the government. In much of the Third World graft is a way of life and nothing can be accomplished without bribing someone. For non-Christians this may be a nuisance but hardly a matter of conscience. What is the Christian missionary to do? He can hardly resort to bribery, but that may be the only way to get what he wants. This means that he is faced with a moral dilemma that requires the wisdom of Solomon and the patience of Job.

What about the question of foreign exchange? In country after country inflation is running wild, in some instances at the rate of 100 to 200 percent a year. In addition the American dollar may be pegged at a rate that has nothing to do with the realities of the situation. In these countries there is a black market in foreign exchange. The official rate for the American dollar may be one hundred pesos, but on the black market the dollar will fetch five hundred pesos. If the missionary deals on the black market, his conscience will give him no peace; and if he is found out, he will probably end up in jail or be expelled from the country. If he insists on doing business through the proper channels, he will find it impossible to make ends meet.

I know whereof I speak, for during the Sino-Japanese War the American dollar in China was fixed at an arbitrary rate of twenty to one for two years. On the black market it was two hundred to one. We missionaries refused to deal on the black market, so the purchasing power of our funds from home dropped 90 percent. At one time the gatekeeper, paid in kind rather than cash, had a higher income than I did! The only way to make up the difference was to sell some of our possessions.

From time to time, when inflation gets completely out of hand, governments recall the old currency and replace it with new. In 1979 the government of Zaire did this and one mission lost $30,000 in the process.

4. Many countries in the Third World are characterized by political insecurity and the only way to maintain order is to settle for some form of dictatorship. In these places the missionary is a marked man. It is taken for granted that he is against all forms of oppression. Consequently the government regards him with a certain degree of suspicion; and, if he is an American, there is always the sinister shadow of the Central Intelligence Agency in the background.

In many countries today all foreign nationals are under surveillance of one kind or another. To remain for any length of time they must have a residence permit. To engage in missionary work they must have a work permit. A short-term missionary who spent six weeks in north Thailand in 1980 was required to get a work permit before he could hold Bible classes for church leaders! Other missionaries must secure a travel permit if they wish to visit another city. Even with all permits in good shape, missionaries are often required to report once a month to the local police station. Before they leave to come home on furlough, they have to check in with the police to have their passports stamped: "No Objection to Return." Then they must be back in the country within a year or they lose their residence permit.

5. Under colonial rule the missionaries usually did as they pleased. They had their own work, developed their own programs, and made their own decisions. They did not need anyone else's approval. That is no longer so. The governments in these newly independent countries are conscious of their recently acquired authority and see to it that all foreigners toe the line. Evangelism and church planting remain fairly free of government control; but educational and medical work, where they still exist, are another matter. Mission schools at the elementary level have been taken over by the government, though in Zaire they were returned to the churches after several years of failure on the part of the government.

Medical work must be integrated with the national health system. This means that the hospitals have to work closely with the Department of Health in the host country. This invariably involves a great deal of red tape, supervision, interference, getting permission for new programs, and making detailed reports.

In spite of the paucity of qualified medical personnel (most of the young people who receive medical education in foreign lands do not return to practice), many of these countries are now requiring missionary doctors and nurses to take exams before they can practice medicine. At the present time the Overseas Missionary Fellowship has ten new missionary nurses in Thailand waiting for permission to begin medical work. To get permission they must take the Nursing Registration Examination (in English), but in order to do that they have to secure permanent visas. Applications for the visas have been made several times, only to be turned down. A missionary doctor in the hospital at Manorom was somehow permitted to take the medical exam and thereafter proceeded to work in the hospital. When the government got wind of this, he was stopped on the grounds that he did not have a work permit! This kind of treatment is exceedingly frustrating, especially to medical personnel who have spent so much time, energy, and money to qualify for a medical career.

Missionaries in Thailand are working under conditions which are extremely irksome. It is virtually impossible to procure a permanent visa. The Overseas Missionary Fellowship, the largest mission in Thailand, has not been granted one in the last three years. This may be a blessing in disguise; each visa costs $2,500! The only visas being given are visitors' visas, good for one year but with the possibility of renewal for a second year.

6. Increasingly mission agencies are coming under government supervision. In India all foreign funds, whether used by church or mission groups, must be reported to the government. In Bangladesh all mission agencies—missions, relief agencies, and the Bible society—are now required to register with the Ministry of Social Welfare. Each agency has to fill out reams of papers and reports covering all its activities for the past ten years. Of the seventy groups involved, thirty-five have been cleared; the other thirty-five will probably not get clearance. No agency has actually been turned down, however, and nothing to that effect has been put in writing; so everyone continues with business as usual pending the outcome. Each mission leader had to appear before the various secretaries of the Ministry of Social Welfare and was bombarded with all kinds of questions. From now on, all visas, work projects, and financial expenditures must be approved by the Ministry.

Bangladesh is a Muslim country, so the mission agencies there may be in for a rough time in the days ahead. It is quite possible that only those agencies engaged in social or relief work will be permitted to remain.

7. Another problem area is finance. For the first time ever, American missionaries making over $20,000 must pay federal income tax. In addition many of them also have to pay income tax to the country in which they work. In Sweden the income-tax rate is between 35 and 40 percent. This is to some extent offset by the fact that residents, as well as citizens, can apply for an allowance for housing and family. Fortunately the United States has a mutual tax agreement with most countries whereby the American abroad pays only the higher of the two amounts. The host country is the first to receive payment. If

one's tax in Sweden is $1,000 and his tax in the United States is $800, he pays the full tax in Sweden and nothing to the United States government. If, on the other hand, his United States tax is $1,200 and his Swedish tax is only $1,000, he pays $1,000 in Sweden and $200 to the United States.

When one remembers that some of the larger missions have almost a thousand missionaries in their membership, it becomes clear that keeping track of the income-tax and social-security payments is a major operation. In 1979 The Evangelical Alliance Mission sent out four sets of instructions to every missionary in twenty-four countries, and the instructions differed from country to country.

To make matters worse, the United States government is now requiring mission agencies to file reports covering all aspects of the total operation. In addition, thirty-five state governments are also asking for full disclosure of all financial transactions other than direct fund-raising. Even some of the larger cities, among them Los Angeles, are making similar demands. One mission reports that half of its office space is given over to the accounting department!

Nationalism and Church/Mission Relations

The great new fact of our time is the existence of a large number of independent churches in the Third World. Some of them received their independence back in the 1930s and 1940s, long before the governments became independent. Most of them, however, achieved their independence after World War II. The churches with the longest history were naturally the first to gain independence. Some of the more progressive missions saw to it that "their" churches were given independence as soon as they were ready for it. Others dragged their feet and gave it only after church/mission tension had heated to the boiling point.

The advent of independence was a good thing; nevertheless, it sometimes resulted in increased tension between church and mission. In some instances the missions were to blame.

They were too slow to see the handwriting on the wall and come to terms with the realities of the developing situation. In other cases the church leaders were to blame. They were more interested in self-government than in self-support. This did not please the mission leaders, who insisted that true independence could not be achieved without complete self-support. One might have thought that independence would bring complete harmony between church and mission, but it did not. A certain amount of friction and misunderstanding still exists, much of it connected with the use of foreign funds and mission property. The church leaders feel that all mission property should be handed over to them. Mission funds, including the salaries of the missionaries, should be channeled through the church; and, of course, no restrictions should be placed on how the church spends foreign funds.

Some missions are prepared to go along with these demands. Others are not sure that this is the best way to solve the financial problems of the church. They feel that the churches should be willing to acknowledge some degree of responsibility. They believe that if the missions are accountable to their churches in the United States, the national churches should be willing to acknowledge some accountability to the missions.

Another serious problem is the inability, or the unwillingness, of missionaries to relinquish leadership positions. In theory the churches are independent, but in practice the missionaries engage in back-seat driving, much to the distress of the national leaders, who feel that *all* authority should be in their hands. Veteran missionaries especially find it difficult to adjust to the new day. It is high time that national churches be recognized for what they are: sovereign, independent bodies. Wherever they exist, missionaries should be willing to work not only with them, but under them. In the future missionaries *must* be willing to be servants of the church.

These two factors (friction over funds and the unwillingness of missionaries to be servants), more than anything else, have been responsible for the call for moratorium which has been sounded in recent years. Of the two problems, the first is probably more difficult to solve. As long as missionaries are present, there will be foreign money available. This is bound to lead to jealousy. Whether we acknowledge it or not, money plays a large part in human affairs. Touch a man's pocketbook and you touch the apple of his eye. This is true of Christians as well as non-Christians, of churches in the West as well as in the East.

As the standard of living rises in the Third World, this problem will gradually disappear. In Japan it has long since ceased to exist. Many Japanese pastors are better off than American missionaries, and the situation in South Korea is not far behind. In other parts of the world, particularly Africa, the churches are extremely poor; they are still finding it difficult to pay their full-time workers a living wage, and that makes Western missions still appear to be wealthy institutions.

As long as this disparity remains, tensions will continue to plague church/mission relations. Two things can be done to alleviate the situation. Missionaries should make a genuine effort to simplify their lifestyle and so narrow the gap. In addition, mission agencies should give more time and thought to community development in order to raise the standard of living, particularly among the Christians.

CHAPTER 17

The Resurgence of the Non-Christian Religions

During the first half of the twentieth century we were informed by mission leaders that the non-Christian religions were about to break up under the impact of Western science and technology. Nobody talks that way any more. Today the picture has changed completely. Far from breaking up, these religions are on the move and are showing signs of new vitality. They are even making inroads in Europe and North America.

Christian leaders in India, for instance, are not convinced that Hinduism is moribund.

> Far from believing that Christianity will convert Hinduism in the foreseeable future, they are afraid that in India Christianity may be swallowed up in the all-embracing arms of the "mother of all religions," to become just another sect within the family of sects. Hindus themselves think their religion is not only the most ancient in the world but also the most modern and the best suited to resolve the problem of the world's many conflicting faiths.[1]

1. "The World's Great Religions. Part I: Hinduism," *Life*, 7 February 1955, p. 79.

Islam

Like every other great religion, Islam has had its periods of advance and retreat. During the heyday of Western imperialism it suffered at the hands of the great European powers. Today the situation is reversed. "Changes that in Christianity took centuries have been compressed into one generation for Muslims. These have left some Muslims gasping and troubled, and others exhilarated and alive with hope."[2] Robert Miller states that the Muslim revival is due to three major factors: (1) the influence of modern education, (2) the recovery of economic and political power, and (3) the pressure of Muslim laity for social reform.

Whatever the reason, Islam is on the march and its leaders intend to spread the faith throughout the world. In 1976 delegates from forty-four countries met in Karachi for the first International Shariat Congress for the promotion of Islam. They openly called on Muslim governments to quietly arrange for the "peaceful withdrawal" of Christian missionaries. Already several countries, Bangladesh and Indonesia among them, have tried to put this policy into effect. Some Muslim countries have never permitted Christian missionaries on their soil. During the past decade others have expelled them.

The last time the Muslims invaded Europe was in 1453 when their armies captured Constantinople. Today another invasion is under way, but this time it is peaceful. Muslims from Turkey, Pakistan, the Middle East, and North Africa are pouring into Europe in search of employment, higher wages, and a better life. Islam, with twenty-five million adherents, is now the second largest religion in Europe. In 1976 the world's first Festival of Islam was celebrated in England. It lasted for three months and had a profound effect on the people. Referring to the festival the Anglican Bishop of Guildford said: "Islam is now well and truly planted in the soil of Britain. Britain has become one of the leading Islamic centers, with

2. Robert E. Miller, "The Renaissance of the Muslim Spirit," *Christianity Today*, 16 November 1979, p. 18.

over 300 mosques and one million Muslims."[3] With their numbers increasing, Muslims are demanding, and receiving, recognition for their faith. In 1973 the Belgian Parliament recognized Islam as one of the official religions to be taught in the schools. Austria did the same in 1976.

With their fabulous wealth, derived from oil revenues, some Muslim countries, particularly Libya and Saudi Arabia, are subsidizing the spread of Islam all over the world. A $16 million mosque is to be built in Chicago and a $20 million one planned for Rome will rival St. Peter's Basilica. Robert Nicklaus stated:

> Petrodollars are on the way to making Islam the world's richest religion. Some of the top Arab leaders reason that Allah has been generous in pouring his black gold on the sons of Islam, so they might convert the world. The evangelistic use of petrodollars is certain, because the richest and most powerful of all Arab leaders also happens to be the chief guardian of the Muslim religion, King Faisal of Arabia.[4]

Pakistan, one of the poorest countries in the world, in 1973 set up the International Muslim Bank with initial capital of $1 billion to spread Islam around the world.

Africa, where Christian missions have met their greatest success, is now a target area for Muslim advance. A $12 million mosque is being erected in Chad. An Islamic university is being planned for Uganda and another for Niger. Eight million dollars have been set aside to establish an Islamic center in Senegal. Leaders in Saudi Arabia have unanimously agreed to make Liberia the center of Islamic activities in West Africa. Some four hundred Muslim students are studying at a new missionary training center in Libya, and the first thirty-six missionary teachers have been graduated from a new training academy in Mecca. A continent away, in Japan the Muslims are printing a million copies of the Koran for free distribution to homes and hotels.

3. Kerry Lovering, "Islam's Bid for Renewal," *Africa Now*, July-August 1977, p. 2.
4. Robert Nicklaus, "Global Report: Middle East: Oil, Politics and Islam," *Evangelical Missions Quarterly*, April 1975, p. 72.

Hinduism

There is reason to believe that Hinduism is the oldest religion in the world, but it was not until the nineteenth century
that any major reforms occurred. Modern Hinduism has seen
three attempts at reform: the Brahmo Samaj, the Arya Samaj,
and the Ramakrishna Movement. All three were directly influenced by Christianity.

Hinduism, generally regarded as the most tolerant of all
religions, is experiencing a renaissance in India and it is now
talking of winning the world. It has already invaded the West
in the form of Transcendental Meditation. Yoga is now practiced in many of the larger cities of the United States. In the
process Hinduism has incorporated certain Christian truths
into its system.

> Hinduism simply absorbed most of the Christian message, as
> it had previously absorbed Buddhist ideas, and along with the
> *Mahabharata* and the *Ramayana* the gurus began to teach the
> Sermon on the Mount. Many Hindus now list Christ as Vishnu's
> 10th incarnation, and some claim that Jesus actually lived in
> India from his 19th to his 30th years.[5]

It is common knowledge that Oriental religions, Hinduism
in particular, have in recent years had a strong appeal for the
Western mind. "The fascination of the East is exercising an
increasing influence upon Occidentals—especially in intellectual circles where Vedanta philosophy is capturing the minds
and imaginations of many men and women."[6]

Now that Hinduism has been stripped of its more offensive
crudities and has been given an air of respectability by the
Vedanta Movement, it is not surprising to learn that the new
gurus intend to propagate their religion by all means at their
disposal. As a matter of fact a missionary movement is already
under way.

5. "Hinduism," p. 80.
6. Abingdon Press *Newsletter*, December 1956.

With Swami Vivekananda's preaching, the ancient religion of the Hindus has been released from the stigma of a crude and superstitious creed, and it has positively stepped in to a new phase of evangelism that has been termed "Aggressive Hinduism" by Sister Nivedita. The term connotes the fresh missionary zeal infused into Hinduism. . . . Hindus are no longer ashamed of any constituent of their religious faith and philosophy of life. On the other hand they are found in the roles of bold exponents of "the Hindu view of life" even before the universities, scholars, and savants of Europe and America, and many among their Western audience are found to be really interested in the hoary culture of the Hindus.[7]

Buddhism

Following the advent of independence in the late fifties and early sixties, the Buddhist leaders of Asia naturally assumed that they would play a decisive role in the formation of the new societies about to emerge. This, however, did not happen, the principal reason being that Communism has been unusually successful in Southeast Asia and the Far East, the heartland of Buddhism. China, Mongolia, North Korea, Vietnam, Laos, and Cambodia, where for hundreds of years Buddhism was the dominant religion, are now under Communist control.

China is beginning to relax its restrictions against religion. It remains to be seen to what extent Buddhism can effect a comeback. The Panchen Lama is now studying politics in Peking. The Dalai Lama, who fled Tibet after a revolt broke out against the Chinese Communists in 1959, has been in North India ever since. There is reason to believe that China would "welcome" him back to Tibet. His return would certainly give the Communist regime in Tibet a much-needed boost.

In Sri Lanka the Constitution of 1972 promised preferential treatment for Buddhists, but this position was eroded following the defeat of Prime Minister Bandaranaike in 1977. Over ten thousand technicians and intellectuals, including Buddhist monks, left the country. In the three countries of

7. Belur Math, *Cultural Heritage of India* (Calcutta: Ramakrishna Centenary Committee, 1936), p. 611.

Indochina the Buddhists, along with other religious groups, have suffered various forms and degrees of persecution.

In Japan Soka Gakkai, the fastest growing Buddhist sect, has made a deal with the Japanese Communist Party whereby the Communists have agreed to defend freedom of religion and Soka Gakkai has agreed not to oppose Communism.

This does not mean that Buddhism is about to roll over and die. Far from it. In recent decades Buddhism has invaded the West. Meditation centers and educational institutions in Europe and North America continue to grow. It is in the West, especially in North America, that Buddhism's prospects are the brightest. A Society for Buddhist Studies was established at Columbia University in 1975. That same year a study center was founded in Denver, and for the first time in history a Buddhist leader was appointed chaplain for the California State Senate. The first Vietnamese Buddhist temple in the United States was built in Los Angeles in 1976. Zen Buddhism from Japan has been popular in the West, especially among university students. Nichiren Shoshu, also from Japan, is attracting an increasing number of adherents. In 1979 the Dalai Lama paid a historic visit to the United States, where he met with Christian and Buddhist leaders. There are at present between one and two million Buddhists in the United States, most of them of Japanese descent.

Factors Involved in the Resurgence

1. The collapse of the vast colonial system following World War II was a body blow to Christian missions. For almost two hundred years Protestant missions had been identified with Western imperialism. In many instances the colonial administrations looked with favor on the humanitarian work of missions and gave them both moral and material support. This was particularly true in Africa, where the missions for many years were the sole purveyors of modern education and trained a steady stream of skilled personnel needed to fill the many offices created by the colonial administration. The missions believed they were performing a worthwhile service by edu-

cating the nationals, and were gratified that their graduates were able to find well-paying jobs. On their part the colonial administrators were happy to have the missions contribute in this way to the success of their enterprise.

In British colonies English soon became the language of business, education, politics, and the professions. Likewise French became the *lingua franca* of the French colonies. Anyone wishing to get ahead was obliged to learn either French or English, which were taught only in mission schools.

For these and other reasons the connection between the missionary enterprise and Western colonialism was much closer than most people realize.

Now that the colonial system has been dismantled, all the fringe benefits enjoyed by Christian missions have disappeared. French and English are still in great demand but they can be acquired in the secular universities. Young people wanting a modern education are no longer obliged to attend a mission school. Indeed, most mission schools have long since been nationalized and are now part of the tax-supported school system.

2. Since the coming of independence the governments in the Third World have done everything in their power to encourage and support the spirit of nationalism among their people. Patriotism, almost a dirty word in the West, suddenly became the cornerstone of national reconstruction. Each ex-colony now has its own constitution, national anthem, parliamentary system, armed forces, and flag. In the General Assembly of the United Nations the last and least of these ex-colonies now has as much voting power as the two super powers, the United States and the Soviet Union. The peoples of the Third World are justifiably proud of these accomplishments.

To some extent in Africa, but to a much greater extent in Asia, Christians are often the objects of discrimination, in contrast to their privileged status under colonial rule. To be a patriotic Thai one must be a Buddhist. To be a patriotic Indian one must be a Hindu. To be a patriotic Pakistani one must be a Muslim. The peoples of the Third World have become aware of their national heritage.

3. With few exceptions the governments in the Third World believe that religion, being an integral part of culture, is a fit subject to be taught to children in the tax-supported school system. This is quite different from the situation here in the United States, where Bible reading and the Lord's Prayer have been banned from the classroom. There are several reasons for this situation. First, there seems to be an innate fear of establishing a "civic religion." Moreover, the recitation of the nonsectarian Lord's Prayer, we are told, is a violation of the First Amendment, which says that Congress shall not establish any religion. A third argument is that here in the United States we have a pluralistic society. Not everyone is a professing Christian. There are several million Jews and a smaller number of Buddhists, Hindus, and Muslims. To force them to recite the Lord's Prayer would be an act of cultural aggression unworthy of such an open, tolerant country as America.

Personally I have never been impressed with any of the above reasons. To suggest that reciting the Lord's Prayer is tantamount to "establishing a religion" in the sense in which our Founding Fathers used the term is ridiculous. The argument based on our being a pluralistic society is equally far-fetched. There are scores of countries in which there is a greater racial, religious, and cultural mix than in the United States, and they have not encountered any insurmountable obstacles. No; the decision of the Supreme Court was just another indication of the increasing secularization of American society. To invoke the First Amendment is simply a smoke screen.

In these other countries the governments require that all children be taught religion in the schools. The subject, which is usually called Religious Knowledge, is compulsory through grade school and even into high school. How do the schools get around the problem of pluralism? Quite simply. They teach the religion of the parents. If the student comes from a Muslim background, he is taught Islam, the Koran being the main textbook. If he is from a Christian home, he is taught Christianity, and the Bible is the main text. This seems to work well and it has several advantages. It enhances the importance of religion in the eyes of the people, and it acquaints the student with an important ingredient in his own cultural heritage.

From the point of view of the government, the greatest benefit is the fact that the students are now less vulnerable to the "proselytizing" activities of the Christian missionaries. In colonial times education was under the control of the missions, and the schools were regarded as an evangelistic as well as an educational facility. This being so, Christianity was the only religion they taught.

It is true that mission schools did a much better job in education than in evangelism. Only a small percentage of students ever became Christians, especially in India, China, and Japan. Now, however, mission schools have disappeared and so has the opportunity to influence for Christ a whole generation of students. This is a serious loss from our point of view.

4. Here in the United States we have separation of church and state—the government would not think of supporting, much less subsidizing, the churches. In the Third World things are different. Three great religions are dominant in Asia—Hinduism, Buddhism, and Islam—and each of them, in one way or another, receives moral and material support from the government.

Persons belonging to the Scheduled Classes, formerly known as Untouchables, receive preferential treatment from the Indian government to compensate for the despicable treatment they received for over two thousand years. Christians from an Untouchable background, however, are no longer recognized as belonging to the Scheduled Classes, so they are not eligible for government handouts. When one remembers that 60 percent of today's Christians come from that background, it is apparent how discriminatory such a practice is. It is not surprising that some Christians have returned to the Hindu fold in the hope of getting much-needed government help.

Buddhism is the state religion in Thailand, where there are more Buddhist temples than Christian converts. Every family is encouraged to provide one son for the Sangha—the religious order. One can enter the Sangha on a permanent basis and become a lifetime monk, or he can enter for a shorter period of a year or less. A government employee who enters the Sangha for a short period gets paid for the time he spends in the Sangha and is guaranteed his job when he returns to civilian life.

In other countries of Southeast Asia, Buddhism, the dominant religion, can also count on government support. In Burma the government has allocated large sums of money for the building and repair of Buddhist temples. In contrast, Christian churches are often modest, unpretentious buildings, as bare on the inside as they are plain on the outside.

5. In some countries the dominant religion has been made by government action the state religion. As such it is backed up by all the power and paraphernalia of the government at all levels, local, provincial, and national. This is almost universally true of the more than forty Muslim countries of the world. In them there is no such thing as the separation of church and state. In fact, church and state—or mosque and state, to be more correct—are one and indivisible. In all such countries religious minorities are barely tolerated, and it is always with the understanding that they not engage in any "proselytizing" activities. They must keep their religious convictions strictly to themselves. Any attempt to share their faith is met with immediate opposition.

For over two thousand years Buddhism has been the dominant religion of Burma. In August, 1961, it was declared to be the state religion. When the Christians raised objections, the government, the following month, passed a constitutional amendment protecting the rights of religious minorities. Until it was abolished in 1962, the Government Sasana Council aided the resurgence of Buddhism. Pagodas were rebuilt, centers for study and meditation were established, and Buddhist missionaries were sent into the hill country to convert the animistic tribes.

In Nepal Hinduism is the state religion, and it is unlawful for anyone to convert from Hinduism to any other religion.

Those who accept Christian baptism are given a one-year prison term. The one who administers baptism is liable to a seven-year term. In India two states passed anticonversion laws which were later struck down by the Supreme Court. In 1979 the Indian Parliament considered a law which would punish anyone for using fear, inducement, or coercion to gain converts. Now that Indira Gandhi is back in power that measure is probably a dead issue.

Wherever a religion is strongly entrenched, the people tend to identify with that religion. Job opportunities and other benefits may depend on it, and Christian converts are at a serious disadvantage when it comes to employment or promotion.

6. A growing sense of solidarity is in evidence in the non-Christian religions. World fellowships are being formed and world councils are being organized. Buddhism, once confined to Southeast Asia, is now spreading to other parts of the world, including Western Europe and North America. The World Fellowship of Buddhists was formed in 1950 and a world congress is convened every two or three years. The Muslims likewise hold their International Islamic Colloquiums every few years. These world assemblies attract scholars and leaders from all over the world and greatly enhance the international image of the religion.

The Sixth Great Buddhist Council, commemorating the twenty-five-hundredth anniversary of the Enlightenment of Buddha, was held in Rangoon from 1954 to 1956. One outcome of the council was a new version of the *Tripitaka*, the Buddhist Scriptures, and translations into several modern languages.

7. For centuries the great ethnic religions of Asia were world-renouncing. In recent years a change has taken place. Taking their cue from Christian missions, they are actively engaged in various kinds of social service. The Ramakrishna Movement in India (Hindu), Soka Gakkai in Japan (Buddhist), and devotees of the Aga Khan (Muslim), are opening and maintaining schools, hospitals, clinics, and day-care centers.

8. In some countries these non-Christian religions have gone beyond social service and are engaged in political activities. In

India the fanatical Hindus, known as the Mahasabah, are dedicated to the proposition that India, which they call Hindustan, should be reserved for Hindus only. During the 1960s the Buddhist monks in Vietnam participated in antigovernment activities and succeeded in bringing more than one regime to its knees. Several monks, to dramatize the situation, burned themselves to death in the streets of Saigon. This is a new departure for a religion which through the centuries has been known for its emphasis on meditation and compassion. In Japan Soka Gakkai has organized a political party, Komeito, which is now the third largest party in the country. What shall we say about the Muslim "students" and others who held fifty Americans hostage in Iran for 444 days in 1979-81? More and more religious leaders are becoming engaged in political action.

9. These religions are now carrying on missionary work, some of them for the first time, and are using methods and techniques learned from Christian missionaries. The Ahmadiyya Movement of Islam has opened missionary training centers in various parts of the world, including England and the United States. In the fall of 1979 we had an Ahmadiyya missionary address a class in Islam at Trinity Evangelical Divinity School. He made no secret of the fact that he is an "evangelist" out to win converts to Islam. The leader of the movement said on one occasion: "We need men to take it upon themselves to spread the message of Islam everywhere. The number of missionaries in the field is not enough. I am thinking of asking every Ahmadi family to dedicate one member to the service of Islam." The Black Muslims in the United States are on the march, making converts wherever they can. Their most famous convert is Muhammad Ali, whose conversion seems to be genuine. The two million Muslims in the United States and Canada represent a fourfold increase in the past decade.

The Ramakrishna Mission, based in India, has opened centers in the leading cities of the West, where it is known as the Vedanta Society. The centers are usually located near a major university and are manned by well-educated swamis whose main message is that there is truth in all religions, including

Christianity. Their approach is dialectical rather than polemical. Their evident otherworldliness (spirituality, if you like) has a fascination for our youth, who are fed up with the materialism of the West. The centers have a dual objective: to minister to the spiritual needs of Hindu students and to present Hinduism as the coming world religion. Its eclectic approach has a strong appeal to intellectuals both East and West.

CHAPTER 18

The Charismatic Movement

In the 1950's in an article in *Life* magazine Henry P. Van Dusen, then president of Union Theological Seminary in New York, referred to the Pentecostals as "the Third Force" in Christendom and predicted that in the second half of the century they might become the first force in American church life.

Since then the charismatic movement has grown beyond all expectations and today is the most vital force in world Christianity. Both here in North America and throughout the world the Pentecostal churches are outstripping all others as far as numerical growth is concerned. In the United States the Assemblies of God in 1979 registered a gain of .7 percent; in overseas operations the rate was 5 percent.

The Pentecostal Movement

The Pentecostal movement began in Los Angeles in the Azusa Mission in 1906. From there it spread to St. Louis and then to Chicago. Pentecostal missionaries went from Chicago to Italy and Brazil. About the time that it began in Los Angeles it also appeared in Norway, where it has continued to flourish.

Most of the Free Churches in Norway today are Pentecostal in character.

Here in North America several large Pentecostal denominations have developed. The largest is the Assemblies of God, with headquarters in Springfield, Missouri. Others are the Church of God (Cleveland, Tennessee), the Church of God (Anderson, Indiana), and the International Church of the Foursquare Gospel, headquartered in California. In Canada there is the Pentecostal Assemblies of Canada.

One of the outstanding characteristics of the Pentecostal churches is their commitment to world missions. The Assemblies of God have over 1,200 missionaries working in more than a hundred countries. Their overseas membership is 9.5 times as great as the membership in the American churches. One local church in Seoul, Korea, has over 150,000 members; another in Chile has 70,000.

It is in Latin America that the Pentecostals have had their largest gains. Today they represent almost 70 percent of all evangelicals in that part of the world. In Chile the figure is 90 percent. They have also done exceedingly well in Brazil, where the largest churches are almost all Pentecostal. They have not been so successful in other areas, however, notably in the Muslim countries.

The Neo-Pentecostal Movement

It is necessary to make a distinction between the "classical" or "mainline" Pentecostals and the more recent brand known as Neo-Pentecostals. This movement began in Roman Catholic circles at Duquesne University in February, 1967. From there it spread to Notre Dame University in Indiana the following month. About the same time it appeared at Michigan State University. In the intervening years it has penetrated all parts of the Roman Catholic Church. Each year a conference of Roman Catholic charismatics, attended by some forty thousand persons, is held at Notre Dame University. Now known as the charismatic movement, it has infiltrated Protestant churches of all denominations, including most of the conservative churches as well.

The thrust of the movement is to bring the twentieth-century church back to its first-century heritage. David Womack, formerly an Assemblies of God missionary in Latin America, stated it quite clearly:

> We will define Pentecostalism as that theological position that calls for all the doctrines, the religious experiences, the fundamental practices, and the basic priorities of the apostolic Church. It is no coincidence that Pentecostal theology has predominated during the two periods of the most rapid church growth in history. The whole evangelical church must purge itself of its complicating vestiges of medieval and Reformational religion and return wholeheartedly to the purity and simplicity of purpose of apostolic Christianity, or else forever give up any hope of total world evangelization.[1]

Not surprisingly, a movement of such distinction and dimension has stirred up a great deal of controversy. As always, there are those who support the movement and rejoice that God has once more visited His people in power. There are others who vigorously oppose it, teach and preach against it, and exclude from their fellowship anyone in any way sympathetic towards it.

Unfortunately the greatest opposition has come from the conservative evangelicals, many of whom maintain that certain spiritual gifts, speaking in tongues among them, were temporary in nature and ceased with the apostles. Since then any manifestation of supernatural power must be psychological at best or demonic at worst. This has been a particularly sensitive issue among the faith missions belonging to the Interdenominational Foreign Mission Association. No Pentecostal mission may join the IFMA.

The problem goes deeper, however. Within the faith mis-

---

1. David A. Womack, *Breaking the Stained-Glass Barrier* (New York: Harper & Row, 1973), p. 57.

sions themselves there are missionaries who have had a charismatic experience of one kind or another, and this has caused dissension and turmoil in their ranks. A majority of the faith missions have taken a definite stand against the movement. They will not accept any candidate who has had a charismatic experience. They find it more difficult to deal with veteran missionaries who have recently become charismatics. Some of the more "progressive" faith missions have endeavored to come to terms with the phenomenon, acknowledging its presence in their midst but at the same time trying to keep it under control. If a person speaks in tongues in his own private devotions, for his own edification, he may remain in the mission; but if he becomes a crusader and considers his experience a norm by which to judge his fellow missionaries, he must leave. The missions which have adopted this position have alienated some of their ultraconservative supporting churches. Other missions have lost council members over the issue. The charismatic movement has been a thorn in the flesh of the faith missions. The same is true of the Bible colleges in the United States and Canada, most of which are interdenominational and therefore vulnerable to reprisals from their supporting constituencies.

Features of Neo-Pentecostalism

1. Neo-Pentecostalism cuts across denominational lines. The movement runs the gamut from the Plymouth Brethren to the Episcopal Church, from the Quakers to the Salvation Army, from storefront churches to the powerful Roman Catholic Church. According to a *Christianity Today*–Gallup poll taken in 1979:

> About one-quarter of those who reckon themselves to be Pentecostal-charismatic are Roman Catholics and two-thirds are Protestants. . . . Likewise, the major Protestant denominations are represented roughly according to their size: Baptists constitute 21 percent of all charismatics; Methodists, 8 percent; Lutherans, 6 percent; and Presbyterians, 4 percent; other

smaller bodies plus classical Pentecostals make up approximately one-third of all Pentecostal-charismatics.[2]

2. Charismatics are remaining in their churches. For the first half of the century the Pentecostals were a distinct group with their own denominations, and those who became Pentecostals left the mainline churches to join Pentecostal churches. That has not been true in recent years. Present-day charismatics have no desire to join the Pentecostal churches. They prefer to remain where they are and bear whatever witness they can.

> Neo-Pentecostalists have a dilemma as to whether they should remain in their old denominations, as a witness in isolation from their fellow charismatics, or should join a Pentecostal denomination and lose the entree into their own denomination, towards which they often feel a heavy responsibility and within which they may carry on a Pentecostal mission.[3]

This has raised some eyebrows in Pentecostal and conservative circles alike. It came as something of a shock to classical Pentecostals to find people with the gift of tongues showing no desire to join them in their corporate witness to the rest of the world. Because of this some Pentecostals have questioned the genuineness of the Neo-Pentecostal movement.

Evangelicals also have their problems with the charismatics. They find it difficult to understand how a born-again, charismatic Roman Catholic priest can continue to celebrate the mass every Sunday morning when he must know that Christ offered the perfect sacrifice when He offered Himself without spot as the Lamb of God slain before the foundation of the world (Rev 13:8). How can he continue to believe that the elements are really the body and blood of Jesus? Another problem has to do with lifestyle. Many of these charismatics,

2. Kenneth S. Kantzer, "The Charismatics Among Us," *Christianity Today*, 22 February 1980, p. 25.

3. Kenneth S. Kantzer, "Charismatic Renewal: Threat or Promise?" in *Theology and Mission*, ed. David J. Hesselgrave (Grand Rapids: Baker, 1978), p. 29.

at least in the early stages of their spiritual pilgrimage, show little or no change in their manner of life. The old habits—drinking, smoking, swearing, and so on—remain. Their life-style does not conform to that usually associated with conservative evangelicals.

3. The movement has a strong evangelistic thrust. Invariably, when a person is filled with the Holy Spirit, he begins immediately to share his faith with others. Without any effort on his part he acquires a love for others and a passion for souls that compels him to go out into the highways and byways with the gospel of Christ. Timid souls who were never able to speak to others about Christ now have a holy boldness that enables them to share the gospel with all and sundry, and it is amazing the number of persons they lead to the Lord.

4. In any charismatic group there is a feeling of warm Christian fellowship. There is in every heart a new sense of love, joy, and peace. The fruit of the Spirit is seen among them, in many instances for the first time. This is most obvious when they get together for their own meetings, usually once a week. Roman Catholic priests and nuns, Presbyterian elders, Methodist ministers, Lutheran laymen, Baptist believers, Salvation Army officers, Episcopalians—all find a unity in Christ that surpasses anything ever dreamed of in the ecumenical movement. They could not care less about church union. They have all kinds of theological differences, but they have one thing in common—life in Christ. Because they are born-again believers, they are members of the body of Christ, and their love for one another is something to behold. This is one thing that has attracted people from the mainline denominations, where there is plenty of liturgy and worship but little Christian fellowship.

5. The gift of tongues, so characteristic of the mainline Pentecostals, is a nonissue with the charismatics. Only a small fraction of them speak in tongues. Among the charismatic Catholics the ratio is one in ten; among the Lutherans one in seven; among the Methodists one in ten; and among the Baptists one in sixteen. Obviously the gift that is supposed to be *the* sign of the baptism of the Holy Spirit is a negligible factor among

them. Many charismatics, if they exercise the gift of tongues at all, do so only in their own private devotions.

Why the Charismatic Movement Is So Popular

1. Existentialism in philosophy and theology, with its emphasis on personal experience, has created a climate in which this kind of experience-oriented movement can thrive and grow.

2. The mainline denominations, while outwardly prosperous, are in a state of spiritual decline. The United Methodist Church lost a million members during the past decade, and other denominations did not do much better. Those who continue to attend church services derive little spiritual help. The liturgy tends to be mechanical. The hymn-singing is not exactly inspiring. The eighteen-minute sermonette, seldom based on Scripture, may challenge the mind but does nothing for the soul.

Many church members today are searching for spiritual reality. This is especially true of the youth. In church they hear much about love, joy, peace, power, and a lot of other fine things; but few church members have personally experienced any of them. Consequently, when our youth go to a charismatic meeting, they are deeply impressed by the sincerity of the participants. Never before have they seen so many people literally filled with love and ready and willing to sing and shout about it. Here, for the first time, they find spiritual reality, and they love it.

3. Another factor is the new openness on the part of the Roman Catholic Church. Prior to Vatican II Catholics and Protestants went their separate ways. To the Catholics we were heretics. To us they were apostates. Pope John XXIII changed all that. Today we are "separated brethren" and they are reading the Bible! Protestants are still barred from the mass, except by dissident bishops; but Catholics are encouraged to read the Bible and pray with their Protestant friends. This is a giant step forward. Roman Catholic charismatics no longer incur the wrath of the hierarchy when they fellowship with Prot-

estant charismatics. In fact, not a few priests and some bishops are themselves charismatics.

4. The moral decadence of Western civilization cries out for spiritual power great enough to cope with the social evils that abound on every hand—alcoholism, drugs, divorce, juvenile delinquency, violence, vandalism, corruption, graft, pornography, and abortion, all on an unprecedented scale. In the face of these gargantuan problems the Christian church is virtually helpless. If people want help in these areas, they look to the schools, the courts, the hospitals, the politicians, the lawyers, the psychiatrists. They do not even think of the church. It has neither the expertise nor the power to deal effectively with the social evils of the day.

When the charismatics come along with their marvelous accounts of bodies healed, lives changed, families reunited, alcoholics rehabilitated, and drug addicts cleaned up, both the church and the world have to sit up and take notice. Here are people with *power*—power to solve the problems that no one else has been able to solve.

The world will never be evangelized, nor will Western civilization ever be cleaned up, unless we experience a genuine, heaven-sent, Holy Spirit–revival that will set the church on fire and send her members out to win the world.

Why Evangelicals Object to the Charismatic Movement

Theological Reasons

1. Pentecost, say the evangelicals, was a unique, once-for-all event, never to be repeated. This being so, the speaking in tongues described in Acts 2 was a unique experience not to be repeated in later church history.

2. The term *baptized* in the Holy Spirit used by Paul in 1 Corinthians 12:13 refers to the incorporation of the believer into the body of Christ and has nothing to do with the spiritual gifts found in the same chapter. This baptism occurs only once, when the person repents, believes the gospel, and is regenerated by the power of the Holy Spirit. It has no ref-

erence to the "second blessing" some persons profess to have received.

3. Certain spiritual gifts enumerated in 1 Corinthians 12 were temporary and others were intended to be permanent. The temporary gifts, speaking in tongues among them, ceased with the apostles. This view is based on 1 Corinthians 13:8.

4. Pentecostals maintain that the gift of tongues is the only sure proof of the filling of the Holy Spirit. Everyone, therefore, should have, or seek to have, this gift. The New Testament, on the other hand, clearly teaches that tongues is only *one* of the gifts and not the most important at that.

5. Pentecostals base everything on their experience instead of on the Word of God. They interpret the Scriptures in the light of their experience rather than judging their experience by the Scriptures. This can lead to highly undesirable results.

Pragmatic Reasons

1. The gift of tongues, say the evangelicals, leads to spiritual pride. Persons with this gift tend to regard themselves as more spiritual than those who do not have it. Some of them become crusaders, accosting mature Christians and berating them for their failure to receive it. Such persons are then regarded as second-class citizens in the kingdom.

2. Evangelicals are Christocentric in their theological orientation. Christ gets more attention in their teaching and preaching than do the other two persons of the Trinity. The Pentecostals make more of the person and work of the Holy Spirit and have a tendency to exalt Him rather than Christ.

3. Pentecostalism leads to excesses. Witness the stereotype of the old Pentecostalism represented by the "Holy Rollers" of bygone days. Morever, some Pentecostal preachers have doubtless raised the gift of healing to the status of a cult. They appear to be more interested in healing the sick than in saving the lost. They have become heavily involved in "faith healing," both in large crusades and over the air. Not all the "cures" have been genuine, and some have even been faked.

4. Pentecostalism is divisive. It has wrecked some churches and divided others right down the middle. It has even split denominations.

5. The Pentecostal experience often ends in disillusionment. At first the experience is very exhilarating and people get carried away with their new-found power. But after a few years they tire of the same emphasis in all the services and begin to hunger for a more balanced treatment of New Testament doctrine.

An Objective Appraisal

In a matter so controversial, it is difficult, if not impossible, to be objective. Nevertheless, a few observations might help to place the whole problem in a more objective perspective. I might add at this point that I have never spoken in tongues, nor can I claim to be a charismatic; but I have had sufficient fellowship with charismatics to know that some of the criticism leveled against them is not entirely fair.

Although we grant that the Pentecostals may be slightly off base theologically, that is no reason for us to avoid and oppose them altogether. They are born-again members of God's family and are therefore our brothers and sisters in Christ. They love the Lord, they love the Word, and they love one another. Moreover, they give generously to the Lord's work and support the program of the local church. It is common knowledge that the Pentecostals are the fastest-growing Christian group in the world.

When it comes to the pragmatic reasons for evangelical opposition, the following remarks are in order. There is a certain amount of truth in all five accusations, but at best they are only half-truths.

1. Anyone who has gone farther in the Christian life than someone else may give the impression that he is lifted up with pride, especially if he insists on sharing his experience with his friends. However, this is not *necessarily* a matter of pride. If his experience has helped him, he owes it to his brother to share it with him. It often happens that the nominal church

member who attends a Billy Graham crusade and is thoroughly converted returns home to tell his family and friends about the wonderful thing that has happened to him. In some cases his friends and family may be church members in good standing. They will naturally resent his remarks and challenge his right to claim an experience to which they are still strangers. Such persons may indeed be accused of "spiritual" pride.

2. Pentecostals do emphasize the person and power of the Holy Spirit, but so did the early Christians. The Holy Spirit is mentioned by name fifty-five times in the Acts of the Apostles. The apostle Paul declared that his entire ministry was in the demonstration of the Spirit and of power (1 Cor 2:4; cf. Rom 15:19). The Old Testament was the dispensation of the Father. The Gospels represent the dispensation of the Son. With Pentecost began the dispensation of the Holy Spirit. He came to promote, empower, direct, and consummate the entire program of the Christian church. If the Pentecostals have overemphasized the ministry of the Holy Spirit, we have gone to the other extreme and all but ignored His presence and His influence.

3. Pentecostalism has indeed led to excesses, but should it be condemned on that account? Has not the doctrine of the second coming of Christ been abused by fanatics who sold all their earthly goods, dressed themselves in white robes, and ascended a nearby mountain to meet the Lord, who was supposed to return on a particular day? This has been done not once but many times in the last century, but we do not reject the doctrine on that account. The devil as an angel of light has more than one way to undermine the truth of the Word. We must not judge a doctrine by the behavior of a few advocates who obviously have been the tools of the devil.

4. Pentecostalism has been divisive, but again, we must be careful not to reject it on that account. Truth as well as error has a way of dividing churches. Jesus was accused of "stirring up the people" by His subversive teaching (Lk 23:5). Every reformer in church history has been accorded similar treatment. Sooner or later he and his followers have become *personae non gratae* in their own churches. John Wyclif and the

Lollards, John Hus and the Bohemian Brethren, Menno Simons and the Anabaptists, John Wesley and the Methodists, John Darby and the Plymouth Brethren were all rejected, sometimes persecuted, by the religious hierarchy of the day, not because they championed error but because they preached a different brand of truth.

Charismatics have split churches, but does all the blame lie with them? Does not some of it rest with us? Much depends on how the situation is handled. Some churches have accepted the charismatics and given them a degree of freedom. These churches have invariably grown both in grace and in numbers. Other churches, regarding the charismatic movement as demonic in nature, have adamantly rejected it and they have split, losing some of their most spiritual members.

5. It is, of course, true that a small number of Pentecostals have been known to give up Pentecostalism and return to the more traditional forms of Christian experience; but this phenomenon is not peculiar to the Pentecostal movement. Christians seeking God's best are often attracted to another group that seems to offer what they are seeking. After a time in the new group they change to another or revert to the original one. Denominational loyalty seems to be on the wane. More and more people are moving from one church to another until they find one in which they can be "comfortable." This is particularly true in the large urban centers where families come and go with increasing frequency.

How to Cope with the Situation

1. Let us recognize that many of God's choicest servants experienced a "second work of grace." Adoniram J. Gordon, founder of Gordon-Conwell Theological Seminary; Reuben A. Torrey, the great evangelist; J. Hudson Taylor, father of the faith mission movement; and A. B. Simpson, founder of the Christian and Missionary Alliance, all experienced a second work of grace which was as dramatic and dynamic as their conversion experience. So profound was Hudson Taylor's ex-

perience that, even after fifteen years in inland China, he exclaimed: "God has made me a new man!"[4]

The Keswick Movement of our day goes back to 1875 in England. Its leaders included such spiritual giants as F. B. Meyer, Andrew Murray, Bishop Taylor Smith, Bishop Handley Moule, W. H. Griffith Thomas, W. Graham Scroggie, and a host of others. The Keswick message was introduced to this country by Alan Redpath and Stephen Olford. Not all evangelicals, however, agree with the Keswick message. To them it is a perversion of Christian doctrine and therefore to be rejected. The well-known Martyn Lloyd-Jones, when asked what he thought of the Keswick Movement, replied: "I refused to speak there. I was unhappy about the so-called Keswick message concerning sanctification. I considered it unscriptural and have tried to show why in my volumes on Romans 6 and 8. To me, sanctification is a process, and the Keswick formula 'Let go and let God' is quite unscriptural."[5]

There are others who say the same thing about regeneration. It too is a process; it involves infant baptism, catechetical classes, confirmation, and first communion. For a person to "decide for Christ" at an evangelistic rally (as an addition to this process) and thereby pass instantly from death to life in a conversion experience is regarded by them as a "second work of grace" and therefore not acceptable. Evangelicals, however, consider such a conversion experience both scriptural and valid.

In this respect we are in danger of setting up a chain reaction. Liberal churches reject the evangelicals because of their belief in a "second work of grace" known as conversion. Evangelical churches, on their part, reject the charismatics because of their belief in a "second work of grace" known as the "baptism" in the Holy Spirit. It is almost universally true that a person without the experience denies the validity of the doc-

4. Dr. and Mrs. Howard Taylor, *Hudson Taylor's Spiritual Secret* (London: China Inland Mission, 1932), p. 110.
5. "Martyn Lloyd-Jones: From Buckingham to Westminster: An Interview by Carl F. H. Henry," *Christianity Today*, 8 February 1980, p. 32.

trine. Conversely, a person who has had the experience always regards it as scriptural.

2. We should search our own hearts and lives to ascertain whether or not we need a new infilling of the Holy Spirit. The church is practically powerless against the rising tide of evil in society, evil which was once confined to the world but is now beginning to appear in the church. If the church is to keep itself unspotted from the world, to say nothing of winning the world to Christ, it must have the power of the Holy Spirit. When the Holy Spirit does begin to move in power, however, we raise all kinds of objections. Someone has said: "For years we have been praying for the fire of heaven to fall; but when it does, we immediately call for the fire engine."

3. We must be sure that we teach and preach the whole counsel of God, including the doctrine of the person and work of the Holy Spirit. I was brought up in a Christian group that excelled in the private and corporate study of the Scriptures. Their exaltation of the person and work of Christ was beautiful, but in ten years I never heard a message or participated in a Bible study on the person or power of the Holy Spirit. He was acknowledged as the third person of the Trinity, but beyond that He was virtually unknown.

4. It is the ultradispensationalists who have the greatest problem with the charismatic movement. They fight it tooth and nail, and they do so in all sincerity, thinking all the time that they are champions of the truth. They have certain well-defined ideas of what God's program is for this dispensation. They insist that all things be done "decently and in order." I am a dispensationalist, but I do not want to carry my dispensationalism so far that I place almighty God in a theological straitjacket and tell Him what He may or may not do in this dispensation. God must remain sovereign. The Holy Spirit must be free to move in power, to work His will, to empower His servants, and to renew His church.

5. We must be careful not to attack the movement head on. That is like throwing gasoline on a fire. There are diversities of spiritual gifts and these are administered by the Holy Spirit

as He wills (1 Cor 12:11). We should give heed to Gamaliel's advice to the Sanhedrin: "Refrain from these men, and let them alone; for if this counsel or this work be of men, it will come to nought; but if it be of God, ye cannot overthrow it; lest haply ye be found even to fight against God" (Acts 5:38-39). We must also remember the solemn warning of our Lord: "Whosoever speaketh a word against the Son of man, it shall be forgiven him; but whosoever speaketh against the Holy Ghost, it shall not be forgiven him, neither in this world, neither in the world to come" (Mt 12:32).

6. Let us remember that the charismatics are our brothers and sisters in Christ. They may be theologically naive. They may have more zeal than knowledge. They may have engaged in some excesses. They may even have divided churches. That is no reason why they should be excluded from the fellowship of the Christian church and obliged to form splinter groups of their own. They need us and we need them. Some of us were rejected by the mainline denominations when we experienced the new birth and were so excited about it that we wanted to share it with others. It would be a mistake for us to reject our charismatic brethren because they have experienced what they describe as the "baptism" in the Holy Spirit and in the glow of that marvelous event want to share it with us. We may even learn from them.

> Despite some unhappy theology, the charismatic movement overall bears marks of genuine spiritual renewal, and though it or sections of it may have lessons to learn in doctrine, it has its own lessons to teach concerning practice.
>
> Doubtless they are not unique, and could be learned elsewhere. But when God has brought new life to so many along charismatic channels, it would be perverse conceit on the part of non-charismatics to be unwilling to look and learn.[6]

---

6. J. I. Packer, "Charismatic Renewal: Pointing to a Person and a Power," *Christianity Today*, 7 March 1980, p. 19.

Bibliography

Adeney, David H. *The Unchanging Commission*. Chicago: Inter-Varsity, 1955.
Allen, Roland. *The Ministry of the Spirit*. Grand Rapids: Eerdmans, 1962.
————. *Missionary Methods: St. Paul's or Ours?* Grand Rapids: Eerdmans, 1962.
————. *The Spontaneous Expansion of the Church*. Grand Rapids: Eerdmans, 1962.
Anderson, Gerald H., ed. *Asian Voices in Christian Theology*. Maryknoll, NY: Orbis, 1976.
Anderson, Gerald H., and Thomas F. Stransky, eds. *Christ's Lordship and Religious Pluralism*. Maryknoll, NY: Orbis Books, 1981.
————. *Mission Trends No. 1: Crucial Issues in Missions Today*. Grand Rapids: Eerdmans, 1974.
————. *Mission Trends No. 2: Evangelization*. Grand Rapids: Eerdmans, 1975.
————. *Mission Trends No. 3: Third World Theologies*. Grand Rapids: Eerdmans, 1976.
————. *Mission Trends No. 4: Liberation Theologies in North America and Europe*. Grand Rapids: Eerdmans, 1978.
————. *Mission Trends No. 5: Faith Meets Faith*. Ramsey, NJ: Paulist Press, 1981.
Anderson, Rufus. *To Advance the Gospel: A Collection of the Writings of Rufus Anderson*. Edited by R. Pierce Beaver. Grand Rapids: Eerdmans, 1967.
Beaver, R. Pierce. *Ecumenical Beginnings in the Protestant World Mission: A History of Comity*. New York: Nelson, 1962.
Beyerhaus, Peter. *Missions: Which Way? Humanization or Redemption*. Grand Rapids: Zondervan, 1971.
————. *Shaken Foundations: Building Mission Theology*. Grand Rapids: Zondervan, 1972.

Braaten, Carl E. *The Flaming Center: A Theology of the Christian Mission*. Philadelphia: Fortress, 1977.

Brierley, Peter, ed. *U.K. Protestant Missions Handbook*. Vol. 2. London: Evangelical Missionary Alliance, 1977.

Bryant, David. *In the Gap: What It Means to Be a World Christian*. Downers Grove, IL: Inter-Varsity, 1979.

Cervin, Russell A. *Mission in Ferment*. Chicago: Covenant Press, 1977.

Chaney, Charles L. *The Birth of Missions in America*. South Pasadena, CA: William Carey Library, 1976.

Cho, David J. *New Forces in Missions*. Seoul: East-West Center for Missions Research and Development, 1976.

Clark, Dennis E. *The Third World and Mission*. Waco, TX: Word Books, 1971.

Coggins, Wade T. *So That's What Missions Is All About*. Chicago: Moody, 1975.

————, and Edwin L. Frizen, Jr., eds. *Evangelical Missions Tomorrow*. South Pasadena, CA: William Carey Library, 1977.

Cook, Harold R. *An Introduction to the Study of Christian Missions*. Chicago: Moody, 1954.

————. *Missionary Life and Work*. Chicago: Moody, 1959.

Corwin, Charles. *East to Eden? Religion and the Dynamics of Social Change*. Grand Rapids: Eerdmans, 1972.

Coxill, H. Wakelin, and Kenneth Grubb, eds. *World Christian Handbook, 1968*. Nashville: Abingdon, 1968.

Dayton, Edward R., and David A. Fraser. *Planning Strategies for World Evangelization*. Grand Rapids: Eerdmans, 1980.

DeRidder, Richard B. *Discipling the Nations*. Grand Rapids: Baker, 1975.

Detzler, Wayne A. *The Changing Church in Europe*. Grand Rapids: Zondervan, 1979.

Douglas, Donald E., ed. *Evangelical Perspectives on China*. Farmington, MI: Evangelical China Committee, 1976.

Douglas, J. D., ed. *Let the Earth Hear His Voice*. Minneapolis: World Wide Publications, 1975.

Engstrom, Ted W. *What in the World Is God Doing? The New Face of Missions*. Waco, TX: Word Books, 1978.

Fairbank, John K., ed. *The Missionary Enterprise in China and America*. Cambridge: Harvard University, 1974.

Falk, Peter. *The Growth of the Church in Africa*. Grand Rapids: Zondervan, 1979.

Fenton, Horace L. *Myths About Missions*. Downers Grove, IL: Inter-Varsity, 1973.

Fleming, Bruce C. E. *Contextualization of Theology: An Evangelical Assessment*. South Pasadena, CA: William Carey Library, 1980.

Fuller, W. Harold. *Mission-Church Dynamics*. South Pasadena, CA: William Carey Library, 1980.

Gerber, Vergil, ed. *Discipling Through Theological Education by Extension*. Chicago: Moody Press, 1980.

————. *Missions in Creative Tension: The Green Lake Compendium*. South Pasadena, CA: William Carey Library, 1971.

Gibbon, Edward. *The Triumph of Christendom in the Roman Empire*. New York: Harper & Row, 1958.

Glasser, Arthur F., et al., eds. *Crucial Dimensions in World Evangelization*. South Pasadena, CA: William Carey Library, 1976.

Goddard, Burton L., ed. *The Encyclopedia of Modern Christian Missions: The Agencies*. Camden, NJ: Nelson, 1967.

Goldsmith, Martin. *Don't Just Stand There: The Why and How of Mission Today*. Downers Grove, IL: Inter-Varsity, 1975.

Griffiths, Michael M. *Give Up Your Small Ambitions*. London: Inter-Varsity, 1970.

Grunlan, Stephen A., and Marvin K. Mayers. *Cultural Anthropology: A Christian Perspective*. Grand Rapids: Zondervan, 1979.

Hancock, Robert L. *The Ministry of Development in Evangelical Perspective*. South Pasadena, CA: William Carey Library, 1979.

Hardin, Daniel C. *Mission: A Practical Approach to Church-Sponsored Mission Work*. South Pasadena, CA: William Carey Library, 1978.

Harr, Wilbur C., ed. *Frontiers of the Christian World Mission Since 1938*. New York: Harper & Row, 1962.

Hastings, Adrian. *African Christianity: An Essay in Interpretation*. London: Geoffrey Chapman, 1976.

_____. *A History of African Christianity, 1950-1975*. Cambridge: Cambridge University, 1979.

Hay, Ian M. *Now Why Did I Do That? The Biblical Basis of Motivation*. Scarborough, Ontario, and London, England: Sudan Interior Mission, 1977.

Hedlund, Roger E. *World Christianity: South Asia*. Monrovia, CA: Missions Advanced Research and Communication Center, 1979.

Henderson, W. Guy. *Passport to Missions*. Nashville: Broadman Press, 1979.

Hesselgrave, David J. *Communicating Christ Cross-Culturally*. Grand Rapids: Zondervan, 1978.

_____. *Planting Churches Cross-Culturally: A Guide for Home and Foreign Missions*. Grand Rapids: Baker, 1980.

_____, ed. *Dynamic Religious Movements: Case Studies of Rapidly Growing Religious Movements Around the World*. Grand Rapids: Baker, 1978.

_____, ed. *New Horizons in World Mission: Evangelicals and the Christian Mission in the 1980s*. Grand Rapids: Baker, 1980.

_____, ed. *Theology and Mission*. Grand Rapids: Baker, 1978.

Hodges, Melvin L. *The Indigenous Church and the Missionary*. South Pasadena, CA: William Carey Library, 1978.

Hoekstra, Harvey T. *The World Council of Churches and the Demise of Evangelism*. Wheaton, IL: Tyndale, 1979.

Hogg, William R. *Ecumenical Foundations: A History of the I.M.C.* New York: Harper & Row, 1952.

Hoke, Donald E., ed. *The Church in Asia*. Chicago: Moody, 1975.

Hopkins, Paul A. *What Next in Mission?* Philadelphia: Westminster, 1977.

Horner, Norman A. *Rediscovering Christianity Where It Began: A Survey of Contemporary Churches in the Middle East and Ethiopia*. Beirut: Near East Council of Churches, 1974.

Howard, David M., ed. *Declare His Glory Among the Nations*. Downers Grove, IL: Inter-Varsity, 1977.

———. *The Great Commission for Today*. Downers Grove, IL: Inter-Varsity, 1976.

———. *Student Power in World Evangelism*. Downers Grove, IL: Inter-Varsity, 1970.

Johnston, Arthur P. *The Battle for World Evangelism*. Wheaton, IL: Tyndale, 1978.

———. *World Evangelism and the Word of God*. Minneapolis: Bethany Fellowship, 1974.

Johnstone, Patrick J. *World Handbook for the World Christian*. South Pasadena, CA: William Carey Library, 1976.

Kane, J. Herbert. *Christian Missions in Biblical Perspective*. Grand Rapids: Baker, 1976.

———. *A Concise History of the Christian World Mission*. Grand Rapids: Baker, 1978.

———. *A Global View of Christian Missions*. Grand Rapids: Baker, 1971.

———. *Life and Work on the Mission Field*. Grand Rapids: Baker, 1980.

———. *The Making of a Missionary*. Grand Rapids: Baker, 1975.

———. *Understanding Christian Missions*. Grand Rapids: Baker, 1974.

———. *Winds of Change in the Christian Mission*. Chicago: Moody, 1973.

Kato, Byang H. *African Cultural Revolution and the Christian Faith*. Jos, Nigeria: Challenge Publications, 1976.

———. *Theological Pitfalls in Africa*. Kisumu, Kenya: Evangel Publishing House, 1975.

Kendall, Elliot. *The End of an Era: Africa and the Missionary*. London: SPCK, 1978.

Kitagawa, Daisuke. *Race Relations and Christian Mission*. New York: Friendship, 1964.

Koch, Kurt E. *Wine of God: Revival in Indonesia, Formosa, Solomon Islands, and South India*. Grand Rapids: Kregel, 1974.

Kraft, Charles H. *Christianity in Culture*. Maryknoll, NY: Orbis, 1979.

Kraus, C. Norman. *Missions, Evangelism and Church Growth*. Scottdale, PA: Herald Press, 1980.

Lacy, Creighton. *The Word-Carrying Giant: The Growth of the American Bible Society (1816-1966)*. South Pasadena, CA: William Carey Library, 1977.

Latourette, Kenneth Scott. *A History of the Expansion of Christianity*. 7 vols. New York: Harper & Row, 1937-1945.

Liao, David C. E., ed. *World Christianity: Eastern Asia*. Monrovia, CA: Missions Advanced Research and Communication Center, 1979.

Lindsell, Harold, ed. *The Church's Worldwide Mission*. Waco, TX: Word Books, 1966.

Luzbetak, Louis J. *The Church and Cultures*. Techny, IL: Divine Word, 1963.

McCurry, Don M., ed. *The Gospel and Islam: A 1978 Compendium*. Monrovia, CA: Missions Advanced Research and Communication Center, 1979.

———, ed. *World Christianity: Middle East*. Monrovia, CA: Missions Advanced Research and Communication Center, 1979.

McGavran, Donald. *The Clash Between Christianity and Cultures*. Grand Rapids: Baker, 1974.

———. *The Conciliar-Evangelical Debate: The Crucial Documents, 1964-1976*. South Pasadena, CA: William Carey Library, 1977.

_____. *Eye of the Storm: The Great Debate in Mission*. Waco, TX: Word Books, 1972.

McQuilkin, J. Robertson. *How Biblical Is the Church Growth Movement?* Chicago: Moody, 1973.

Mathews, Basil J. *Forward Through the Ages*. New York: Friendship, 1951.

Mbiti, John S. *Concepts of God in Africa*. London: SPCK, 1975.

Mellis, Charles J. *Committed Communities: Fresh Streams for World Missions*. South Pasadena, CA: William Carey Library, 1976.

Murray, Andrew. *Key to the Missionary Problem*. Fort Washington, PA: Christian Literature Crusade, 1979.

Neill, Stephen. *Call to Mission*. Philadelphia: Fortress, 1970.

_____. *Colonialism and Christian Missions*. New York: McGraw-Hill, 1966.

_____. *A History of Christian Missions*. New York: Penguin, 1964.

_____. *Salvation Tomorrow*. New York: Abingdon, 1976.

_____, et al. *Concise Dictionary of the Christian World Mission*. London: Lutterworth, 1970.

Nelson, Marlin L. *The How and Why of Third World Missions: An Asian Case Study*. South Pasadena, CA: William Carey Library, 1976.

_____, ed. *Readings in Third World Missions: A Collection of Essential Documents*. South Pasadena, CA: William Carey Library, 1976.

Nicholls, Bruce J. *Contextualization: A Theology of Gospel and Culture*. Downers Grove, IL: Inter-Varsity, 1979.

Nida, Eugene A. *Religion Across Cultures*. New York: Harper & Row, 1968.

Parshall, Phil. *New Paths in Muslim Evangelism: Evangelical Approaches to Contextualization*. Grand Rapids: Baker, 1980.

Peters, George W. *A Biblical Theology of Missions*. Chicago: Moody, 1972.

_____. *Church Growth in the Acts of the Apostles*. Grand Rapids: Zondervan, 1980.

_____. *Saturation Evangelism*. Grand Rapids: Zondervan, 1970.

Scherer, James A. *Missionary, Go Home: A Reappraisal of the Christian World Mission*. Englewood Cliffs, NJ: Prentice-Hall, 1964.

Schmitt, Karl M., ed. *The Roman Catholic Church in Modern Latin America*. New York: Knopf, 1972.

Shorter, Aylward. *African Christian Theology: Adaptation or Incarnation?* Maryknoll, NY: Orbis, 1977.

_____. *African Culture and the Christian Church*. Maryknoll, NY: Orbis, 1974.

Smalley, William A., ed. *Readings in Missionary Anthropology II*. South Pasadena, CA: William Carey Library, 1978.

Song, Choan-Seng. *Christian Mission in Reconstruction: An Asian Analysis*. Maryknoll, NY: Orbis, 1977.

Stott, John R. W. *Christian Mission in the Modern World*. Downers Grove, IL: Inter-Varsity, 1975.

_____, and Robert T. Coote, eds. *Gospel and Culture*. South Pasadena, CA: William Carey Library, 1979.

Taber, Charles R. *The Church in Africa*. South Pasadena, CA: William Carey Library, 1978.

Training for Missions. Grand Rapids: Reformed Ecumenical Synod, 1977.

Trueblood, Elton. *The Validity of the Christian Mission*. New York: Harper & Row, 1972.

282   *Bibliography*

Turner, Harold W. *Religious Innovation in Africa. Collected Essays on New Religious Movements*. Boston: G. K. Hall, 1979.

VanderWerff, Lyle C. *Christian Mission to Muslims—The Record: Anglican and Reformed Approaches in India and the Near East, 1800-1938*. South Pasadena, CA: William Carey Library, 1977.

Venn, Henry. *To Apply the Gospel: Selections from the Writings of Henry Venn*. Edited by Max A. Warren. Grand Rapids: Eerdmans, 1971.

Verkuyl, J. *Contemporary Missiology*. Grand Rapids: Eerdmans, 1978.

Wagner, C. Peter. *Frontiers in Missionary Strategy*. Chicago: Moody, 1972.

———. *Look Out! The Pentecostals Are Coming*. Carol Stream, IL: Creation House, 1973.

———. *Our Kind of People: The Ethical Dimensions of Church Growth in America*. Atlanta: John Knox, 1979.

———. *Stop the World, I Want to Get On*. Glendale, CA: Regal, 1973.

———, ed. *Church/Mission Tensions Today*. Chicago: Moody, 1972.

———, and Edward R. Dayton, eds. *Unreached Peoples '80*. Elgin, IL: David C. Cook, 1980.

Wakatama, Pius. *Independence for the Third World Church: An African's Perspective on Missionary Work*. Downers Grove, IL: Inter-Varsity, 1976.

Warren, Max A. *I Believe in the Great Commission*. Grand Rapids: Eerdmans, 1976.

———. *The Missionary Movement from Britain in Modern History*. Naperville, IL: Alec R. Allenson, 1965.

———. *Social History and Christian Mission*. Naperville, IL: Alec R. Allenson, 1967.

Webster, Douglas. *Yes to Mission*. New York: Seabury, 1966.

Willis, Avery T. *Indonesian Revival: Why Two Million Came to Christ*. South Pasadena, CA: William Carey Library, 1977.

Wilson, J. Christy. *Today's Tentmakers/Self-Support: An Alternative Model for Worldwide Witness*. Wheaton, IL: Tyndale, 1978.

Wilson, Samuel, ed. *Mission Handbook: North American Protestant Missions Overseas*. 12th ed. Monrovia, CA: Missions Advanced Research and Communication Center, 1980.

Winter, Ralph D. *The Twenty-Five Unbelievable Years, 1945-1969*. 7th ed. South Pasadena, CA: William Carey Library, 1974.

———, ed. *Evangelical Response to Bangkok*. South Pasadena, CA: William Carey Library, 1973.

Wong, James, et al. *Missions from the Third World*. Singapore: Church Growth Study Centre, 1973.

Subject Index

Abortion, 221
Abraham, 19, 26
ACTION, 73
Acts, Book of, 29-30
Adam, 26, 167
Adeney, David, 194
Africa, 67, 91, 95-96, 128, 174, 236, 249, 252, 253; Black, 5, 86-88, 200, 204; churches of, 78, 103, 105, 187, 193, 246; East, 233
Aga Khan, 257
Ahmadiyya Movement of Islam, 258
Albania, 89
Alcoholism, 219
Ali, Muhammad, 258
Alienation, 158, 168-69
All Africa Conference of Churches, 175
Ambedkar, B. R., 203
American Bible Society, 83, 118
American University in Beirut, 96
Amin, Idi, 233
Ananias, 53
Anglicans, 82, 95
Angola, 87, 91
Animism, 87, 199
Annas, 203
Antioch, 60
Architecture, church, 197
Armed forces, 224
Arya Samaj, 250
Asia, 127, 187, 195, 204, 237, 253; East, 192; missions in, 77, 80-81, 179, 230; Southeast, 233

Assemblies of God, 75, 105, 261, 262
Associated Missions of the International Council of Christian Churches, 74
AT&T, 159
Atlantic Charter, 176
Augustine, 169
Augustinians, 78
Austria, 249
Authentic humanity, 169

Babel, Tower of, 26
Babylon, 20
Bandaranaike, Sirimavo, 251
Bangladesh, 243, 248
Bangui Evangelical School of Theology, 117
Barnabas, 53
Batak Church, 105
Battle of Britain, 5
Belgian Parliament, 249
Berlin Congress on Evangelism, 82
Bible School Movement, 96
Black Muslims, 258
Bliss, Daniel, 96
Boer, Harry, 16, 45
Bolivia, 240
Bonhoeffer, Dietrich, 161
Brahmo Samaj, 250
Brazil, 85, 105, 107, 114, 262
Bright, Bill, 56
British East India Company, 99
Brown, Edith, 101
Brunner, Emil, 46

283

Brzezinski, Zbigniew, 225
Buddhism, 82, 144, 251-52, 255-56, 257; Zen, 252
Bulgaria, 89
Burma, 80, 182, 235, 256
Byrne, Jane, 217

Cain, 26
Cairo, 157
Calcutta, 157
Cambodia, 168, 234, 251
Campus Crusade for Christ, 55-56, 83
Canada, 234
Canadian Council of Churches Commission on World Concerns, 74
Caracas, 157
Cardenas, Gonzalo Castillo, 133
Carey, William, 16, 47, 95, 100
Carmichael, Amy, 101
Carr, Canon Burgess, 173
Carter, Jimmy, 132, 217, 222, 223, 224
Castro, Fidel, 224, 236
Celsus, 39
Central Intelligence Agency, 124-25
Chad, 236
Charismatic movement, 261-75
Chicago, 217
Chicago Tribune, 132, 217
Chile, 85, 262
Chilean Pentecostal Church, 189
China, 61, 80, 90, 103, 106, 110, 130, 132, 157, 186, 192, 198-99, 241, 251; churches of, 113, 178, 207-8
China Inland Mission, 96, 101
China Revolutionary Party, 132
Christian and Missionary Alliance, 75, 81, 117-18, 209
Christianity Today, 264
Christ's mission, 142-43
Church: architecture of, 197; essential nature of, 45-49; function of, 45; music in, 197
Church growth, 201-12
Church Growth Canada, 83
Churchill, Winston, 5
Church Missionary Society of England, 95
Church of God (Anderson, Indiana), 262

Church of God (Cleveland, Tennessee), 262
Church of South India, 105
Colonialism, 181, 186-88, 215, 236-37, 252-53; collapse of, 122-23; missionary under, 239-40, 242
Communism, 80, 89-91, 168, 234-35, 251; in the United States, 158-59
Congregational missionaries, 96
Congress of the United States, 217, 223
Conservative Baptists, 75
Constantine, 55
Contextualization: factors which prompted the call for, 187-88; guidelines for, 196-99; reasons for, 186-87
Copts, 86
Cornelius, 42
Costas, Orlando, 151
Cuba, 91, 181
Cultural mandate, 46
Cultural Revolution, 90, 91, 113, 130
Curriculum, 191
Czechoslovakia, 89

Daktar, 64
Daniel, 20, 26
Danish-Halle Mission, 73, 94
Darby, John, 272
David, 20, 145
Decline of the West, 215-31
Dehumanization, 157-58, 166
Democracy, 126, 127
Department of Energy, 223
Detzler, Wayne A., 82
Dictatorship, 127
Diem, Ngo Dinh, 124
Discipleship Training Centre, 194
Divine Word Fathers, 78
Division of Overseas Ministries, 74
Dominicans, 78
Dorcas, 53
Duquesne University, 262
Durant, Will, 42, 84, 147, 205

Eastern Orthodox, 74
East Germany, 89
Economic decline of the West, 221-23

Education: public, 218; theological, 188-90
Egypt, 20
Elymas, 53
Energy, Department of, 223
England, 82
Equal Rights Amendment, 100
Estonia, 89
Ethics Committee, 217
Ethiopia, 86, 91, 182
Eurocommunism, 234
Europe, missions in, 81-83
European Evangelical Alliance, 82
Evangelical Alliance Mission, 244
Evangelical Church of Vietnam, 81
Evangelical Foreign Missions Association, 74, 117, 201
Evangelical Free Church of America, 75
Evangelical Missionary Society of the Evangelical Churches of West Africa, 78
Evangelism, 40-41, 150-51
Exchange, foreign, 240-41
Exxon, 159

Faisal, 249
Faith Mission Movement, 96
Far East (Peffer), 99
Fellowship of Missions, 74
Festival of Islam, 248
Finance, 109-19, 243-46
First Amendment, 219, 254
Ford Motor Company, 223
Foreign exchange, 240-41
Foreign students, 229
Fourth World, 110, 111, 115
Frabicius, Philip, 94
France, 82
Franciscans, 78
Francke, August, 94
Frazier, William B., 155
Freytag, Walter, 155
Fuller School of World Mission, 201

Gallup, George, 226
Gandhi, Indira, 127, 257
Gatu, John, 173
General Motors, 219

Germany, State Church in, 82
Ghana, 87, 114
Gibbon, Edward, 42, 147
Glasser, Arthur F., 185
Glover, Robert H., 208
Goforth, Jonathan, 209
Gomorrah, 19, 26
Good News for Modern Man, 83
Gordon, Adoniram J., 272
Gospel: meaning of the word, 35-36; proclamation of, 41-43; universal appeal of, 39-40
Gospel mandate, 46
Government Sasana Council, 256
Graham, Billy, 82, 84
Great Britain, 186, 215-16. *See also* England
Great Commission, 16-17, 29, 32, 39, 40, 45, 47, 79, 139, 141; Protestant Reformers' view of, 15
Greater Europe Mission, 76, 82
Green, Michael, 60
Guildford, Bishop of, 248
Gutierrez, Gustavo, 161
Guttmacher Institute, 221

Halle, University of, 94
Harnack, Adolf von, 148
Hatfield, Mark O., 226
Herrnhut, 95
Hesselgrave, David J., 155
Hezekiah, 20
Hinduism, 82, 111, 144, 247, 250-51, 255, 256
Hippocrates, Oath of, 221
History of the Christian Church, 191
Hitler, Adolf, 168
Hoffman, Nicholas von, 216-17
Humanity, authentic, 169
Humanization, 155-71
Hungary, 89
Hus, John, 272

IBM, 159, 181
Idolatry, 195
Imperialism, theological and ethical, 182
Incarnation, 20
Income tax, 243

Independence for Third World
    churches, 244-45
Independents. *See* Separatists
India, 61, 77, 103, 105, 110, 111, 127,
    130, 194, 219, 237, 239, 243, 257,
    258; missions in, 80, 94, 170-71
Indigenous church, 185, 236-38
Indonesia, 81, 105, 207, 233, 248
Industrialization, 157-58
Interdenominational Foreign Mission
    Association, 74, 117, 201, 263
International Islamic Colloquiums, 257
International Muslim Bank, 249
International Shariat Congress, 248
Iran, 182, 228, 237
Iraq, 182
Islam, 88-89, 192, 248-49, 255
Israel, 19, 27
Italy, 82

Japan, 62-63, 104, 107, 192, 207, 217,
    222-23, 246; Buddhism in, 252;
    churches in, 103, 116; missions to,
    80; Muslims in, 249
Jeremiah, 20
Jesuits, 78
Jinnah, Mohammed Ali, 237
John, 47, 139
John Paul II, 90
John the Baptist, 43, 139
John XXIII, 267
Jonah, 18-19, 26
Jones, E. Stanley, 149, 193
Jones, Tracey K., 155
Joseph, 26
Josiah, 20
Judgment, 19
Judson, Adoniram, 6, 100

Kato, Byang, 87, 200
Kennedy, Bobby, 217
Kennedy, John, 217
Kenya, 87
Keswick Movement, 273
Khomeini, Ayatollah, 228, 237
King, Louis L., 117
King, Martin Luther, 217
Kingdom, 29
Komeito, 258

Koran, 192
Korea, 77, 114; North, 91; South, 67,
    80-81, 130, 178, 246

Lama, Dalai, 251
Lama, Panchen, 251
Latin America, 127, 129-30, 192, 262;
    missions in, 78, 84-86, 204
Latourette, Kenneth Scott, 79, 81, 147
Latvia, 89
Lausanne Committee for World
    Evangelization, 66
Lausanne Congress on World
    Evangelization, 82, 131, 175
Lausanne Covenant, 175
Libya, 88, 249
Lilje, Hans, 81
Lithuania, 89
Living Bible, 83
Lloyd-Jones, Martyn, 210, 230, 273
London Missionary Society, 95, 177
Lot, 19
Luke, 30
Lusaka Assembly of the AACC, 174
Lutheran Church–Missouri Synod, 75
Lutherans, 82
Lydia, 60

McGavran, Donald, 201
McNeill, William H., 215
Madras Conference of the Inter-
    national Missionary Council, 185
Mahasabah, 258
Malaysia, 237, 239
Manasseh, 19
Mandate, 46
Manifest Destiny, 126
Mao Tse-Tung, 90, 168
Mariam, Mengistu Haile, 229
Mar Thoma Church, 77
Martial law, 130-31
Marx, Karl, 159, 168
Marxism, 91, 130, 158-59, 192
Maryknollers, 79
Mauritania, 88
Mbiti, John, 88
Methodists, United, 85, 181, 267
Michigan State University, 262

Middle East, 127
Military decline of the West, 223-25
Miller, Robert, 248
Miracles, 210-12
Mission: effect of the decline of the West on, 227-31; meaning of, 148-50; nature of, 143-45; priority of, 151-53; purpose of, 142-43
Missionaries, early, 94-98
Missionary: definition of, 139; image of, 98-100; unwillingness to give up leadership, 179, 245; vulnerability of the American, 123-24
Missionary enterprise in the early church, basic assumptions of, 42
Missionary message, 35-43
Missionary support, 114-19
Mission funds, 245-46
Mission Handbook, 74
Mission Trends, 162, 163
Moody, D. L., 98, 207
Moody Bible Institute, 97-98
Moody Monthly, 221
Mooneyham, Stan, 68
Moral decline of the West, 219-21
Moratorium, 173-84, 245
Moravians, 94-95
Mordecai, 26
Morrison, Robert, 100
Mortenson, Vernon, 153
Moses, 26
Mott, John R., 96, 104, 209
Mozambique, 91
Muggeridge, Malcolm, 131
Music in church, 197
Muslims, 87-89, 258
Muslim world, 88-89, 204

Nacpil, Emerito, 174
Nationalism, 187-88, 233-46
National Missionary Society of India, 77
Nehemiah, 20, 26
Neill, Stephen, 51, 76, 133, 170
Neo-Pentecostal movement, 262-67
Nepal, 256-57
Newbigin, Lesslie, 46
Newsweek, 124
Newton, John, 206

New Tribes Mission, 75
New York Stock Exchange, 222
Nichiren Shoshu, 252
Nicklaus, Robert, 249
Nietzsche, Friedrich, 203
Nigeria, 86, 87
Nixon, Richard M., 217
Noah, 19, 26
Non-Aligned Nations, 236
North America, missions in, 83-84
Norway, 262
Notre Dame University, 262

Oath of Hippocrates, 221
Oil revenues, 249
Olford, Stephen, 273
Oliver, Dennis, 83
OPEC, 223
Operation Mobilization, 66
Opium War, 186
Organization of Petroleum Exporting Countries (OPEC), 223
Oriental religions, 52. *See also* Buddhism; Hinduism; Islam
Overseas Missionary Fellowship, 242, 243

Pakistan, 237, 249
Park Chung Hee, 131
Parshall, Phil, 195
Paul, 16, 30, 40, 43, 52, 56, 98, 121, 206; churches planted by, 41, 211-12; his philosophy of history in Romans 9-11, 31; his understanding of the cross, 22
Paul III, 202
Peace Corps, 73, 115, 228
Peffer, Nathaniel, 99
Pentecost, 30, 208
Pentecostal Church, 212
Pentecostal movement, 261-62
Persia, 20
Peter, 17, 40, 43, 47, 53, 141
Peters, George, 87, 200
Petrodollars, 249
Philip, 35, 40, 53
Philippi, 60
Philippines, 80, 81, 130, 131
Phillips, J. B., 53

Phnom Penh, 205
Pickett, J. Waskom, 203
Pilate, 22
Poland, 89
Political decline of the West, 216-17
Politics and nationalism, 234-36
Poverty, 112-13
Presbyterians, United, 66, 85, 181
Prisons, 218-19
Prodigal son, 21
Protestant missionaries, 15, 74
Protestant Reformers, 15
Protestants, 74, 86
Public education, 218

Radhakrishnan, Sarvepalli, 55
Ramakrishna Mission, 258
Ramakrishna Movement, 250, 257
Redpath, Alan, 273
Religious Affairs Bureau (China), 90, 178
Religious decline of the West, 225-27
Resurrection, 48, 49-56
Revelation, Book of, 31-33
Rhodesia, Northern, 95
Ro, Bong Rin, 179, 230
Roman Catholic Church, 74, 82, 225, 231, 262; in Black Africa, 86; in Poland, 90; Pentecostalism in the, 267-68
Roman Catholic missions, 78-79
Romans, 59
Romans, Book of, 30-31
Rumania, 89
Russia. *See* Soviet Union

SALT II, 224
Sangha, 256
Sanhedrin, 47
Sapphira, 53
Saudi Arabia, 88, 249
Scheduled Classes. *See* Untouchables
Scherer, James, 68, 173
Schwartz, Christian F., 94
Scotland, 96
Scudder, Ida, 101
Separatists, 86
Shalom, 160
Sider, Ron, 68

Simon Magus, 53
Simons, Menno, 272
Simpson, A. B., 272
Sixth Great Buddhist Council, 257
Skoglund, John E., 48, 208
Slessor, Mary, 101
Social decline of the West, 217-19
Society for Buddhist Studies, 252
Sodom, 19, 26
Soka Gakkai, 252, 257, 258
Solzhenitsyn, Alexander, 229-30
Somalia, 88, 182
Sorensen, 95
South Africa, 86
Southern Baptist Board of Foreign Missions, 75
Southern Baptists, 75, 85
Sovereignty of God, 206-8
Soviet Union, 89, 166, 216, 224, 234
Speer, Robert E., 15
Spirit in church growth, 208-10
Sri Lanka, 251
State Church (in Germany), 82
Stephen, 53
Stewart, James S., 23
Stott, John R. W., 149, 163, 166
Student Volunteer Movement, 96
Sudan, 86, 181
Suenens, Leo, 82
Sunday observance, 197
Sung, John, 107, 209
Support, missionary, 114-19
Swain, Clara, 101
Sweden, 243-44
Syncretism, 199-200
Syria, 88
Syrian Christian College, 96
Syrophoenician woman, 37
Systematic theology, 192

Taiwan, 114, 130, 178, 237
Tanzania, 86
Taylor, J. Hudson, 96, 272
Television, 220-21
Temple, William, 102
Teresa, Mother, 240
Terrorism, 225
Thailand, 81, 239, 241, 243, 255-56
Theological education, 188-90

Third World, 5, 54, 61, 80, 110, 133, 157, 228, 231, 240, 253, 254; church leaders in the, 104-6; churches of the, 63, 67, 102-8, 113, 176, 178, 182, 186, 187, 191-92, 193, 244; democracy in the, 123; missions in the, 77-78, 118-19; national Christians in the, 106-8; politics in the, 129-31, 241
Thoburn, Isabella, 101
Three Self Movement, 90, 178
Time, 124
Tito, Marshall, 236
Tongue-speaking, 263, 266-67, 268-69
Tower of Babel, 26
Transcendental Meditation, 250
Trinity Evangelical Divinity School, 258
Tripitaka, 257
Tyndale Publishing House, 66

Uganda, 87, 233
Ultradispensationalists, 274
United Church of Canada, 83
United Church of Christ, 181
United Kingdom, 234. *See also* Great Britain
United Methodist Church, 85, 181, 267
United Nations, 66, 110, 215, 236, 253
United Presbyterian Church, 66, 85, 181
United States, 61, 96, 118, 124, 157, 216, 254; poverty level in the, 111
United States Steel, 223
Untouchables, 111, 170-71, 203, 255
Uppsala Report, 161, 164
Urbana Missionary Convention (1979), 75
Urbanization, 157
Uruguay, 114
U.S. Catholic Mission Council, 79
U.S. News and World Report, 69

Van Dusen, Henry P., 261
Vatican, 79
Vatican II, 82, 85, 267
Vedanta Movement, 250
Vedanta Society, 258
Vellore Christian Medical College and Hospital, 101
Venn, Henry, 185
Vietnam, 81, 227; North, 91; South, 91, 127
Vivekananda, Swami, 251
Voice of Islam, 89

Wagner, C. Peter, 182-83
Ward, William, 95
Wells, H. G., 167
Wesley, John, 67-68, 272
West, decline of the, 215-31
Western missions, 177-81, 238-44
Whately, Richard, 51
White Fathers, 78, 181
Wilson, Woodrow, 176
Womack, David, 263
Woman's Union Missionary Society, 100
Women in missions, the role of, 100-2
Women's Liberation Movement, 100
World Christian, 57-69
World Fellowship of Buddhists, 257
World Hunger Conference, 110
Wyclif, John, 271
Wycliffe Bible Translators, 75, 182

Yang, David, 190
Year of Mission, 83
Yemen, 182; South, 88
Yugoslavia, 89, 234

Zaire, 86, 241, 242
Zambia, 95
Zenana Bible and Medical Mission, 100
Ziegenbalg, Bartholomaus, 94
Zinzendorf, Count, 94

Scripture Index

Genesis

1:1—57
1:28—46
2:17—166
chapter 3—26
3:19—168
chapter 4—26
chapter 6—26
chapter 11—26
chapter 12—26
12:3—19, 26
chapter 18—26
18:32—19
22:18—26
28:14—26
chapters 39-47—26

Exodus

chapters 1-12—26
9:16—27

Deuteronomy

7:7-8—19

Nehemiah

chapters 1-6—26

Esther

chapters 1-10—26

Psalms

2:8—27
24:1—26, 58
51:4—165
63:3—20
66:1-7—27
67:1-2—27
72:8, 11—27
76:10—6
103:8—20
103:19—26
127:1—212
145:9—20
145:16—26
145:17—27

Isaiah

28:21—18
43:3—28
43:10—27
43:11—28
44:1-2—27
45:22—28
46:10—207
49:6—28
49:7—28
52:10—27
54:5—28
55:7—20
55:8—6
56:6-7—28
61:1—141

61:3—206
66:19—28

Jeremiah

3:17—28

Ezekiel

33:11—18

Daniel

chapter 9—26

Jonah

2:9—17
chapters 3-4—26

Habakkuk

2:14—28
3:2—18

Zechariah

4:6—212

Malachi

1:11—28

Matthew

1:21—142
4:4—145

291

4:23—143
5:5—29
5:5-11—29
5:44—149
5:45—20
6:9—58
6:9-10—28
8:11—29
9:12—205
10:9-10—109
10:22—196
10:40—140
11:5—93
11:20-24—211
11:25—29
11:25-26—169
11:28—36, 39, 169,
    206
12:4—145
12:32—275
chapter 13—186,
    202, 204
13:19—202
13:38—29, 38, 202
14:14—145
15:26—37
16:19—140
20:25-28—29
20:28—142
21:32—29
24:14—32, 39
25:31-36—29
25:32—26
chapter 28—15
28:5-7—50
28:18—59, 140
28:18-20—38, 39
28:19-20—29
28:20—36, 45

Mark

2:5—54
2:10—52
6:34-44—145
7:27—37
8:1-9—145
8:36—166
8:36-37—152

11:17—38
16:15-18—38

Luke

1:33—29
1:71—142
4:16-19—143
4:16-21—141
4:18-19—146
4:24-29—60
6:20—29
9:1—52
10:1—52
10:9—52
10:17—52
10:27—144
10:31-32—145
12:15—67
15:21—165
16:8—69
17:11-19—146
17:21—29
18:24-25—93
18:25—29
19:10—142
22:25-26—143
22:27—142
23:5—271
24:45-49—38
24:49—52, 141

John

1:6—140
1:9-10—37
1:14—139
1:18—139
1:29—37
3:16—20, 21, 36, 39
3:17—38, 139
3:19—167
3:36—162, 167
chapter 4—197
4:10—20
4:24—176
4:37-38—206
4:42—37
5:19—20, 140, 169

5:22—52
5:27—52
5:28-29—59
5:29—26
6:26—145
6:32—20
6:51—38
8:12—38
8:31-32—29
8:31-36—167
8:36—169
10:24-25—210-11
11:25—50
12:24—149
12:32—29, 38
12:49—20, 169
13:13-14—143
14:1—36
14:6—170
14:11—140
14:12—147, 211
15:5—140
16:8—38
16:28—140
16:33—169
17:2—52
17:4—140
17:21-23—38
17:23—140
18:11-17, 22
18:33-38—29
19:10-11—22
20:19-23—38
20:21—38, 139
20:22—141
20:23—140
20:28—49
20:31—211

Acts

chapters 1-8—30
1:3—38
1:4-8—38
1:7—207
1:8—29, 30, 38, 40,
    45, 47, 53, 141,
    208
1:22—48

chapter 2—268
2:4—47
2:44-45—147
3:1-10—53
3:6—109
4:2—48
4:13—94
4:18-20—47
4:27-28—17, 22
4:33—53
5:1-10—53
5:14—211
5:28—40, 43, 47
5:38-39—275
6:8—53
chapter 8—32, 40
chapters 8-12—30
8:1—40
8:4—35
8:6—53
8:19—53
8:20-23—53
8:35—35
9:20—43
9:36-42—53
9:42—211
chapter 10—40
10:9-20—40
10:38—21, 52, 141, 211
11:13-14—42
11:19—40
chapter 13—32
chapters 13-28—30
13:10-12—53
13:12—54
13:38-39—36
13:46—41
14:17—20
15:12—53
chapter 16—32
16:16-18—53
16:31—156
17:24-28—58
17:25—21
17:30—40
17:31—26
18:6—41

chapter 19—32
20:35—119
26:8—49
26:18—87
26:22-23—50
28:28—41
28:31—43

Romans

1:1—35
1:2—150
1:4—52
1:8-15—30
1:14—40
1:16—30, 35, 41, 52, 53, 150
1:25—167
1:26-27—167
2:16—30, 35
3:23—40
3:25—22
4:25—36
5:12—58
chapter 6—273
6:23—21
chapter 8—273
8:7—162, 167
8:32—21
chapters 9-11—31
10:9—36
10:9-11—40
10:12-13—31, 39
10:13—39
10:14—42
10:14-15—31
10:17—41
11:25—37
11:26—31
13:8-10—29
14:7—165
15:18-19—56, 212
15:19—31, 271
15:23-33—30

1 Corinthians

1:17—43
1:20-23—94

1:22—51
1:23-24—51
1:26—93
1:26-27—40
2:1—52
2:1-5—30
2:2—36
2:4—52, 271
3:6—206
3:9—206
4:20—53
9:1—48
9:16—43, 151, 170
9:18—142
9:20-22—142
9:22—133, 170
chapter 12—269
12:11—275
12:13—268
13:8—269
15:1-4—36
15:45-49—58

2 Corinthians

3:17—55
4:4—153
5:15—39
5:19—22, 163
5:21—22
8:9—109, 116

Galatians

1:8—50, 196
2:5—50, 52, 150
2:14—30
3:28—39
6:2—147
6:9-10—148

Ephesians

chapter 1—6
1:11—207
1:19-20—53
1:20-23—29
1:21—38
1:21-22—58

2:1—167
2:8—20
3:8—152, 170
3:15—58
4:6—58
4:18—162, 167

Philippians

1:15-18—196
2:5-11—169
2:9-11—38
2:10-11—59
2:11—59
3:10—53

Colossians

1:4—145
1:5—53
1:23—41
2:14-15—29, 169

1 Thessalonians

1:3—145
1:9—87
4:14—36

2 Thessalonians

3:16—21

1 Timothy

1:11—177

1:15—142
2:1-2—66
2:4—17, 40
6:15—59

2 Timothy

2:3—195
3:15—25
3:17—148
4:2—152
4:5—152

Titus

1:15—161
2:7—148
2:10—148
2:14—148
3:1—148
3:3—167
3:8—148
3:14—148

Hebrews

1:1-3—27
1:2—38
3:1—16, 140
5:8—141, 169
9:12—38
9:27—58, 170
11:7—19
12:2—141
12:14—194

James

1:5—20
1:17—21
2:14-26—145
2:15-16—149
4:6—20

1 Peter

2:24—22
3:18—22, 36

2 Peter

3:18—189

1 John

2:2—38
3:8—139
3:17—147
3:23—145
4:9—22
4:14—20, 38

Revelation

2:5—84
5:19—32
11:15—32, 59
13:8—49, 265
21:24—33
22:2—33
22:17—33, 39

266.02
K16c

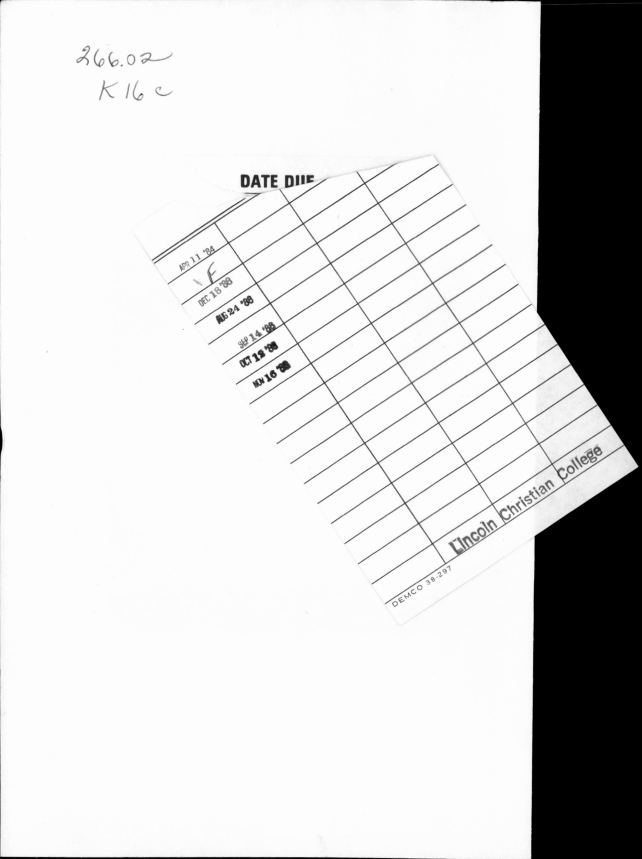

DATE DUE

APR 11 '84			
DEC 18 '88			
AUG 24 '88			
SEP 14 '88			
OCT 19 '88			
NOV 16 '88			

Lincoln Christian College

DEMCO 38-297